TRUE**CANADIAN**

STORIES OF
CANADIAN
BATTLEFIELDS

TRUE **CANADIAN**

STORIES OF
CANADIAN
BATTLEFIELDS

Ed
Butts

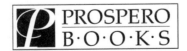

PROSPERO
B·O·O·K·S

Library and Archives Canada Cataloguing in Publication

Butts, Edward, 1951–
   Stories of Canadian battlefields / Ed Butts.

Includes bibliographical references.
ISBN 978-1-55267-525-0

   1. Battles—Canada—History. 2. Battlefields—Canada. 3. Canada—History,
Military. I. Title.

FC226.B88 2007   971   C2007-901539-5

This collection produced for Prospero Books.

Key Porter Books Limited
Six Adelaide Street East, Tenth Floor
Toronto, Ontario
Canada M5C 1H6

www.keyporter.com

Printed and bound in Canada

07 08 09 10 11 5 4 3 2 1

Contents

Introduction

The land now called Canada had battlefields long before the first Europeans stepped ashore and began to claim real estate in the names of far-off monarchs. While the newcomers brought many evils—diseases, land hunger, rotgut alcohol, and even new reasons for going to war, such as trade rivalries—they did not bring war itself. The various Native nations fought each other over the territories from which they took their food and other necessities of survival. They raided their neighbours for plunder and prisoners. They went to war to gain honour and prestige. When horses first appeared on the Canadian prairies generations before the first Europeans ventured onto the sea of grass, warriors of various tribes learned horsemanship, and used that advantage to dominate their unmounted neighbours. Though the stories of these Native battles live on in Native lore and legend, they are for the most part undocumented, and therefore are mentioned here only in passing.

When the Europeans came to Canada they brought their wars with them. They soon had the Natives embroiled in wars that began on the other side of the Atlantic, and were settled in European capitals with treaties in which the Natives had no say. To most Europeans, and later Canadians of European descent, the Natives were "savages" to be used and then brushed aside.

Canadian battles were fought by armies of thousands, as in the struggles between France and Britain. Others, like the tragic fight at Seven Oaks, involved small numbers of combatants, but nonetheless made profound impressions on Canadian history. Canadian battlefields were scenes of dramatic acts of heroism, like General Isaac Brock's death at Queenston Heights. They were also places of national shame, such as the victory at Batoche of a modern, well equipped army over a handful of desperate, poorly armed defenders.

Early Canadian battles were fought with flintlock muskets and the bayonet. Those weapons gave way to the repeating rifle and the Gatling gun. The well-trained "regulars" of the British and French armies were replaced by the Canadian militia; the citizen soldiers who effectively quashed William Lyon Mackenzie's rebellion, but were no match for the American-based Fenians who'd had hard training in the Civil War.

Canadians may be excused for looking back with a degree of pride at the War of 1812, when Canadian militia stood side by side with British redcoats to throw back one invading American army after another, and emerge as the only "winners" of that regrettable conflict. The sites of Canadian battlefields in that war are well marked today by parks, monuments and plaques. But it must be remembered that battlefields were far from being places of glory, regardless of the propaganda that followed a fight. A battlefield was a framework for fear, pain and death. It was said that a field of battle could be smelled for miles away after the clash of arms, because it stank of blood, vomit, excrement and urine. For the common soldier, death in battle was a dirty death. But many a soldier must have prayed for a quick death wound, rather than one that would land him in the hell of a military hospital, where the surgeon's chief tool was the bone saw, and anaesthetic was unknown. Generals got the glory, but the ordinary soldier was "cannon fodder." The Canada we know today owes as much to those common soldiers as it does to the generals honoured by monuments.

Acknowledgements

T he stories in this book by no means represent all of the battles fought in Canadian history. I do hope the selections I have made, and my descriptions of the conflicts, will encourage readers to look further into this fascinating aspect of Canada's past. Many other Canadian authors have written books and articles about battles that took place on Canadian soil. A few have even devoted books to single battles, providing thrilling and informative minute-by-minute accounts of the struggles that shaped Canadian destiny. I am indebted to all of those authors. I'd like to thank Paula Sloss and Jordan Fenn of Key Porter Books for trusting me with this project. I must also thank my daughter Melanie for her patience while I was holed up in my room. Special thanks, once again, go to the staff of the Guelph, Ontario, Public Library.

For my Mum and Dad, Ted and Patricia Butts:
Veterans of the Second World War

War Over Fish
and Furs

In the sixteenth century, France and England looked on in envy as Spanish conquistadores looted the empires of the Aztecs in Mexico and the Incas in South America of fortunes in gold and silver. Privateering captains like Francis Drake and Henry Morgan would relieve the Spanish of vast quantities of that treasure, and the armed forces of both England and France would seize Caribbean islands originally claimed by Spain, so they could get in on the incredibly lucrative sugar trade. But the French and the English, while probing the more northerly coasts of America in search of a sea route to the Orient, stumbled across commodities that were, in the long run, even more valuable than gold and silver. One was fish—in particular, cod. The Grand Banks off the island of Newfoundland, claimed for England by the Italian navigator John Cabot, were so rich in cod, it was said a man could step out of a boat and walk to shore on the backs of teeming fish. The nation that controlled that important food supply held a major card in European power struggles. In 1585 a proposal was put forward in England for a raid on the Spanish fishing fleet in Newfoundland,

"To starve his [King Philip's] country and possess his mariners and shipping, wherin consists his chief strength." In 1587 Francis Drake and John Hawkins again proposed attacking Spain's fishing fleet, though in neither case were the attacks actually made. Basque fishermen protected themselves by obtaining passports from the Lord Admiral of England. Just to be safe they obtained a second passport from the English fishing admirals at St. John's as added security for the return voyage, when their holds would be full of valuable dried and salted cod.

The other commodity was beaver. European gentry had fallen in love with hats and other fashionable items made from the felt that was manufactured from the soft underhairs of beaver fur. No lady or gentleman of the upper class could appear in public without a beaver hat. To be really fashionable, one had had to own several of them, and change hats throughout the day. Capes, coats and ladies' dresses were also adorned with beaver fur. The pelts of a rodent found in the millions in the wilderness of what would one day be called Canada were practically worth their weight in gold. An English pirate named Eric Cobham made his fortune not by plundering treasure ships in the Spanish Main, but by hijacking French fur cargoes in the Gulf of St. Lawrence. (Pirates were also known to steal cargoes of salted cod, because they could be sold at a tidy profit on the black market.)

To get beaver pelts, one had to trade with the Natives. So the French, from their base at Quebec, and the English, from posts in what is now New England, lured the Natives in to trade their beaver pelts for guns, coloured beads, cheaply manufactured domestic goods, and alcohol. The goods the Europeans traded were not nearly as valuable as the pelts, so of course the profit was enormous (ironically, the Natives believed they were getting the better of the deal). The Dutch were in on this lucrative business for a while, but were eventually muscled out of the way by the English.

Competition led to conflict, with Native trappers spreading out looking for more beaver as their own territories were trapped out. The Iroquois, who did business with the English, clashed with the Huron, who dealt with the French. The explorer and adventurer Samuel de Champlain made an implacable enemy of the Iroquois when he accompanied a Huron attack on one of their towns. The Iroquois–Huron war ultimately resulted in the destruction of the Huron nation. Some tribes set themselves up as middlemen, trading European goods to tribes farther afield in return for beaver pelts. This created more rivalries.

In the quest for beaver pelts, the white traders probed ever deeper into the continent. They set up trading posts, mapped previously unmapped territories, and sparked violence as whites and Natives alike battled over the trade. Battles large and small were fought from the Great Lakes and the St. Lawrence Valley to the distant shores of Hudson Bay. A battle might involve two Native war parties in a brief, bloody skirmish, or it could have the armies of England and France facing each other with muskets and cannon. Thus did a fashion trend in Europe bring war and bloodshed to the forests and fields of far-off Canada.

Battle of the
Long Sault

Canada's Thermopylae

Heroic "last stands" in which outnumbered defenders bravely fight to the last man against overwhelming odds are the stuff of which legends are made. None of the many battles fought by ancient Sparta are as well remembered as the three-day standoff at the pass of Thermopylae in 480 BC, in which three hundred Spartans under their king, Leonidas, defied the might of the Persian Empire. The thirteen-day siege of the Alamo at San Antonio, Texas, in 1836, which saw David Crockett, James Bowie, William Barret Travis, and about 180 others make a hopeless attempt to fight off a huge Mexican army has inspired numerous ballads, novels and films. Even Colonel George Armstrong Custer's famous "Last Stand" at the Little Bighorn in 1876 (it wasn't a last stand at all, because the Sioux and Cheyenne were the defenders) has entered the realm of heroic mythology.

Canadians, too, have a "Thermopylae" in their history. It is a story that was at one time familiar to every Canadian schoolchild, and was even used during the two World Wars to encourage young men to enlist in the Canadian army. Today, however, it is largely forgotten, at least in part because twentieth-century revisionists cast doubts on the actual motives of the central character.

Adam Dollard des Ormeaux (b. 1635) probably arrived in the fledgling settlement of Ville-Marie (Montreal) in 1658. Almost nothing is known of his life prior to his encounter with destiny. He was an officer in the garrison and was apparently well-respected. His acquisition of thirty *arpents* (10 hectares) of land indicates that he may have planned to settle there after completing his military service. One story claims that Dollard had committed an indiscretion back in France and came to Canada in hopes of redeeming himself through some great deed. However, the story may be apocryphal.

By the spring of 1660 the French colonists along the St. Lawrence and their Huron and Algonquin allies were well entangled with the English and Dutch colonists to the south, and the powerful Iroquois Confederacy in a struggle over the fur trade. The Iroquois had trapped out most of the beaver in their country south of Lake Ontario, and had been making hunting and raiding expeditions north of the Great Lakes and into the Ottawa Valley. In April of that year there were rumours circulating that large numbers of Iroquois planned to descend the Ottawa River and attack the settlements of Montreal and Trois-Rivières. Such rumours were common, however, and it is not certain how much credence was given them.

Adam Dollard went to Governor Paul Chomedey de Maisonneuve with a plan to go up the Ottawa River with sixteen men and intercept the Iroquois. At the Long Sault, a series of dangerous rapids, canoe traffic had to go ashore and portage past the white water. Just what Dollard's intentions were has been the subject of much debate.

Dollard's admirers insist that the young Frenchman was volunteering for what amounted to a suicide mission by which he hoped to spare New France from the wrath of the Iroquois. Others argue that he was a glory hound who probably hoped to reap a tidy profit hijacking Iroquois fur canoes. The Iroquois themselves regularly ambushed the fur convoys of the French and their Native allies, and if that was indeed Dollard's intent, it would be the first time the French had carried this kind of guerilla warfare to the foe. It might also have been his plan to simply ensure safe passage for a fur fleet the explorer Pierre-Esprit Radisson would be bringing down the river.

Whatever his motives, Dollard was certainly no coward. To head out into the howling wilderness with a mere handful of men and knowingly place oneself in harm's way took more than a little nerve. This was especially true when one was aware that the Iroquois warriors were known for their ferocity in battle, and were not known for kind treatment of prisoners. While a lucky few might be adopted into the tribe, most captives were enslaved or tortured to death. The Native perception of torture was not the same as that of the Europeans, who regularly tortured victims to punish, humiliate, or extract information. To the Iroquois, as well as their Huron and Algonquin enemies, death by torture was a test of the victim's courage.

Some of the men in Montreal who were more experienced in wilderness warfare were against Dollard's idea. They wanted him to wait until after the spring planting had been done so that more men would be available for the expedition. But Dollard evidently was concerned that he would then have to give up command to someone of higher rank. He prevailed upon Maisonneuve to let him take his men up the Ottawa. Maisonneuve finally gave Dollard's scheme his approval.

The seventeen men left Montreal near the end of April. All were bachelors. The oldest of them was thirty-one. The rest were in their twenties. They supposedly swore an oath to stand together and fight to the death if necessary. Such melodramatics were not uncommon for the period. It did not necessarily mean that they expected to die.

The band travelled by night to avoid detection, but at Île Saint Paul they ran into a party of Iroquois. After a brief skirmish in which neither side suffered any casualties the Iroquois fled, leaving behind their canoe and possessions. This minor success boosted the morale of at least one Frenchman who had spoken of turning back.

Dollard and his men were not expert canoeists, and it took them eight days to travel up the Ottawa River to the Long Sault (near present-day Carillon, Quebec). They found an old Algonquin stockade about 152 metres (500 feet) from the riverbank, and there set up their camp. They began to repair the somewhat ramshackle defensive works, but considering the time the men had before they would actually encounter the enemy, they seem to have gone about the work at a leisurely pace.

Meanwhile, a band of forty Hurons led by chief Anahotaha, and four Algonquins including chief Mitiwemeg arrived at Montreal. They, too, had been stalking the woods in search of Iroquois. When they learned of Dollard's expedition, they asked Maisonneuve to write them a letter that they could take to Dollard, expressing their desire to join forces with him. Maisonneuve wrote a letter of introduction, in which he warned Dollard not to trust the loyalty of these would-be allies.

The Huron–Algonquin party reached the Long Sault, raising Dollard's force to sixty-one men. Soon after, two Hurons

Anahotaha had sent out to scout the territory reported that they had seen Iroquois. The enemy, they said, had been spying on the stockade.

Now that their position was known to the foe, many of the Hurons feared that the Iroquois would attack in force. They wanted to return to Montreal immediately. They changed their minds when Anahotaha berated them as cowards. The men now stepped up the repair work on the stockade. But they were taking a dinner break on the riverbank when a fleet of canoes bearing two hundred Iroquois warriors swept into view.

There was a ragged exchange of shots as the Iroquois landed and the defenders took cover behind their walls. Then an Iroquois chieftain approached unarmed, indicating that he wanted to parley. He asked for a truce, and Dollard agreed on the condition that the Iroquois retreat to the other side of the river. Even as Dollard spoke, his men were hurriedly trying to patch up the stockade with whatever materials were at hand. So lax had they been in their preparations, they hadn't even dug a well.

The Iroquois chieftain was aware that Dollard was playing for time. He returned to his warriors, and the men in the stockade braced themselves for an attack. Then the forest erupted with blood-chilling war cries and the crash of musket fire as the Iroquois hurled themselves at the fort.

The gunpowder of that time produced an incredible amount of smoke, so the little stockade soon would have been shrouded in an acrid fog. Given the noise, the lack of visibility, and the knowledge of what would happen if the Iroquois breached their walls, the experience for the men in the fort must have been frightful indeed. But they threw back that first assault without taking a single casualty. The Iroquois withdrew, dragging their wounded and leaving behind many dead. Dollard's men infuriated them by cutting off the head of a slain chieftain and mounting it on a stockade pole.

The Iroquois settled in for a siege, a type of warfare with which Native fighters usually had little patience. They built a stockade of their own. They would feint an attack to draw the defenders' fire, then withdraw back into their fort. This went on for seven long days, during which the Iroquois sent runners to war parties that had been raiding along the Richelieu River to the south.

Conditions within Dollard's stockade were squalid. The air was rank with the stench of human waste. The men grew weary from lack of sleep. Food and ammunition were running low. They dug a shallow well, but because it was on a hill it produced little more than mud. A few times the men made sorties under the cover of their comrades' guns to fetch water from the river, but this was extremely dangerous and they were able to bring back only small amounts. By the seventh day, Anahotaha's Hurons were on the verge of mutiny.

Then the ranks of the attackers were more than doubled with the arrival of another five hundred warriors. The situation in Dollard's stockade was now hopeless. Anahotaha called for a truce. He sent two warriors bearing gifts to parley with the Iroquois. The Huron chief was obviously not in much of a position to negotiate, but owing to the peculiar nature of Native warfare, there was always the slim chance that he could buy his companions' freedom with promises of more gifts.

The emissaries found that there were a considerable number of adopted Hurons among the Iroquois. Some of them now moved toward Dollard's stockade, calling on the Hurons within to join them. Most of Anahotaha's men (some accounts say all) immediately leapt over the walls and deserted. The chief remained with the Frenchmen, as did Mitiwemeg and his Algonquins.

Angry, and alarmed that another attack was imminent, Dollard ordered his men to open fire. A volley of lead tore into the front rank of the Iroquois and the backs of the turncoat Hurons. Anahotaha allegedly admonished Dollard for breaking the truce.

Informed by the deserters that they faced but a few weakened defenders, the Iroquois launched an all-out attack. They advanced behind body-length wooden shields that protected them from musket balls. Dollard's men fired as fast as they could reload their guns, but for every Iroquois who fell there were a dozen to take his place. The attackers reached the palisade and began hacking at the timbers with axes. The Frenchmen made two crude grenades by packing pistol barrels with gunpowder and attaching fuses, and hurled them into the mass of shrieking warriors. Still the Iroquois pressed their attack.

Then Dollard played what would be his last card. He lit the fuse on a keg of gunpowder (or some kind of homemade bomb) and attempted to throw it over the wall. Instead of falling among the Iroquois, the bomb struck the top of the palisade, fell back into the fort, and exploded. In the enclosed space, Dollard's bomb killed several of his own men.

Now the Iroquois scaled the walls and poured into the stockade. Others poked their muskets through unmanned loopholes and fired into the small compound. With no chance to reload their guns, the defenders who were still standing fought furiously with swords and axes. Anahotaha and any Hurons who had stayed with him, Mitiwemeg and his Algonquins, and Dollard and several Frenchmen were killed in the melee. The remaining handful of defenders killed their own wounded to spare them from the torture stake. They tore into the Iroquois with swords and knives with such ferocity that the warriors momentarily abandoned any notion of taking prisoners. They finished the Frenchmen off with a volley of musket fire. Then nothing could be heard but the roaring waters of the Long Sault.

The Iroquois found four Frenchmen who were wounded but still alive. These unfortunates would be taken back to Iroquois towns for death by torture. One other Frenchman who was still alive but too badly wounded to be taken on the trail was burned on the spot. The bodies of the dead were stripped, mutilated and tied to stakes along the riverbank. Disappointed that they did not have enough French prisoners to distribute among their communities, the Iroquois seized the Hurons who had so cravenly deserted their chief and marked them for death. Several of these men eventually escaped. One of them reached Montreal, where he told a shocked Maisonneuve all that had happened at the Long Sault. As word of the disaster spread, all of New France braced itself for a major Iroquois invasion. *Habitants* fled to the forts, where gates were barred and the big guns readied for action. But no invasion came that year.

It is not known just how many Iroquois died at the Long Sault. The "heaps of bodies" described in some accounts is quite likely an exaggeration. But Pierre Radisson came upon the scene eight days after the battle, and he reported that there were signs of a ferocious struggle. "There was not a tree but was shot with buletts [sic]," he wrote. Radisson also noted that the Iroquois had left behind many of their canoes, which suggests they didn't have enough men to take them all away.

It has been suggested that the Iroquois abandoned their plan to attack New France that year because they were satisfied with killing Dollard and his men and plundering the stockade. But the belongings of a mere seventeen Frenchmen and the few Natives who had fought alongside them would not have gone far amongst several hundred warriors. It is far more likely that they withdrew because they had taken too many casualties, even if the number was not as high as some chroniclers put it.

The Native concept of warfare was entirely different from that of Europeans. Courage was admired, but the idea of sacrificing great numbers of men to achieve an objective would have been considered insane. After the carnage at the Long Sault, it simply would not have made sense to the Iroquois to attack larger, stronger posts, especially with all element of surprise lost.

Adam Dollard's detractors have said that he and his men went down in a blaze of glory because they had no other choice. They were surrounded and could do nothing *but* fight to the last man. Surrendering and throwing themselves upon the not-so-tender mercy of the foe was not an option.

But the fact remains that the seventeen Frenchmen left the comparative security of Montreal to venture into dangerous territory. That they were caught in a trap in no way diminishes their heroism. The Iroquois wars would continue for many years, but in 1660 the French settlements gained a respite because of the bloody clash at the Long Sault: Canada's Thermopylae.

The Battle for Newfoundland

Blood on the Rock

In the days when international disputes were settled by tall ships, broadsides, muskets and bayonets, the island of Newfoundland sat like a sentinel between the open Atlantic and the Gulf of St. Lawrence. The gulf was the gateway to the St. Lawrence River, which was the highway to the Great Lakes and the heart of the North American continent. Newfoundland was also the base for the fishing fleets that came every year to harvest the bounty of the Grand Banks. Fishermen from the British Isles, France, Spain, Portugal and other nations swarmed over the Banks to fill the holds of their ships with cod. For hungry Europe, the Grand Banks were a treasure as valuable as an Aztec gold mine.

Officially, the "New-founde-lande" was "discovered" in 1497 by John Cabot, who claimed the island for England. However, the Vikings had been there five hundred years before Cabot came along. Why the Scandinavian warriors left after a brief period of settlement is not known. They might have lost a battle with the Beothuk, the Native people of Newfoundland who were later exterminated by European guns and diseases. There is evidence, too, that between the time of the Viking settlement and the time of John Cabot's landing, Basque fishermen had been visiting the Grand Banks regularly, keeping the secret of the rich fishing grounds to themselves.

Fishing the Grand Banks meant much more than the hard work of hauling in cod with nets and jigging lines. The catch had to be taken ashore to be gutted, cleaned, salted and dried before it could be transported back to Europe. All that work called for a large labour force. Those people had to be housed and fed. At first settlement on Newfoundland was discouraged. Workers came and went with the fishing season. Fishermen would even burn settlements along the shore because they took up valuable space needed for drying fish. This, of course, led to clashes between fishermen and settlers. Eventually a law forbade settlement within nine-and-a-half kilometres (6 miles) of the coast.

John Cabot had claimed Newfoundland for England, but in those times just planting a flag on a piece of real estate usually wasn't enough. Claims had to be backed up with guns, and England couldn't guard the entire island against interlopers. So, while the English fishery centred around communities between St. John's and Ferryland on the east side of the Avalon Peninsula, the French built their own fortified station at Placentia on the other side of the peninsula. Soon the two were fighting over who would be masters of Newfoundland.

In 1628 the Marquis de la Rade, commanding three ships and four hundred men, went marauding along the Avalon coast, capturing ships and attacking St. John's and other communities. The English retaliated by seizing six French fishing boats and sending them to England as prizes. In 1665 during the Anglo–Dutch War, the famous Dutch admiral Michiel de Ruyter captured St. John's.

He later stated that if there had been six mounted guns protecting the harbour, he would not have tried to enter the port.

That very year Christopher Martin, vice-admiral of the Newfoundland convoy, erected a small but strong fort called the Castle on the south side of the Narrows of St. John's harbour. In 1673, with only thirty men, Martin drove off an attack by the Dutch pirate, Captain Jacob Everson, who led a fleet of four ships. The Castle and other defensive works the English added were successful again in the early summer of 1696, when a French fleet commanded by the Chevalier Nesmond tried to enter the harbour. However, St. John's defences were designed to protect the port from attack by sea. Nobody expected an attack by land.

On November 1, 1696, a column of four hundred men that included eighty Canadians and twenty-five Native warriors from Quebec set out from Placentia to march 112 kilometres (70 miles) across the Avalon Peninsula and take the settlement at Ferryland by surprise. The leader of this expedition was Pierre Le Moyne d'Iberville, a Canadian-born adventurer whose name already struck terror into English hearts. In a series of campaigns from 1686 to 1694, d'Iberville all but drove the English from James Bay and Hudson Bay, capturing their posts and sending their stocks of furs to France. He proved himself to be a brilliant commander, courageous and sometimes ruthless. In one assault on an English fort d'Iberville found himself all alone against seventeen Englishmen. He fought them off until his comrades came to his assistance. On his way to Newfoundland in 1696 d'Iberville also captured an English ship and Fort William Henry at the mouth of the Pemaquid River on the Atlantic coast.

D'Iberville easily captured Ferryland, the inhabitants all having fled to Bay Bulls. He confiscated all of the port's stock of dried cod, and then burned the place to the ground. He then joined forces with Jacques-Francois de Mombeton de Brouillon, the governor of Placentia, who had arrived with two warships and three hundred soldiers. Brouillon was a petty, bad-tempered bureaucrat who insisted on doing things his way, and stubbornly refused to listen to the advice of others. Though the two commanders did not get along, their combined strength was enough for them to wreak havoc on the isolated English fishing ports. They travelled north, looting and burning every English port in their path. Finally they reached St. John's, the fortified English capital.

Here, d'Iberville and de Brouillon quarrelled. D'Iberville wanted to attack the town of Carbonear and Carbonear Island in Conception Bay first. He reasoned that because Carbonear and the island were the most well defended places in Conception Bay, if they fell the rest of the Conception Bay communities would have to capitulate. Seizing the island would also deny uprooted Englishmen a place to which they could flee. With Conception Bay cleared of the English, d'Iberville argued, they could then turn their attention to St. John's. But de Brouillon insisted on attacking St. John's first. Because d'Iberville would need the warships to assault Carbonear Island, he had no choice but to go along with the mulish governor.

The English tried twice to stop the French advance on St. John's, but both times they suffered heavy losses and were forced to retreat into a primitive fort. The French plundered the town, and loaded the booty onto the ships. D'Iberville did not want to waste time and men attacking the fort, so he resorted to an act of cruelty to frighten the defenders into surrendering. Among the prisoners the French had taken was a man named William Drew. D'Iberville allowed one of his warriors to scalp the unfortunate Drew. Then he sent

Drew to the fort to show the other English his bloody skull and deliver the message that they would all suffer the same fate if they did not surrender immediately. The English gave up on November 30, on the condition that they would not be molested, and would be allowed to sail back to England. D'Iberville did not realize that the women in the fort had hidden valuables under their dresses.

D'Iberville wanted to move on right away to Carbonear, but de Brouillon decided he would rather spend the winter in St. John's. The commanders quarrelled again. Then, in a huff, de Brouillon left, taking his ships with him.

D'Iberville burned St. John's to the ground. Then he took the town of Harbour Main, where he seized three boats to use in the attack on Carbonear Island. There, on January 24, he found that the English had had time to prepare for him. About two hundred people from communities around Conception Bay had fled to the island. Abbé Baudion, a monk who was with d'Iberville, described what the Frenchmen saw when they reconnoitered the small isle:

"It is scarped with high cliffs, except one landing at the west point, a pistol shot from the boom made of sloops. On the isle are four cannon, six pounders, besides which, only two sloops at a time can land, and then only in calm, which is not frequent in the winter."

When d'Iberville tried to enter the island's harbour, he was driven back by cannon fire. He circled the island looking for a landing place, but could not find one. He then landed at Carbonear and sent a message to the people on the island, demanding their surrender. They refused. The following day d'Iberville sent a party of his men to capture the tiny community of Mosquito between

Carbonear and Harbour Grace. As the boat passed Carbonear Island, the English fired at it with cannons. The boat passed safely, but it was clear the island would be difficult to take.

On January 26 some prisoners told d'Iberville of two possible landing places on the island, The next day he sent scouting parties to investigate, but bad weather, rough seas and ice on the rocks prevented them from landing. On January 31 d'Iberville attacked again. The French were within pistol range and were ready to jump ashore when a sentry saw them and fired. Abbé Baudion recorded:

"They tried two landings at east and north points of the isle; a pistol-shot off, a sentinel called in a trembling voice: 'Que vive?' Montigny (one of d'Iberville's officers) was close enough to lay his hand on the rock...but in vain. The sentinel seeing that we withdrew, fired on us, without wounding anyone. The guard did not perceive us until we were already some distance off."

D'Iberville was frustrated by his failure to capture Carbonear Island. He seized a sloop full of Englishmen trying to reach the island, then he turned his attention to ransacking more communities on Conception Bay. One fishing port after another was captured and burned. In some places d'Iberville left men to keep watch over the dried fish and other goods he had seized. When he returned to Carbonear on February 10 he learned that four of his men had been captured by the English and were being held on the island. D'Iberville might have admired this bit of derring-do on the part of the English as the sort of thing he would have done, had he been in their place. But if so, he kept his admiration to himself, and instead sent his men off to continue the campaign of looting and burning.

D'Iberville made several more attempts to get the people on the island to surrender, but the English were defiant. Then he tried to get them to agree to a prisoner exchange. After two days of haggling the English agreed. On February 18 a boat rowed out with Montigny and a few soldiers, and the men the English had asked for, one of whom was the brother of Captain Nicholas Peddle, believed to be the man in command on the island. An English boat that came out to meet them, but none of the French prisoners were in it. Montigny angrily demanded to know why the English had not kept their end of the deal. The English said they first wanted to see if he had brought the men they'd asked for. They wanted Montigny to release their captain's brother to them right away, but the Frenchman would not. He said he would go with them to the island to get the French prisoners they were holding, but the English did not want to allow a party of armed Frenchmen on their shores, so the negotiation broke off.

Then the English captain and several of his men came out to speak to Montigny. The Frenchman was furious with them for doubting his word of honour and for not keeping their end of the bargain. At Montigny's scathing remarks, one Englishman started to draw his sword. Montigny drew his own sword, forced the English into his boat, and took them back to Carbonear.

D'Iberville sent some of his prisoners to the island with another order that his men be released. The English refused, and said they would fire on any French boat that approached. D'Iberville left forty of his men to keep watch on Carbonear Island, then went off to complete his campaign of destruction. When he returned he told the islanders that if they released his men, he would permit them to fish for the summer. Again they refused. The prisoners were finally released for a ransom. D'Iberville had destroyed thirty-six settlements, killed two hundred people, taken over seven hundred prisoners, and seized two hundred thousand quintals (nine million kilograms) of dried cod. Carbonear Island and remote Bonavista were the only places still in English hands. D'Iberville wanted to finish the job of completely driving the English from Newfoundland, but he received orders calling him to France. That summer an English fleet carrying two thousand soldiers arrived at St. John's. The commander convinced the disheartened English fishermen to return to their outports and rebuild.

Under the Treaty of Ryswick, signed in September of that year, France was obliged to return all the territory d'Iberville had captured. In 1705, however, the French violated the agreement. Daniel d'Auger de Subercase, the new governor at Placentia, led another expedition to drive the English from the island. Commanding 450 men, including one hundred Native warriors from Canada, he captured Petty Harbour and Bay Bulls. Then he moved on St. John's.

The English had improved St. John's defences and had built Fort William on a site overlooking the harbour, putting in a permanent garrison. At the time of de Subercase's attack, the fort was commanded by Lieutenant John Moody. The man at the head of the French force was the same Montigny who had been with d'Iberville. He approached St. John's overland undetected. On the night of January 21 he ordered his men to lie in the snow until a half hour before dawn, so as not to alert the English. The tactic worked, and the citizens of the town did not realize they were under attack until the French were upon them. But the French soldiers had suffered from the extreme cold, and took out their fury on the helpless civilians, murdering many men, women, and children in cold blood. The citizens who survived the massacre were locked up in the church. While the French soldiers indulged in an orgy of rape, pillage, and slaughter, they did not press their attack against Fort William, giving Lieutenant Moody time to prepare his defences.

Moody had but forty men in the fort, and another twelve in the Castle under Lieutenant Robert Latham. For two weeks de Subercase besieged these strongholds, but could not crack their defences. He sent Moody letters urging him to surrender, or he would not be able to restrain the Indians. Moody refused. The French governor sent a letter to Latham, telling him to come out of the Castle because Moody was about to surrender. Latham did not fall for it. On March 5 de Subercase put the town to the torch and left for Placentia with two hundred prisoners. Meanwhile, Montigny took raiding parties out to destroy small settlements. Montigny went to Carbonear and found that once again the people had fled to Carbonear Island. His men plundered the abandoned town, but all of Montigny's attempts to capture the island failed. He finally had to withdraw, knowing that English soldiers would soon arrive. Because of those two successful stands against the French, Carbonear Island has been nicknamed the Gibraltar of Newfoundland.

Five years later the French tried once again to expel the English from Newfoundland. They captured St. John's on New Year's Eve of 1707 after taking Fort William in a surprise attack that lasted about half an hour. Eight English soldiers were killed, and seven wounded. Three French soldiers died. The English commander, Major Thomas Lloyd, was wounded three times and was in his dressing gown when captured. The French were unable to hold the port, and left in April.

The Treaty of Utrecht, signed in 1713, required France to give up all claims to Newfoundland. French fishermen could fish the Grand Banks, and dry and salt their cod along the coast from Cape Bonavista to Pointe Riche. But France had to abandon Placentia. For the next fifty years there was relative peace in Newfoundland, though pirates like the infamous Bartholomew Roberts (Black Bart) would sometimes raid outports to pillage stores and recruit crewmen from the fishing fleets for their ships. Some Newfoundland fishermen were forced at the point of a cutlass to join pirate crews, but many willingly sailed off under the black flag.

Then came the Seven Years War which saw France lose most of her empire in North America to the British. The French decided that if they could capture St. John's, they would have an extra card to take to the negotiating table. On May 8, 1762, a fleet of four ships carrying eight hundred soldiers, including about 160 Irish mercenaries, sailed out of Brest and managed to evade the Royal Navy blockade. The French believed that by taking along the Irish, they could convince Newfoundland's Irish fishermen to join them. They had good reason for thinking that way. The Irish had never been happy under English rule, and had often rebelled. In Newfoundland society there was a wide gap between the wealthy merchant class, who were mostly English and Protestant, and the fishermen, of whom many were Irish and Catholic. The merchants paid low prices for the fish, and charged high for their goods. The fisherman was almost always in debt to the merchant, on whom he depended for supplies and equipment.

In command of the French fleet was Charles-Henri-Louis d'Arsac de Ternay, who had been admitted to the Knights of Malta before he was fifteen and became captain of a ship before he was thirty. His orders were to capture St. John's and "to cause as much harm as possible to the English...(and to advance) if possible as far as Île Royale (Cape Breton Island) to assault the English there." The commander of the land forces was an aristocrat, Colonel Joseph-Louis-Bernard de Cleron d'Haussonville. The expedition was arranged in absolute secrecy. Only de Ternay knew where they were going.

On June 23 the French ships dropped anchor off Bay Bulls, twenty-nine kilometres (18 miles) south of St. John's. They flew the British flag to deceive those on shore. The next day d'Haussonville landed with his infantry unopposed and set off for St. John's.

Overlooking the city of St. John's is the 152-metre (500 feet) high Signal Hill. From there it was possible to use lights or fires to signal to ships far out to sea. The women of St. John's would go there to watch for their menfolk coming home with the fishing fleets. However, despite the geographic advantages, no serious attempts had been made to establish permanent fortifications there. St. John's was still protected by Fort William, which had fallen into disrepair and been rebuilt several times.

Fort William at that time was garrisoned by only fifty men under Major Walter Ross. One warship, the frigate H.M.S. *Gramont,* was in harbour. When that ship's skipper, Captain Patrick Mouat, learned of the approaching French force, he sent out a longboat with a message for the British base at Halifax. Then he scuttled the *Gramont* and took his crew to join Major Ross's tiny force in Fort William. When d'Haussonville arrived at St. John's on June 27 and demanded immediate surrender, Ross did so, rather than have his men massacred. De Ternay sailed his ships into St. John's.

The French re-floated the scuttled warship and added it to their fleet. Then they set about destroying all British installations, including the fisheries. Every ship that was in the harbour, or that entered the harbour during their occupation, was sunk, as well as those in outlying ports; in all some 460 vessels of various sizes. The cost of the damage amounted to over a million pounds, an incredible sum at that time. The local Irish did not join the invading force, but evidently many of them did pounce on the opportunity to rob the homes and stores of the English merchants.

De Ternay thought the British would wait until spring of the following year to try to re-take St. John's, so he and his men established themselves in the city. Then they went after that nuisance of two earlier campaigns, Carbonear Island. The British had fortified the island in 1745 and manned it with a garrison of about fifty men. But by 1762 the defences had fallen into disrepair and only a skeleton crew of a few elderly men were on hand as caretakers. When d'Haussonville showed up with his infantry, the Gibraltar of Newfoundland was taken without even a fight.

By August Sir Jeffrey Amherst, the conqueror of Louisbourg and Commander-in-Chief of all British forces in North America, had received news of the St. John's situation at his headquarters in New York City. For an officer who had a reputation for acting slowly and cautiously, he was swift to take action against the French. He wasn't going to wait until spring. He wanted de Ternay thrown out of St. John's before the snows came.

Amherst appointed his brother, Lieutenant-Colonel William Amherst as commander of 1,500 British troops and colonial auxiliaries from the garrisons of New York, Halifax and Louisbourg. They were to assemble at Louisbourg and board a fleet of ships commanded by Rear Admiral Lord Alexander Colville for transport to Newfoundland. By the last week of August Royal Navy squadrons sent out by Colville had blockaded St. John's harbour and were patrolling the Avalon Peninsula coast.

On September 13 Colonel Amherst's troops landed at Torbay, sixteen kilometres (10 miles) north of St. John's. The French marched out to oppose them, but after a sharp clash they retreated into the fort, the English having only four men wounded.

D'Haussonville had placed a company of soldiers and a mortar on Signal Hill. Those troops were well dug in, but the English were able to move in close under a cover of fog. They overran the French position, but lost about thirty men in the battle. Then the British put guns on Gibbet Hill, which gave them a perfect place from which to fire into the fort or the French fleet sitting in the harbour.

De Ternay, d'Haussonville and their officers held a council of war. De Ternay wanted to put all of the soldiers on the ships and get out immediately. D'Haussonville and the other officers insisted on staying and fighting. They were expecting reinforcements. If the situation became too desperate, they could transport the infantry to the ships in longboats under the cover of naval guns.

De Ternay destroyed the boom he had placed across the harbour entrance, and spiked all guns covering the harbour. Then he prepared his ships to get underway at a moment's notice. The night of September 15 a thick fog rolled in, forcing the British fleet to put out to open sea. De Ternay took advantage of the pea souper to slip out of harbour and make his escape. But he left d'Haussonville and the infantry behind.

With British guns bearing right down on him, d'Haussonville was in a difficult spot. He planned to blow up the fortifications and retreat, but to where is unknown. Perhaps he would have tried

25

making a dash overland to some port where he might seize a ship. Then he received a letter from William Amherst.

> "I know the miserable state your garrison is left in and I am fully aware of your design of blowing up the fort on quitting it; but have a care, as I have taken measures to effectually cut off your retreat, and so sure as a match is put to the train, every man of the garrison shall be put to the sword. I must have immediate possession of the fort in the state it now is, or expect the consequences. I give you half an hour to think about it. I have the honour to be, Sir, your most obedient and humble servant."

D'Haussonville replied that he would fight until the fort was entirely destroyed and he had no more gunpowder. But such a show of bravado was in keeping with the military code of honour. After a short bombardment, he surrendered the fort in relatively good condition on September 18.

The British were annoyed that de Ternay had made a clean get-away, and considered his flight shameful. But they somewhat made up for the disappointment with the capture of two French ships that were bringing reinforcements for d'Haussonville. The fight that took place on Signal Hill was the last battle of the Seven Years War to be fought in North America.

De Ternay did not have an easy time reaching France. He was chased several times by Royal Navy vessels, and once had to hide in a Spanish port to avoid British patrols. By the time he sailed into Brest he had also captured an English privateer. When d'Haussonville was finally paroled back to France, he lodged an official complaint about de Ternay's sudden departure from St.

John's. However, no disciplinary action was taken against de Ternay, because he had saved his fleet, which almost certainly would have been destroyed had it remained in harbour much longer. De Ternay eventually rose to the rank of rear admiral, and saw action in the Revolutionary War when France entered the conflict as an American ally.

The British were slow to grasp the significance of installing guns on Signal Hill, even though the French guns up there could have caused them problems if d'Haussonville had decided to fight to the end. Not until the 1790s was Signal Hill extensively fortified. The guns the British placed there certainly discouraged a French naval attack on St. John's in 1796. By their very presence, the guns on Signal Hill ended the spilling of French and English blood on Newfoundland.

The First Battle
of Louisbourg
The Gibraltar of New France

I t was said that when King Louis XV of France saw the accounts for the construction of the fortress of Louisbourg on Île Royale (Cape Breton Island), he looked out a window of his palace at Versailles, expecting to see the walls of the fortress rising above the western horizon. Louisbourg was indeed costly. In the twenty years required to build it, the French royal treasury spent thirty million *livres,* (about fifty million dollars), an astronomical sum in that day. But Louisbourg was meant to be impregnable. At the end of The War of the Spanish Succession (also called Queen Anne's War), France had been obliged to agree to the terms of the Treaty of Utrecht, signed in 1713, that saw her lose some of her Acadian colonies to the British, and give up all claims to Newfoundland and Hudson Bay. France had, however, retained Île Royale, Île St Jean, and fishing rights on the Grand Banks. Louisbourg, with its excellent harbour, was to be the main North American port for the French fishing fleet, as well as the merchant fleet and the French navy. It would stand as a sentinel over the entrance to the Gulf of the St. Lawrence, the gateway to the St. Lawrence River and the colony of Quebec. Just as the British guns on a massive rock controlled the Straits of Gibraltar, so would the guns of Louisbourg control the gateway to Quebec.

To the other nations of Europe, especially France's traditional foe, England, Louisbourg was a thing of awe. It was as imposing as the mighty fortress at Dunkirk, that "pistol aimed at England's head," which the French had been required to dismantle under the terms of the treaty. Louisbourg's walls were three metres (10 feet) thick, and rose nine metres (30 feet) above a deep ditch. The walls had emplacements for 148 cannon, including forty-two pounders that were the most powerful artillery of the day and could smash wooden battleships to rags and splinters.

On three sides of Louisbourg the ocean itself provided a moat. A foaming surf pounded relentlessly against jagged rocks and sheer cliffs. The sea approach to Louisbourg was a maze of deadly shoals and reefs, with only one safe channel through to the harbour. Gun emplacements within the harbour could make that channel a gauntlet for any attacker. The redoubt on Battery Island alone had thirty guns, and at the northeast arm of the harbour the Royal Battery had twenty-eight big guns. Added to them would be the guns of French warships in the harbour—enough combined fire-power to blow an enemy fleet out of the water before it even came within range of the fortress' main artillery. From Louisbourg's twenty-metre- (66 foot) high lighthouse, enemy ships could be seen in plenty of time for the garrison to prepare for battle. Louisbourg had about nine hundred soldiers to man the ramparts, of whom six hundred were well-paid Swiss mercenaries.

The ground on the landward side of Louisbourg was believed to be too marshy to allow an enemy to drag heavy artillery within range of the fortress. Moreover, France's Native allies, the Micmacs, controlled the forests. The warriors were always ready to take English scalps, for which the governor at Louisbourg paid a bounty of one *livre* each. A little over three kilometres (about 2 miles) south of Louisbourg was Gabarus Bay, the only place on the rocky coastline where an enemy might come ashore through the surf. The French had gun emplacements there, to prevent such a landing.

Louisbourg's star-shaped stronghold was constructed from designs made by the Marquis de Vauban, the Marshal of France and the greatest architect of forts in his time. Its blockhouses and bastions were believed to be so strong that if an enemy army did actually make it to shore, the foe could easily be destroyed. Louisbourg's cannon and muskets would mow the attackers down as they stood helplessly before those massive battlements. Within the walls tunnels protected the troops from falling shells and rock splinters caused by artillery fire striking masonry. The largest building inside the walls was the Chateau St. Louis—the Governor's Palace. It stood three storeys high, and in the basement had barracks for the garrison. The Chateau had its own moat and drawbridge, and was actually a fort within a fort.

The fact that Louisbourg was located on a remote coast of an island that was still mostly wilderness was also a deterrent against attack. An enemy would have to travel a long way to get there, and would have to bring a lot of supplies. Even if the enemy established a foothold beneath those walls, there would be little for besieging troops to forage. From all appearances, Louisbourg was indestructible. As one proud Frenchman commented, "Louisbourg will stand forever."

But for all that, Louisbourg was a hollow threat. It was a constant drain on the French treasury. The only profitable enterprise was the local fishery, and the income from that did not nearly offset the costs of keeping the fortress manned, maintained and supplied. The ground in the fort's vicinity was rocky and poor farmland, so almost all food had to be shipped from France, or brought over from Louisbourg's "garden," Île St. Jean. Graft and corruption were rife. Even during construction, contractors cut corners and pocketed money. The mortar that held the stone walls together was of poor quality, being made with sea-sand. Supplies intended for the garrison were pilfered by unscrupulous quartermasters and sold to English merchants in Boston, or even sold to the soldiers at inflated prices. The merchants who established businesses in the town within the walls made small fortunes, selling their wares at many times what the merchandise cost in France.

The governors and officers assigned to Louisbourg hated the place (as did their wives). They used any and every excuse to go back to France. Governors might be absent for up to two years of their time in office. The very isolation that discouraged enemy attack also played against Louisbourg. For the French ladies and gentlemen of the community's upper class, Louisbourg was in the middle of nowhere. It was as far removed from society as a place could be. Boredom was the hallmark of duty in Louisbourg.

If *ennui* was a curse for the aristocratic officer class, it was more than doubly so for the lowly soldiers. Aside from monotonous guard duty, keeping uniforms spit-and-polish clean and muskets in good order, and working on the fortifications, there was little for the soldiers to do. Off-duty soldiers would visit the town's brothels (from which the officers took a share of the profits). But the only other distraction was drink. Drunkenness among the troops was a constant problem at Louisbourg. There were times when not even that diversion was available. Pay ships from France were often late and sometimes did not arrive at all, and soldiers could go many months without being paid. No money meant no over-priced wine or brandy in the taverns. A soldier who was really broke might not even be able to afford the cheap, locally produced *sapinette* (spruce beer). French soldiers were known to sell bits and pieces of their equipment in order to get money for drink. These items disappeared into a black market that eventually saw them reappear in New England. It was hardly surprising that on two occasions the garrison at Louisbourg mutinied.

No open hostility existed between the French soldiers and the better paid Swiss mercenaries, but there was not much in the way of camaraderie, either. Most of these Swiss spoke German, so they tended to keep their own company. They had their own canteen and washhouse, and in the midst of an otherwise all-Catholic town, conducted their own Protestant Sunday services.

The weather also contributed to chronic low morale in the fortress. The short summer was tolerable, once the hellish black-fly season passed. But spring and autumn were cold and wet, with lengthy stretches of dreary fog. Winter was long and bitter, with frequent blizzards howling in from the grey Atlantic. Officers' quarters could be comfortable enough, but heating the big, drafty barracks where the common soldiers slept was difficult. The men slept two or three to a bed on mattresses stuffed with straw (when it was available), with not much more than the heat of each oth-ers' bodies for warmth. Of course, a soldier on guard duty outside simply had to endure the biting cold.

In March 1744 the War of the Austrian Succession (also called King George's War) broke out. Hitherto the French officers and men stationed in Louisbourg had seen no action, although the fortress had been a refuge for Native warriors who attacked English settle-ments at Canso, and even boarded English ships, killing crewmen or carrying them off into captivity. When the English complained about these raids, the governor in Louisbourg said he had nothing to do with them, that the Natives were independent people, quite beyond his control. Now in May the Frenchmen embarked on a raid of their own. Twenty-eight officers and 335 soldiers sailed out of Louisbourg's harbour in the *Caribou* and surprised the British garrison of the small fort at Canso, where the people were not yet aware of a state of war. The *Caribou* had only to open her gun ports and run out the big guns to intimidate the British into surrendering.

The French took the soldiers and civilians of Canso aboard ship as prisoners. Then they burned the entire community to the ground. Not even the poor hovels of the fishermen were spared. The town's stock of salted cod was loaded aboard the *Caribou* for transport back to Louisbourg.

The English prisoners, whose number included several New Englanders, were eventually sent back to Boston on trading ships, but while they were in Louisbourg they took careful note of the conditions there. They even drew charts of the fortifications. Louisbourg, they reported, was not the impregnable citadel everyone believed it to be. They had seen places where, because of poor construction, the walls were already crumbling. They had quickly become aware of discontent among the garrison, and had even witnessed a mutiny that occurred when Governor Louis de Prévost, Sieur du Quesnel de Chagny Pourteville and his officers attempted to sell the fish confiscated at Canso to the hungry soldiers at outrageous prices. They had realized, too, that the garrison at Louisbourg was well under-strength. These men spread the word that Louisbourg could be taken.

Not everyone in New England was so sure about that. Benjamin Franklin wrote to his brother John:

Fortified towns are hard nuts to crack and your teeth are not
accustomed to it. Taking strong places is a particular trade,
which you have taken up without serving an apprenticeship
to it. Armies and veterans need skilful [sic] engineers to
direct them in their attack. Have you any?

The New Englanders did not have any skilled military engineers. But they did have two very determined, ambitious and
resourceful leaders in Massachusetts: Governor William Shirley,
and a businessman and politician named William Pepperrell.
There was no money in the colonial treasury to mount an expedition against Louisbourg, but by issuing bills of credit, Shirley
managed to raise fifty thousand pounds for the venture. He also
put out a call to arms for volunteers. Men came not only from
Massachusetts, but also from New Hampshire, Rhode Island, New
York, New Jersey, Connecticut and Pennsylvania. They were
eager to get revenge for the Indian attacks they knew to have been
backed by Louisbourg, and for the depredations by privateers who
took shelter under Louisbourg's guns. Added incentives for joining the adventure were the bumper of rum given to every man who
signed up, and the possibility of loot at the end of the voyage.

Pepperrell was a wealthy, popular man, born in what is now the
state of Maine, who had made a fortune in shipbuilding and the
fisheries. Historian Francis Parkman said of Pepperrell that his
best qualities were good will and good sense. Another historian,
William Wood, wrote:

There was no military leader in the whole of New England.
So the next most suitable man was the civilian who best
combined the necessary qualities of good sense, sound

knowledge of men and affairs, firmness, diplomacy and popularity. Pepperrell...answered every reasonable test.

Pepperrell and Shirley raised an army of 4,270 men. Few of them had any military experience beyond brawling or—in some instances—fighting Indians in the forest. One observer described them as, "Fishermen in baggy blues and oils, farmers in homespun, backwoodsmen in skins and Indians in full war dress—a motley host in motley array." The only uniforms were worn by officers who could afford them. Every man had to provide his own gun, shot and powder. Had the French in Louisbourg been aware of the ragtag army that was preparing to assail their mighty fortress, they might well have laughed.

While Shirley was recruiting his men, he asked Commodore Sir Peter Warren of the Royal Navy to support the expedition. Warren replied that he could not do so without the permission of the Admiralty in London. Shirley sent a letter to England requesting that permission. In the meantime, he and Pepperrell assembled a fleet of their own. Fishing boats and trading vessels were transformed into "warships" by being equipped with light cannon. The New Englanders' heaviest artillery consisted of eight twenty-two-pounders; pop-guns compared to the monsters at Louisbourg. Only two dozen men had any knowledge of gunnery, and they had to train others in a very short period of time. However, their confidence was such that they took along cannonballs that were too large for their own guns, because they expected to use them when they captured some of the big French guns and turned them on their former owners.

On April 4, 1745, a flotilla of fifty-one vessels set sail for Île Royale. The eleven-day voyage was a nightmare of seasickness for those men who were not experienced sailors. If a single French man o' war had intercepted the fleet, she probably could have sunk every ship. But an unbelievable run of good fortune was to smile upon this most unlikely of military adventures, beginning with the absence of any French vessels in the waters between Boston and what is now called Nova Scotia.

Stormy weather forced the fleet ashore at Canso on April 15, and kept them there for the next few weeks. What at first seemed to be a setback was in fact providential. First, it gave Pepperrell time to drill his men and transform them from a mob into something that resembled an army. More importantly, on May 4 Commodore Warren arrived in his sixty-gun flagship, H.M.S. *Superbe*. With him were the frigates H.M.S. *Eltham*, H.M.S. *Launceston*, H.M.S. *Mermaid*, and several smaller vessels. Warren had received instructions from the Admiralty to give Pepperrell every possible assistance. His arrival greatly cheered the amateur soldiers from New England. The British warships could blockade Louisbourg's harbour, keeping French warships away from their makeshift fleet. Moreover, the ships' big guns, manned by professional gunners, could be brought to bear on the fortress.

Warren sailed for Louisbourg and positioned his formidable fleet outside the harbour, effectively bottling it up. He sent word to Pepperrell that Gabarus Bay was free of ice. Pepperrell's men went back aboard their ships, and were off Louisbourg on May 11.

Commanding at Louisbourg now, following the death of Quesnel, was Governor Louis Dupont, Sieur de Chambon. He was inept as both an administrator and a general. He believed his harbour batteries would keep the English ships at bay, and he had nothing but contempt for Pepperrell's floating militia. Chambon had fewer than six hundred regular soldiers and about 1,200 militia, many of the latter being teenaged boys. Even so, such was his lack of concern that the night before the attack he held a ball in the Governor's Palace.

At Gabarus the French had a mere 120 men, commanded by the governor's son, Mesillac de Chambon. This was the spot Pepperrell had chosen for his landing. Pepperrell executed a feint that threw the small band of defenders off balance, and then stormed ashore with his men and secured a beachhead. Young Chambon regrouped his command and tried to drive the New Englanders back. After seventeen of his soldiers were killed, he retreated into Louisbourg.

Now the New Englanders swarmed ashore, though not without difficulty in the pounding surf. Some of the whaleboats transporting men and stores were wrecked, and men drowned or were pounded to death on the rocks. Nonetheless, by nightfall two thousand men were put ashore, along with thirty-four cannon. They had no draught animals, so by sheer manpower they dragged the heavy guns up the beach and over the rocks until they were in position on that marshy ground the French thought could not support artillery. The Frenchmen's Native allies were nowhere to be seen.

Meanwhile, Commodore Warren's ships were bombarding Battery Island. The officer in command there, Captain Louis d'Aillebout, had 225 men to man his guns and reply to the British shelling. He would hold his position for most of the duration of the siege. When the New Englanders tried to take the fortification by storm, they were beaten back with 189 casualties.

Early in the confrontation, Governor Chambon became concerned that the Royal Battery might be too easily overrun. He ordered the officer in command there to spike the guns and withdraw into Louisbourg. That would prove to be a costly mistake. A group of New Englanders led by Colonel William Vaughan, while on a mission to destroy some storehouses, found the abandoned gun emplacements. The French had not done a very thorough job of spiking the cannon, and the besiegers soon had them working again. Now they had guns they could use to fire the oversized ammunition they had brought along. One day after the guns had been spiked, they were turned on Louisbourg. One resident of the town later recalled, "The enemy saluted us with our own cannon, and made a terrific fire, smashing everything within range." According to one report, the first shot killed fourteen people.

Now Louisbourg was being bombarded from all sides, including the sea. Cannonballs hammered the walls and crashed down on the buildings within. Hardly a building was undamaged. Explosive shells with fuses in them landed in the streets and sent lethal shards of shrapnel in all directions. The passageways filled with rubble that work crews cleared away at night, only to have more debris blasted down the following day. Still, the French soldiers put on a brave show, shouting taunts at the New Englanders and telling them that French women could hold Louisbourg against such an army.

After a month of siege, Louisbourg was a battered shambles, but even though the walls had been breached in several places, it could not have been taken by storm without the attacker suffering many casualties. Over nine thousand cannonballs and six hundred exploding shells had been fired at the stronghold, and the besiegers were running low on ammunition. The New Englanders were also running out of patience. They were not trained, disciplined soldiers, and they had expected the fortress to fall in a matter of days. Now they were weary of digging trenches and doing the other work that accompanied siege warfare. Their clothes were getting ragged and some were barefoot. Many had fallen ill. They had suffered casualties, not only from the French guns, but also from their own inexperience with artillery. The gunners had a habit of stuffing too much gunpowder into the cannon. Several times big guns exploded, causing carnage among the gun crews.

Commodore Warren was growing impatient, too. The French guns on Battery Island continued to give his fleet trouble, and it seemed no amount of bombardment could silence them. Then the French warship *Vigilant,* mounting sixty-four guns, hove into view. She was carrying reinforcements and fresh munitions for beleaguered Louisbourg. Warren was not about to let the *Vigilant* blast her way through his blockade, which she might well do under covering fire from the fortress. At least one small French ship had already made a successful run. Using the *Mermaid* as bait, Warren lured the *Vigilant* right into the guns of the rest of his squadron and then raked her with broadsides. With sixty of his men dead or wounded and his foremast shot away, the French captain surrendered. In the *Vigilant's* hold the British found a thousand barrels of gunpowder, twenty cannon and four month's supply of food for Louisbourg's garrison. The loss of the *Vigilant* was a crippling blow to the defenders of Louisbourg. Another disaster soon followed. A relief party of 1,300 Frenchmen and Native allies from Quebec tried to reach Louisbourg overland, but it was stopped at the Strait of Canso.

By June 15 Captain d'Aillebout was still holding fast on Battery Island, making it impossible for the British ships to enter the harbour. Then the New Englanders hauled some artillery to a headland from which the fortification could be shelled more effectively. One shot hit d'Aillebout's powder magazine. The captain was finally forced to abandon his post and retreat into Louisbourg. Now the way was open for the British fleet, reinforced by newly arrived ships, to sail into the harbour and blast the walls of Louisbourg from close range. Intendant Francois Bigot of Louisbourg later wrote, "We could have borne all this, but the scarcity of powder, the loss of the *Vigilant,* the presence of the squadron, and the absence of any news from Marin (leader of the relief column from Quebec) spread terror among troops and inhabitants. The townsfolk averred they did not want to be put to the sword and we were not strong enough to resist a general assault."

Pepperrell and Warren were making preparations for a combined assault by land and sea. Before that attack was launched, Warren sent Chambon a letter suggesting it would be in the French commander's best interests to surrender now to the Royal Navy, rather than risk having the ungentlemanly colonials rampaging through the town. Chambon agreed to surrender on the condition that private property would be respected. Warren and Pepperrell both accepted that provision, and Chambon formally surrendered Louisbourg on June 18. To ensure there would be no looting or molestation of the defeated French, Warren arranged to have a company of Royal Marines enter the city first. This angered many of the New Englanders who had joined the expedition in expectation of plunder. Some also felt that Warren was stealing Pepperrell's glory. With their hopes of carrying off booty dashed, now they wanted only to go home. En route to Boston, a party of them took out their frustration on the Acadian settlement of Port-La-Joye (now Charlottetown, Prince Edward Island) which they pillaged and destroyed.

Transportation back to France was arranged for the people of Louisbourg. In his report Chambon claimed to have had fifty men killed and ninety-five wounded. The New Englanders admitted to

130 dead and 300 wounded. The numbers in both claims are suspect. Far from having his thunder stolen by Commodore Warren, Pepperrell was awarded a baronetcy. He was the first American-born British subject to be so honoured.

Warren, who would be promoted to rear admiral, was not finished at Louisbourg. He had the French flag run up over the fortress and Battery Island, and left the approaches to the harbour unguarded. As he expected, one French ship after another sailed into the trap, where they were seized under the guns of the British warships. One had in its cargo a number of gold and silver bars, which the commodore happily confiscated. The loot meant a personal fortune for him, and 850 guineas in prize money for every sailor; more than the average Jack Tar could earn in a lifetime of sailing for the king.

News of the fall of Louisbourg hit the French government like a cannon shot. How could a fortress that had been built at such enormous cost have fallen in a matter of weeks? There were two abortive military expeditions to recover the fortress for the French, but it would be at the negotiating table that Britain agreed to give Louisbourg back to France in 1748—something that the people of New England considered an act of betrayal. In addition to developing a mistrust of English policies that would one day grow into rebellion, the colonists had learned something else: that when they cooperated they could successfully fight professional European soldiers. But before the significance of that fact became apparent, war would again descend upon Île Royale and the fortress of Louisbourg.

The Second Battle
of Louisbourg
Pineapples and Champagne

Though the supposedly impregnable fortress of Louisbourg had fallen fairly easily in 1745, the French government still felt it was vital to the defense of Canada. King Louis XV and his ministers believed the fault lay with the defenders, not with the fortress itself. At the Treaty of Aix-La-Chapelle in 1748, they got it back, to the disgust of the leaders in Britain's American colonies. To keep Louisbourg in check, should war between France and Britain erupt again, the British began work on a fortress of their own at Halifax, Nova Scotia.

Governor Augustine de Boschenry de Drucour, a very capable officer, took over the administration of Louisbourg in 1754. Few people doubted that France and Britain would be at each other's throats before long, and he was determined that when the inevitable attack came, Louisbourg would be unconquerable. For as long as Louisbourg remained in French hands, no British fleet could enter the St. Lawrence River to attack Quebec. Drucour beefed Louisbourg's garrison up to more than three thousand regulars, including a battalion of the French foreign legion. He had another four thousand militiamen and sailors. He added more artillery, bringing the number of big guns up to 219, plus seventeen mortars. To protect Battery Island, Drucour installed artillery on the headland from which the New Englanders had bombarded it in 1745. Gabarus Bay, so feebly guarded when Pepperrell had landed there, was now protected by well-manned trenches and gun emplacements. At any given time, Louisbourg's harbour was occupied by several French warships that bristled with guns. Louisbourg's storehouses were packed with enough food, wine and ammunition to last a year.

The Seven Years War (called the French and Indian War in the United States) began in 1756. Louisbourg was a top priority in the British strategy, but the generals prepared and planned carefully before launching their assault. In February of 1758 a fleet of two hundred ships armed with 1,842 guns sailed from England. Aboard were twenty-five thousand men, land artillery that included the biggest brass and iron guns of the time and a pair of eight-inch howitzers—weapons that could reduce towns to piles of sticks and stones. Commanding the naval forces was Admiral Edward "Old Dreadnought" Boscawen. Major General Jeffrey Amherst, a personal friend of the admiral, commanded the land forces. One of Amherst's senior officers was Brigadier General James Wolfe. Only thirty-one years old, the fast-rising, ambitious Wolfe had earned the envy of some of his fellow officers. One went so far as to suggest to King George II that Wolfe was mad. The king allegedly responded, "Mad, is he? Then I only hope he'll bite some of my other generals."

The British armada first went to Halifax, where troops from the thirteen colonies were added to Amherst's army. To get the men into shape after the long voyage, the officers drilled them and had soldiers and sailors practice amphibious landing operations. Meanwhile, another British fleet commanded by Admiral Charles Hardy blockaded the sea lanes to prevent supplies and reinforcements from reaching Louisbourg. The British put an embargo on all their ports from Nova Scotia to South Carolina to ensure that no word of their operations in Halifax reached the French on Île Royale. By May 29 the fleet was ready to sail again. As dawn broke on the morning of June 2, French sentinels on Louisbourg's ramparts looked in awe at the armed might of the Royal Navy poised outside the harbour.

A heavy sea was running, so several days passed before the British could risk sending men ashore in the whaleboats. Thus, they lost the element of surprise and the French had time to prepare defences. Amherst and his generals went out in a whaleboat to do reconnaissance. They decided that the beach at Gabarus was too well-defended, but thought a landing might be possible at a niche in the rocks called Kennington Cove.

At two o'clock on the morning of June 8, with the sea somewhat calmer, a regiment of light infantry commanded by James Wolfe piled into whaleboats and made for shore. Though naval guns gave them covering fire, they soon had the attention of the French gunners on shore. Men in Wolfe's boat later commented on the incredible calm the young general displayed under enemy fire. He didn't even flinch when the boat's flagstaff was shot off.

As the English boats approached the rocks along the shore, the French ceased firing. They evidently thought the boats would be smashed to pieces, and were content to just watch. But a pair of young officers in one of the boats spotted a tiny gap in the rocks and ordered their oarsmen to row for it. The boat shot through the narrow opening, and the first redcoat soldiers splashed ashore and immediately took cover in the woods. Wolfe's boat followed. Then another, and another. Only one boat was smashed on the rocks. All of the men in it drowned.

Now the French were alarmed to find British soldiers on their left flank. The French did not know that the gunpowder those men carried had been soaked during the landing and was useless. General Wolfe, carrying only his cane, led his men in a daring bayonet charge. The French soldiers panicked and retreated into Louisbourg, leaving behind seventeen cannon, fourteen large swivel guns and two mortars. Seventy French soldiers were taken prisoner. The French had lost their best opportunity to send the British packing.

The British now had a foothold. Wolfe wanted to attack Louisbourg and force a speedy capitulation. He knew that Drucour would try to hold up the British as long as possible, so that winter would set in before they could move on Quebec. Wolfe felt there was no reason they couldn't capture Louisbourg *and* Quebec that year. But General Amherst preferred to move slowly and cautiously. The weather, as far as Wolfe was concerned, was no help. On the very day of the landing an unseasonal snowstorm blew in. It was followed by more days of gales and fog. All of this made the landing of equipment, supplies and more soldiers difficult. It also made the ground a spongy morass, so the British had to build roads to support their siege guns.

Wolfe soon had Louisbourg encircled on the landward side with 1,200 men. He ordered guns moved into position and hoped, with support from the navy, to quickly bombard Louisbourg into submission. But things did not at first go well. Guns became stuck in the mud. Soldiers who had smuggled rum ashore from the ships were found to be drunk on duty. Then the British came under heavy fire from French warships in the harbour and the guns on Battery Island. Before the British landed, Drucour had demolished the Royal Battery so it would not fall into enemy hands as it had in 1745. But he knew that in that earlier siege Battery Island had been a major thorn in the side of the attackers, and he intended it should be so again. This time, however, the British guns subjected Battery Island to a brutal pounding and on June 25, knocked it permanently out of action.

Now the way was clear for the Royal Navy to sail right into Louisbourg's harbour. But the British were too slow. Before they could move in, the French frigate *Arethuse* slipped out of harbour, ran the British blockade, and escaped. Another vessel, the *Echo,* tried to follow, but was captured. The governor's wife, Madame Drucour, and several other ladies were found on board. The British officers showed them every courtesy and had them escorted back to Louisbourg. Meanwhile, the French filled four ships with stones and scuttled them at the harbour entrance. The rest of their ships would now be unable to escape, but the British, they hoped, couldn't get in.

Amherst had his men dig trenches and emplacements for his guns. The work went slowly because the carpenters brought along for this labour fell ill with smallpox. Even so, each night the British guns were moved a little closer to Louisbourg's walls. Wolfe, it seemed, was everywhere, overseeing the positioning of guns and instructing the crews on how to improve their accuracy and firepower. Sometimes French soldiers made sorties to disrupt the British. Governor Drucour personally led one that succeeded in killing several British soldiers. In another of their raids they killed an officer and took two officers and thirty soldiers prisoner. To discourage such actions, and prevent French partisans in the woods and their Native allies from doing much damage, Wolfe led light infantrymen in forays to trouble spots. In one engagement he and his men battled four hundred French troops for almost four hours before the Frenchmen withdrew to the fortress.

Wolfe was, in fact, becoming something of a legend within the walls of Louisbourg. An inhabitant of the town wrote:

"Some people of the garrison express their surprise... (at) the suddenness of Brigadier Wolfe's motions from one Place to another, & their Sentiments of the Effect of his Operations. (They) used to say—There is no Certainty where to find him—but wherever he goes, he carries with him a mortar in one pocket, & a 24 pounder in the other."

Wolfe was rather pleased when one of his officers compared his tactics to those described in the writings of Xenophon, the ancient Athenian soldier who led a Greek army through hostile Persian territory against almost impossible odds. Wolfe replied, "You are right. I had it thence, but our friends (the French) are astonished at what I have shown them, because they have read nothing."

Meanwhile, the commanders of the two armies did not forget that they were officers and gentlemen. General Amherst sent Madame Drucour a basket of pineapples. Governor Drucour responded to this act of gallantry by sending some butter and champagne to Amherst, and a box of sweetmeats to Wolfe.

The British had been bombarding the town, but on Amherst's orders had tried to restrict the shelling to military installations. He did not want civilian quarters targeted. Even so, many shells fell on civilian homes, and on July 21 a cannon shot knocked the steeple off the church, depriving the defenders of an important observation post. Then a shell fired at the French ships still in the harbour struck the magazine of the man o' war *Celebre*. The gunpowder exploded, setting the ship ablaze. Sailors bravely tried to fight the fire, but it was useless. They dove overboard and swam to safety. The flames spread to two more ships, and in the morning nothing was left of them but charred hulks.

Now only two French ships remained in the harbour, the *Prudent* and the *Bienfaisant.*

Under cover of darkness fifty small boats full of British soldiers sneaked into the harbour. Some of the men occupied Battery Island. Others went for the French ships. The *Prudent* was set ablaze. On the *Beinfaisant* the soldiers took the crew prisoner and towed the ship beyond the reach of the fort's guns. They discovered, too, that the ships sunk at the harbour's entrance did not effectively block it.

Inside the fortress, morale was very low. Madame Drucour tried to set an example by personally firing three cannon a day in the name of her king. The admiring people of Louisbourg called her *La Bombardiere*. But her show of defiance was not enough. Men were deserting every day. They gave themselves up to the British and told them how badly the situation within the walls had deteriorated. Drucour had sixteen men caught trying to desert hanged. The barracks and the inner citadel had burned. Several large breaches had been blasted in the walls. The citizens were practically on their knees to the governor, begging him to capitulate. But Drucour still wanted to buy as much time for Quebec as he possibly could.

The British gun emplacements were now as close as 183 metres (600 feet) to the walls and gates of the fortress. That was near enough for the gunners to fire "carcasses," a type of fire bomb.

These lethal devices began to rain down on the town. Within view of the lookouts on the walls, the British regiments were drawing up in battle array, as though preparing for an assault. Out at sea, warships were in position to enter the harbour. Louisbourg was clearly doomed.

On the morning of July 26, Amherst sent Drucour a letter laying out his terms for surrender. If the governor did not accept them, he was prepared to bombard the town from point-blank range and reduce it to dust. Drucour replied that he would consider lowering his flag if his officers were permitted to be returned to France on parole. He wrote, "To answer Your Excellencies in as few words as possible, I have the honour to repeat to you that my resolution is still the same, and that I will suffer the attack you speak of."

This was all bluff, because all but three of Louisbourg's artillery pieces had been destroyed by British cannon fire. Amherst replied that the surrender must be unconditional. Civilians would be allowed to return to France, but soldiers and officers would be taken to England as prisoners of war. Amherst gave Drucour one hour to reach a decision. Then he gave orders for the British guns to be loaded. The hour was almost up when a French officer came out of the fortress and said, "We accept." Some of the French officers had wanted to fight to the bitter end. They burned their regimental colours and had their men smash their muskets, rather than surrender them to the British.

The second capture of Louisbourg had cost the British 195 men. France lost the entire Louisbourg garrison, either killed, wounded or taken prisoner. Britain now had Île Royale, to be renamed Cape Breton Island, and Île St. Jean, which would be renamed Prince Edward Island. To ensure that Louisbourg would never again pose a threat, should the politicians give Cape Breton back to France once more, British engineers completely destroyed the fortress, barely leaving two stones together. In the twentieth century it would be rebuilt in the biggest historical reconstruction project ever undertaken in Canada.

Drucour had held out only three days longer than his predecessor of 1745, but that was long enough after all for the British to put off their designs on Quebec until the following year. That would see James Wolfe, promoted to Major General, take the field against the man with whose name his own would be linked forevermore. He was Louis-Joseph de Montcalm-Gazon; the Marquis de Montcalm.

The Battle of Quebec

Fate of a Nation

Come, each death-doing dog who dares to venture his neck,
Come, follow the hero that goes to Quebec:
Jump aboard of the transports, and loose every sail,
Pay your debts at the tavern by giving leg-bail; [leg-bail—to run away]
And ye that love fighting shall soon have enough
Wolfe commands you, my boys; we shall give them Hot Stuff.
Up the River St. Lawrence our troops shall advance
To the Grenadiers' March we will teach them to dance.
Cape Breton we have taken, and next we will try
At their capital to give them another black eye.
Vaudreuil, 'tis in vain you pretend to look gruff,
Those are coming who know how to give you Hot Stuff.
—From "Hot Stuff" by Sergeant Edward Botwood, 47th
Regiment of Foot, killed at Quebec, 1759

As Sergeant Botwood, the unofficial bard of the British army at Quebec noted in his rousing if artistically suspect verse, General James Wolfe emerged from the Battle of Louisbourg a hero, even though General Jeffrey Amherst was the senior commander. Wolfe, however, did not have the look of a military hero. He stood six-foot-three, but was very thin, which gave him a gangly, awkward appearance. His red hair was wispy and already thinning, though at the time of the siege of Quebec, Wolfe was in his thirty-third year. He had piercing blue eyes, but an over-large nose and a weak chin. Cartoonists of the time caricatured him as a rabbit. Wolfe's health was always frail, and he was frequently bedridden with fevers, scurvy, rheumatism and kidney stones. He was quite likely tubercular. He sometimes said he would prefer death on the battlefield for some great cause to wasting away from illness. That probably explained his fearlessness in the face of enemy fire.

In spite of his health problems, Wolfe was a man of seemingly limitless energy, and had a sharp, enquiring mind. He learned Latin and French, read voraciously, and could engage in intelligent conversation on subjects as diverse as music and military tactics. He was a commoner—the son and grandson of soldiers—and attended boarding school as a boy, but at the age of fourteen he joined the army. Wolfe rose through the ranks quickly. As a sixteen-year-old ensign he distinguished himself at the Battle of Dettingen in Bavaria, and caught the attention of the Duke of Cumberland. Wolfe was a lieutenant at the Battle of Culloden, Scotland, where the English routed the army of Bonnie Prince Charlie. When a superior officer told Wolfe to shoot a wounded Scot, Wolfe refused, saying he valued his honour more than his commission.

Wolfe was a stickler for details, and soldiers under his command had to keep their uniforms clean, their buttons polished and their shoes shined. But he was also a man who always looked for ways to improve things, from the use of artillery to the straps on soldiers' caps. He even came up with the idea of a hospital ship, where sick soldiers could be quarantined from the others.

Wolfe could be moody, short-tempered, and sometimes snobbish. When in North America, he looked down his nose at the army's colonial auxiliaries as unwashed barbarians. More than anything else, Wolfe craved action. While many other English senior officers regarded duty in the howling wilderness of Canada as something to be avoided by any means, Wolfe was ecstatic when Prime Minister William Pitt chose him to lead the expedition against Quebec.

Wolfe's adversary at Quebec, Louis-Joseph, the Marquis de Montcalm, was as different from the English general as a man could be. Born in 1712, Montcalm was an aristocrat, though not an especially wealthy one. He was short and somewhat corpulent. As a boy he had a private tutor, but struggled with his studies. Montcalm went into the army at the age of fifteen as an ensign. When he was seventeen his father purchased him a captaincy. By the time of the War of the Austrian succession he had risen to the rank of colonel. In 1746, at the Battle of Piacenza in Italy, Montcalm received five sabre wounds and was taken prisoner. After being paroled he spent some time recuperating at home and then went back to war with the rank of brigadier general. In 1747 he was wounded again, this time by a musket shot in an engagement in the Swiss Alps.

Because the Montcalms were financially strapped, young Louis-Joseph's family arranged for his marriage to a wealthy young woman named Angelique Louise Talon de Boulay. Arranged marriages were common at the time, but Montcalm's was different from most of them. He and Angelique were actually in love with each other. Montcalm was devoted to his wife, and remained faithful to her for the rest of his life, at a time when most noblemen had one or more mistresses.

Montcalm would have preferred to remain on his beloved estate at Candiac, in Provence, living the life of a country gentleman among his olive trees. But he was not a man who could sit back and live on his wife's money. The army provided a regular income for him, so even when France was at peace, he stayed on the rolls as an officer. In 1756 he was chosen by King Louis xv to take command of the French forces in North America with the rank of Major General. Other generals had been offered the post, but like their English counterparts they were horrified at the prospect of going off to a land of snow and savages. Montcalm himself was reluctant to go. But he was a loyal subject of the king, and the pay for an officer of so high a rank was substantial.

Upon his arrival in Quebec in 1756 Montcalm found the colony in a shambles. The administration was rife with corruption. Intendant François Bigot was a shameless thief who lined his own pocket at the expense of the colony. "What a country!" Montcalm once cried in exasperation. "Here all the knaves grow rich and the honest men are ruined." Colonial officials kept Montcalm in the dark on many issues, because he would not involve himself in graft and embezzlement. The general soon discovered that Canadian-born colonists distrusted officials sent over from France. Many felt their first allegiance was to Canada, not Old France. The Governor General, Pierre de Rigaud de Vaudreuil de Cavagnial, Marquis de Vaudreuil, was Quebec-born and deeply resented Montcalm's presence. He had wanted to command the army himself, and technically he was Montcalm's superior. He considered himself a brilliant strategist, though he had no military experience. He refused to cooperate with Montcalm on military matters.

54

Behind Montcalm's back de Vaudreuil wrote vile letters about him to the government at Versailles. It did not help matters that Montcalm had a hot temper and a tendency to be arrogant, which deepened the rift between him and the governor and his cronies. From the moment he stepped onto Canadian soil, Montcalm was homesick for France and missed his wife terribly. He hated being in Canada, but he would do his duty.

Montcalm had only three thousand regular troops who had been sent from France. The rest of his men, about fifteen thousand, were colonials and militia. Like Wolfe, Montcalm had little regard for colonials. He had even less for his Native allies, whom he considered undependable and cruel.

In spite of all these difficulties, Montcalm made a name for himself as a brilliant general with an impressive string of victories. In 1756 he captured and destroyed the British Fort Oswego on Lake Ontario. In 1757 he captured Fort William Henry. That victory was marred when, against Montcalm's orders and to his disgust, Native allies massacred English men, women and children who had been guaranteed safe conduct to another British fort. In 1758 Montcalm inflicted a stunning defeat on a British force five times the size of his own when he defended Fort Carillon (Ticonderoga).

Montcalm wanted to follow up these successes with further strikes against the British. But he lacked the manpower and the funds to do it. Montcalm's victories only increased de Vaudreuil's envy of him, and the governor's letters to France became even more poisonous. Moreover, de Vaudreuil ignored many of Montcalm's suggestions for improvements to the defenses of the city of Quebec. Montcalm wrote to France himself, pleading for reinforcements. He was refused. The king expected him to hold Quebec with the men he had. Several times Montcalm considered resigning his commission and going home. But he had given his word to his king.

Founded by Samuel de Champlain in 1608, Quebec had been captured by the English adventurer David Kirke in 1629, but was subsequently returned to France. Now Quebec was a city of about twelve thousand people. Its citadel was an intimidating stronghold, built on a stone headland more than ninety-one metres (300 feet) above the St. Lawrence River. With the St. Lawrence below it, and flanked by the St. Charles and Montmorency rivers, fortress Quebec was practically unassailable.

General James Wolfe assembled his army at Louisbourg while he awaited the fleet that would carry him up the St. Lawrence. Like Montcalm, he was having manpower problems. He had been promised twelve thousand regulars. Instead he had nine thousand, some of whom were American Rangers, militia that Wolfe called "the worst soldiers in the universe."

The naval commander of the expedition was Vice-Admiral Charles Saunders. He had the difficult task of taking forty-nine warships and over a hundred transport vessels up the St. Lawrence, a river with which the English were unfamiliar. The English had captured some Canadian river pilots and forced them into service, but they would prove to be unreliable. The man principally responsible for taking soundings and guiding the fleet upriver was a young captain named James Cook, who would one day make his name as one of Britain's greatest sea captains and explorers. Under Saunders's command were 13,500 sailors of the Royal Navy and 5,000 merchant seamen. This Armada left Louisbourg for Quebec on June 4. On board the H.M.S. *Neptune*, Wolfe wrote out his will. Chronic bad health plagued him, and he'd had premonitions of an early death.

The British fleet first appeared off the Isle of Orleans on June 26. The dismayed French had hoped the enemy would be destroyed by the great river, but had not counted on the brilliant river piloting of young Captain Cook. As the British began to pour out of their ships and set up camps on the island, Montcalm could only fume. He had wanted to install batteries at Cap Tourmente, a headland that controlled the approaches to the Isle of Orleans, but de Vaudreuil had opposed the idea. The English would never land there, the governor said. Likewise, Montcalm had proposed building defensive works on Point Levis, a promontory on the south bank of the river that overlooked the city. De Vaudreuil had also turned that idea down. Wolfe quickly saw the importance of Point Levis, and ordered a gun battery put there that could bombard Quebec. The night after the first British vessels arrived, Montcalm sent seven blazing fire ships adrift among the British fleet. But sailors in small rowboats got lines on them and towed them away before they could cause any damage.

Wolfe set up his headquarters at a spot on the east side of the Montmorency River, and began to study Quebec's defenses in search of a weakness. He could not see any. Montcalm had not concentrated his men in the immediate vicinity of the city, as Wolfe had expected he would, but had put them into strongly entrenched positions called the Beauport Shore downstream between the St. Charles and Montmorency rivers, which meant the British would face stiff opposition if they tried to make a landing. If they attempted to make a landing upstream, they would have to sail directly beneath Montcalm's artillery, which would be suicide. Wolfe had previously referred to Montcalm as "The Old Wolf." Now he had to admit that the French general had more of the fox in him. The English general might have felt a little more confident if he had known that within the walls of Quebec, food was already in short supply. The embezzling schemes of Intendant Bigot had left a city about to be locked in a siege woefully ill prepared.

On July 1 the French attacked Point Levis, where British guns were already shelling the city. The assault was made at night, and in the darkness the French soldiers became confused and fired on each other. The British defenders had little trouble repulsing the attack, which left seventy Frenchmen dead. It is still not certain if this action was ordered by Montcalm, or if it was another of de Vaudreuil's blunders. After the failed attack, the British guns resumed bombarding the town. Montcalm wrote to Wolfe, "We do not doubt but you will demolish the town, yet we are determined that your army shall never get footing within its walls. " Wolfe replied, "I will be master of Quebec, if I stay here until the end of November."

Both commanders knew that time was both an ally and an enemy. If Wolfe could not take Quebec before winter set in, he would have to withdraw his entire force. That would mean a humiliating retreat and quite possibly the end of his career. Montcalm calculated that with stalwart defense, and some luck, Quebec could hold on until the threat of winter freeze-up forced the British to leave. Then, if the garrison and the civilian population could make it through a hungry winter, relief would come from France. It would be a waiting game, and Wolfe blinked first.

Wolfe thought that if he could draw Montcalm out of his defensive positions to fight in the open, he could beat him. He tried several manoeuvres to do just that, but Montcalm wouldn't take the bait. Wolfe finally decided on an open attack. On July 31 he launched a frontal assault on the Beauport Shore, Montcalm's defensive sector just west of the Montmorency River. The operation did not go well at all.

Warships that were supposed to support the attack weren't able to get into position. Boatloads of assault troops were stranded when their boats ran aground, and were shot to pieces by French musketry. Wolfe, who led the attack, had his trademark cane swept right out of his hand by a cannonball, and was injured by splinters thrown up by artillery fire. Soldiers spilled out of boats into waist-deep water, soaking their gunpowder. Those who made it to shore attempted to make formations, then stumbled around in confusion. Native warriors fighting for the French swept down on the floundering British, tomahawking soldiers and scalping the wounded. Some of Wolfe's men captured a French gun position, but were unable to hold it. With 450 of his men dead or wounded, Wolfe had to withdraw. The French had sixty casualties. James Wolfe had suffered his first defeat, and the Marquis de Montcalm, from all appearances, was in control of the battle for Quebec.

Things now settled into several weeks of stalemate. The British subjected Quebec to a continuous bombardment, but Wolfe could not get his army up to the citadel or lure Montcalm out. Canadian partisans and Indians were a constant menace. Wolfe had given orders that civilians were not to be mistreated, unless they were bearing arms for Montcalm, and private property was to be respected. Rape was punishable by death. Nonetheless, atrocities did occur. Farmhouses were pillaged. Women were assaulted. Men were beaten or killed whether they'd been taking potshots at the British or not. Wolfe was horrified to learn that the American Rangers had been scalping victims, and issued strict orders against the practice.

The Canadian farmers who had not fled into Quebec found themselves in a very unpleasant position. De Vaudreuil had told them they were duty bound to harass the enemy. If they did not, the Indians would burn them out. If they did snipe at the British, they risked death at the hands of the redcoats. Sometimes, in fits of anger (possibly caused by deteriorating health, but perhaps also due to his frustration at not being able to overcome Montcalm's defenses) Wolfe contradicted his orders against the abuse of civilians, and his men burned barns and slaughtered livestock. Civilians who should have been protected were left to the mercy of marauders. Wolfe allowed many refugees passage through his lines into Quebec, where they would place an even greater strain on the food supply.

Early in August Wolfe learned of some French warehouses at Deschambault, upriver from Quebec. After being bloodied at Montmorency, and with the season slipping by, Wolfe knew he had to take some risks. He had Admiral Saunders send some of his small vessels upstream, past the citadel. Saunders did this successfully, and British raiders burned the French storehouses before Montcalm's troops drove them off. This action proved that it was possible to sneak past the big guns trained on the river. Over the next few weeks more British ships made the run, until a sizable British force was on the river above Quebec. That meant the city would be cut off from Montreal, its only remaining source of supplies. Wolfe believed Montcalm would have no choice to come out. Montcalm still held fast behind his defences.

On September 3, Wolfe began to evacuate the British camps by the Montmorency, on the Isle of Orleans and at Point Levis. Watching from above, Montcalm thought at first that the English general had given up and was preparing to leave. Then he saw that the redcoats were being transported to the south bank of the St. Lawrence, opposite Quebec. Montcalm had not been very impressed with Wolfe's generalship thus far. The attack on the Beauport Shore, in Montcalm's opinion, had been foolhardy. Now it seemed that Wolfe, desperate to crack Quebec's defences before the cold weather came, was gearing up for a major assault. But where would he launch it?

First Saunders made a feint on the Beauport Shore, giving the impression the British intended to attack there again. Then Wolfe raided French fortifications at Cap-Rouge, upriver from Quebec. French cavalry hurried to the aid of the defenders there, but rain put an end to the fighting. The British withdrew.

Wolfe spent the next few days sailing up and down the river in front of Quebec, seemingly at a loss as to what to do next—which in fact he was. Vaudreuil was certain that the British were preparing to leave, and that Wolfe was a desperate, frustrated man, hopelessly looking for a miracle. He wrote to a colleague, "Everything proves that the grand design of the English has failed." In fact, General Wolfe found the weak spot in their defences he had been looking for.

Montcalm had placed a lot of faith in Quebec's physical location atop a headland rising almost straight up from the river. No army, he thought, could scale those heights. One rough path did run diagonally from a tiny cove (now called Wolfe's Cove) to the top. For once, Montcalm made a mistake. He did not think the British would risk sending men up such a path, even if they should find it. He had told Vaudreuil, "I swear to you that a hundred men posted there would stop their whole army." There were sentries at the top, but they were not in a state of high alert. Montcalm decided that the enemy activities across the river and upstream were diversions. The real attack would come at Beauport, so that's where he kept his best troops concentrated.

Wolfe kept his plan to himself until the last minute, not even sharing it with his senior officers. Army camps were notorious rumour mills, and with deserters passing back and forth and spies mingling with camp followers, Wolfe could not take any chance that word might somehow reach the ears of Montcalm. If Montcalm suspected for a moment what Wolfe was up to, he would put enough men at the top of that path to annihilate any army trying to ascend it. Besides Wolfe, the only men who knew of the new plan were Admiral Saunders and a Captain James Chads, who had to organize the landing boats. The other officers were angry at being left in the dark and demanded to know where and when the attack was to be made. Wolfe replied, "It is not a usual thing to point out in the publick orders the direct spot of an attack, nor for any inferior officer not charged with a particular duty to ask instructions upon that point." Then he told them anyway.

The plan was dangerous. The men would have to climb a steep, seventy-six-metre (250 foot) footpath in full battle gear, and somehow drag up a pair of six-pounder cannon. If the enemy at the top should be alerted, the British soldiers below would be sitting ducks. Once the British reached the top they would have a reasonably level open field (the famous Plains of Abraham), hemmed in by forest to the west and north, the city to the east, and the precipice above the river to the south. It was a perfect field on which to fight a classic, European set-piece battle. But if the fight did not go well for Wolfe, he would have nowhere to retreat. Wolfe was gambling everything on one throw of the dice.

At about two o'clock on the morning of September 13, boatloads of British soldiers began moving downriver from the positions they had taken upstream. French sentries along the shore mistook them for a flotilla of supply boats expected from Montreal. At the same time, Saunders staged a diversion along the Beauport Shore, to keep Montcalm's attention focused there. At about four o'clock, the first boats landed on the cove's tiny beach. Wolfe was in one of them.

In the little cove boats and boots crunched on gravel, equipment rattled and men cursed. Wolfe was amazed that the sentries at the top didn't react. In fact, they were asleep. The first men to go up were twenty-four volunteers under Captain William Delaune. Their job was to take out the French sentries. Wolfe said, "There seems scarcely a possibility of getting up, but you must do your endeavours."

Delaune's men scrambled to the top and surprised the sentries. Some shots were fired and a few sentries were killed or wounded, but none got away to warn the city. The racket of a few gunshots in the night would not have been considered a cause for alarm. The British advance party moved on to overpower two nearby gun emplacements. Down below more men were stepping out of boats, and a long line of red uniforms was snaking up the path to the Plains of Abraham. Just how many soldiers Wolfe had with him that morning is uncertain. Estimates run from 3,600 to 4,800.

As darkness gave way to dawn, French militia and Indians in the woods were astounded to see an English army where an English army wasn't supposed to be. Wolfe and his officers were getting their men into formations when the enemy began sniping at them from the trees. Wolfe told the troops to lie on their arms so they wouldn't present such easy targets. A rain shower had started. The men lay on the cold, wet ground, and waited for Montcalm.

When a messenger first brought Montcalm the news of British troops on the plains outside the city, the general did not at first believe him. He thought the man was exaggerating. He said it was undoubtedly a raiding party. They would burn a few houses, and then withdraw. The messenger nervously suggested the general look for himself. From a hilltop Montcalm looked through his telescope and was stunned to see that the man had not been exaggerating. He immediately gave orders for troops to be brought from their defensive positions to the plains. De Vaudreuil, however, would not allow soldiers to be transferred from the Beauport Shore. He believed Wolfe was going to attack there, and no amount of pleading from the officer who carried Montcalm's order could shake him. At about eight o'clock the guns on Quebec's west wall began firing on the British.

When Montcalm first surveyed the British lines he knew that Wolfe did not yet have his entire army with him. There were at that time about two thousand redcoats on the plains. The English general also had no heavy artillery. If the French could strike now, they could drive the English over the heights they had just climbed and into the St. Lawrence, before they could bring their full force into action. Some of the divisions Montcalm had called for were on their way; city garrison troops and militia. But the elite regulars he needed most were still at the Beauport Shore.

Montcalm was furious when he learned that de Vaudreuil had countered his order. He stormed off to the governor's quarters where the two argued bitterly. It took Montcalm an hour to convince de Vaudreuil to give him his battalions. In the meantime, more of Wolfe's troops were climbing the path and falling into line.

Montcalm had about sixteen thousand men under arms in Quebec and its environs, but just how many of them arrived in time for the confrontation with Wolfe's army is uncertain. Historians have placed the number as high as seven thousand and as low as four thousand. However, only a portion of Montcalm's army was made of well trained, professional regulars who were as skilled at fighting and as disciplined under fire as Wolfe's soldiers.

The rest were poorly trained colonials or recruits who had never been in a battle. In a letter to his mother, Wolfe had written, "The Marquis de Montcalm is at the head of a great number of bad soldiers, and I am at the head of a small number of good ones."

By nine o'clock that morning the two armies faced each other at a distance of about a quarter of a mile. They were not yet close enough for musket fire, but from behind clumps of bushes in front of the French line, Canadian militiamen and Native warriors sniped at the British. Here and there a red-coated soldier dropped to the ground. Traditionally British commanders lined their men up four to eight ranks deep. Wolfe had done something entirely new. He had his army stretched in a long formation only two ranks deep. When the men in the front rank fired a volley, they stepped aside to create a gap through which the second rank could fire. By the time the second rank had fired, the first rank was reloaded and ready to shoot again. This doubled the firepower of a single volley. But it also denied men the slight feeling of security that came of spending at least some moments in the rear ranks. To shoot, reload and shoot again, while continually exposed to enemy fire without panicking, required intensive training and nerves of steel. Would Wolfe's soldiers meet the test?

Wolfe waited for Montcalm to make the first move. Resplendent in his red and gold general's uniform, he strode up and down his "thin red line" encouraging his men, telling them not to shoot until they heard the order to do so, no matter how close the enemy came. People who had seen Wolfe in action said that in the heat of battle, Wolfe always seemed to be gripped by a feverish ecstasy, as though he loved it. Such was the case now, as he looked across the field at the general with whom he had matched wits all summer but had never actually seen.

Montcalm wore a dark blue coat and was astride a black horse. He waved a sword as he gave instructions and encouraged his troops. They stood eight ranks deep. Behind them on the walls of Quebec, people had gathered to watch the spectacle. The battle that would decide the fate of Canada was about to begin.

At ten o'clock Montcalm gave the order to advance. With drums rolling and banners snapping in the wind, the French army began to spread across the plains, the regular soldiers in their white uniforms, the colonials and militia in grey or their own homespun clothing. As they moved ever closer to the motionless British, Montcalm tried to keep his centre ranks together. By sheer weight of numbers he should be able to break through that feeble-looking double red line. But some of his colonial troops were veering off and heading for the cover of the woods. Only one of Wolfe's two cannon was working, but it was creating gaps in the French lines as cannonballs did their bloody work. Skirmishers in front of the British lines duelled with those in front of the French lines, until the sharpshooters for both armies fell back. Through it all, the main two lines of British troops stood their ground, not firing, not moving,

Then the action on the British left caught Wolfe's attention. The British skirmishers there were withdrawing in disorder and drawing the fire of French Rangers. One of Wolfe's captains was shot in the chest. Wolfe bent down and pressed the man's hand, telling him he had done well and would recover. Then a bullet struck Wolfe in the right wrist, severing the tendons. Wolfe asked another captain for a handkerchief, bandaged his hand and stuck it in his pocket. Wolfe gave a junior officer a message for one of his brigadiers, then strode back to the centre of the front line. He was shot again, this time in the groin. But it seems the musket ball was almost spent, and his coat absorbed much of the impact. Wolfe staggered, but stayed on his feet.

The French were coming on at the double, shouting and cheering, firing their guns at will. Montcalm, leading on his black horse, was the very picture of the noble general. The distance between the French and the English rapidly grew smaller, and still the redcoats didn't move.

Then, when the French were about seventy-three metres (240 feet) away, the redcoats snapped to attention, and shouldered their muskets. Wolfe stood with his cane raised. The French came on. At about thirty-six metres (120 feet), Wolfe's cane sliced down. British officers shouted "Fire!", and that deceptively fragile-looking red line exploded. Two thousand lead balls slashed into the French ranks, closely followed by two thousand more and then two thousand more. One British officer would call it the most perfectly executed display of gunfire he had ever seen. The French charge halted as though it had hit an invisible wall. Men fell by the score. What had moments before been a proud army was now a reeling, disorganized mob. The surviving French soldiers, stunned, many wounded, turned and fled back to Quebec. The Battle of the Plains of Abraham had lasted between ten and fifteen minutes.

The British lines fired only three complete volleys that day. The fourth volley was incomplete because by that time the French were in full retreat, and General Wolfe was down. He had been shot in the chest, and knew this was his death wound. He refused to let the officers grouped around him call a surgeon. One of the men looked up at the battlefield and cried, "See how they run!" Wolfe asked weakly, "Who run?" The officer replied, "The enemy, sir. They run everywhere!"

Wolfe said, "Go one of you, to Colonel Burton. Tell him to march Webb's Regiment down to the Charles to cut off their retreat from the bridge." Then, according to witnesses who were there, Wolfe said, "Now, God be praised, I will die in peace." Those were his last words. Among the legends that arose surrounding Wolfe's fall was one that he had been shot by a former British sergeant who was fighting with the French. The man had supposedly been demoted for striking a private, and had subsequently deserted to the enemy. He was later captured and sentenced to hang for desertion and treason. Before going to the gallows he confessed to shooting Wolfe as an act of vengeance. Another story claims a fifteen-year-old boy in the French militia fired the fatal shot. But those stories are typical of the mythologies that always grow around dramatic events in history. Dressed in his very conspicuous uniform, Wolfe naturally would have caught the eye of every French sharpshooter on the field.

The Marquis de Montcalm, riding high on his splendid horse at the front of his army would also have been an inviting target, though he quite likely was one of many victims of the murderous volleys the British poured into the advancing French. Montcalm was shot in the stomach, and almost fell from his horse as his charge collapsed. Two soldiers kept him in the saddle as they were swept by the mad retreat through one of the western gates in the walls of Quebec. A woman saw him and shrieked, "Oh my God! My God! The marquis is dead!"

Montcalm heard her and said reassuringly, "It's nothing. Don't be troubled for me, my good friends." The soldiers helped him off his horse and took him to a doctor's house.

With Wolfe dead command should have gone to General Robert Monkton, but he, too, had been wounded and was unable to take charge. Command fell to General George Townshend, an officer who had been highly critical of Wolfe's qualities as a leader. Townshend's first act as commander was to ignore Wolfe's final order, to cut off the French retreat. He decided the men had had enough for one day, so did not pursue the fleeing enemy. Thus, the British had the field, but Quebec was still uncaptured, with a substantial army inside its walls.

But chaos reigned in the fortress. Montcalm was obviously dying, the army was leaderless, and the people were panicking. De Vaudreuil, who had wanted all along to be in sole command, didn't know what to do. He sent a message to Montcalm, whose authority he had undermined for three years and who now lay on his deathbed, begging for advice. Montcalm bluntly replied that de Vaudreuil could fight on or surrender. That night de Vaudreuil fled for Montreal, taking three thousand soldiers with him. He would leave the humiliating act of surrendering Quebec to someone else. For some reason, General Townshend made no attempt to intercept him.

Commandant Jean-Baptiste de Ramezay was now in charge in Quebec. He had always taken de Vaudreuil's side against Montcalm, but now he, too, sought the dying general's counsel on what to do. Montcalm,who in his last hours was attending to personal affairs, told Ramezay, "I will neither give orders nor interfere any further. I have much business that must be attended to, of greater moment than your ruined garrison and this wretched country. My time is short, therefore pray leave me."

Montcalm was indeed running out of time. But he still thought of the soldiers and people who had been entrusted to his care, and sent a letter to Townshend requesting that they be treated humanely and with respect. Montcalm died the day after the battle, with the words, "I am happy that I shall not live to see the surrender of Quebec." He had done his duty, out of a sense of honour toward a king who hardly deserved it.

A French army still sat inside the walls of Quebec, but it was a demoralized and hungry one. An English army was camped just outside the walls, and they were bringing up guns that could now shell the city from a new quarter. The English controlled the river as well as the road to Montreal. The civilian population, blasted out of their homes by weeks of shelling, wanted an end to it. This was France's war, not theirs. Five days after the Battle of the Plains of Abraham, Ramezay surrendered the city.

The capture of Quebec did not end the Seven Years War. Nor did the capture of Montreal the following year. The bloodshed went on until 1763, when Britain and France signed the Treaty of Paris to end hostilities. Quebec (and its people) was a bargaining chip in the negotiations. Britain was willing to give the colony Champlain had founded back to France, but France didn't want it. The French government chose to take instead the tiny but profitable sugar island of Guadeloupe in the Caribbean.

In the short Battle of the Plains of Abraham, the British had fifty-eight men killed and about six hundred wounded and missing. French losses are uncertain. De Vaudreuil claimed 640 killed and wounded, but British officers reported picking up more than 1,500 dead and wounded French soldiers. Quite likely de Vaudreuil downplayed French casualties, and the English exaggerated them.

The two most significant soldiers to fall on that field were, of course, James Wolfe and Louis-Joseph de Montcalm. Wolfe's body was returned to England and buried at Greenwich. Montcalm's remains were interred at the Convent of the Ursuline Nuns in Quebec. Both men, enemies in life, and neither of them Canadian, have become inseparable in Canadian history and legend.

The Battle
of Quebec

1775, A Bloody New Year's Eve

With the stroke of a pen at the Treaty of Paris in 1763, the land that had formerly been New France became part of the British Empire. This included not only the St. Lawrence Valley, but a vast territory in the heart of the continent stretching down from the Great Lakes, through the Ohio Valley to the French-controlled Louisiana Territory. On British maps this entire newly acquired domain was called "Canada." It was to be administered from Quebec City. The British drew a line of demarcation the length of the Appalachian Mountains to the east, and forbade settlers from the thirteen colonies to cross it. This great wilderness, they said, was to be left to the Natives who already lived there. This was not done out of any philanthropical feeling for the tribes. This was fur country. British traders moving in on a bounty that once went to the French sought to make a lot of money, and settlements tended to ruin fur trapping. Nor was it meant to be a permanent arrangement. The British expected to move the boundary westward in stages, and acquire Native lands in a peaceful, orderly manner, so as to avoid the kind of bloodshed experienced in Pontiac's War. Furthermore, all land transactions were to be carried out by agents of the Crown, to prevent the confusion and skullduggery that had resulted when real estate deals between whites and Natives had been handled by local politicians with vested interests.

This situation did not go over at all well in the colonies along the Atlantic seaboard. As far as the colonists were concerned, now that the French had been booted out, that land west of the mountains was *theirs* for the taking, and the Natives would have to either get out or suffer the consequences. A large number of businessmen, whose ranks included George Washington, expected to make a lot of money from land speculation when settlers started moving west. They objected to the idea that London should interfere with what they did in what they considered their own backyard. The causes of the American Revolution had as much to do with avarice as they did with concepts of liberty and equality.

In April of 1775, when gunfire at Lexington and Concord, Massachusetts, touched off the conflict that has come to be called the American Revolutionary War, the population of the thirteen colonies was much divided. About one-third were behind the Patriots (whom the opposition called rebels and traitors). Another third supported the king. They called themselves Loyalists; the opposition called them Tories and traitors. The other third of the population didn't know which side to take, and many of them bent with the prevailing breeze throughout the years of the war.

As the Patriot leaders in the thirteen colonies sought to bring more people to their cause, they also looked north to other British colonies. They tried, and failed, to convince what are now the Canadian Maritime Provinces to join the rebellion. They also tried to convince Quebec to come into the war on the rebel side. They had good reason for believing they would find support in the St. Lawrence Valley. It had been barely a decade and a half since Quebec had fallen to British armies. Wouldn't the French-speaking Canadians welcome an opportunity to throw out their British masters? Moreover, once Quebec had become a British colony, merchants and other businessmen from the thirteen colonies had gone north to establish themselves in Quebec City, Montreal and other towns in Canada. Wouldn't many of them share the views of their rebelling countrymen to the south?

Most of the American-born merchants in Canadian towns did, in fact, support the rebellion, because evicting the British would give them the opportunity to exploit the Canadian population. They held meetings to discuss the pros and cons of "independence." Then they waited for the chance to turn Canada over to the Patriots.

But among Canada's French-speaking population, the call to rebellion, though hotly debated, was in the end generally rejected. After their former king had cast them aside in 1763 and Canada officially came under British rule, the inhabitants had expected the worst: oppression, possibly even deportation, as had happened to the unfortunate Acadians. Instead, they found themselves being governed by men like James Murray and then Guy Carleton who, for the times, were remarkably generous in their treatment of the Canadians. All the Canadians had to do was take the oath of allegiance to the Crown. Though criminal law was now British, the people were allowed to keep their old French civil law and the seigneurial system of land ownership. The Roman Catholic religion was tolerated. At first, in accordance with British law, Catholics were not permitted to hold public office, but eventually they were given full political rights.

Moreover, the governors would not allow the slick Yankee merchants to exploit the Canadians.

All of this infuriated the merchants, most of whom were staunch, Catholic-hating Protestants. They wrote angry letters to London, and actually succeeded in having Governor Murray recalled. But Governor Carleton, his replacement, was just as adamant about protecting the rights of the Canadian population. When those rights were cemented in the Quebec Act of 1774, the Anglo American merchants in Canada protested. Some of them blackened the face of a bust of King George III and hung a rosary made of potatoes around the neck. Carved on the crude wooden crucifix were the words, "Behold the Pope of Canada and the English fool."

The Canadians really had nothing to gain by joining the rebellion. If there were some officials from England who treated them like inferiors, they at least were no worse than the officials from France who had treated them like inferiors. How might they fare under an American government? In the early years of the Revolution, few people besides the Patriots themselves believed it had much chance of succeeding. How might the English react if the Canadians threw in with the Patriots, and then the Patriots *lost*? Would the people then endure the kind of persecutions that had not materialized after 1763? As far as most French-speaking Canadians were concerned, this was an English quarrel. Why should they become involved at all?

When Canada did not join the rebellion as "the fourteenth colony," Patriot leaders decided the Canadians would have to be brought into the rebel fold by force. To do that the rebels would have to capture Montreal and Quebec. Such an accomplishment would also deprive the British of a stronghold from which they could wage war. The most optimistic of the Patriots even envisioned American ownership of the entire continent.

The way for invasion was opened in May 1775 when American forces captured the British forts at Ticonderoga and Crown Point on Lake Champlain. The following month the American Congress approved a plan to invade Canada. The Americans would move up the Richelieu River capturing British posts, until they reached Montreal. With that town in their hands, they would have the British cut off from the Great Lakes, and could go on to capture Quebec. The Americans would send an army of three thousand led by General Philip Schuyler and his second-in-command, General Richard Montgomery.

In Canada Governor Guy Carleton had but eight hundred British regulars strung out in various garrisons. He had been obliged to send two regiments to Boston to assist General Thomas Gage, who was under siege. Carleton desperately sent out a call to the Canadians for volunteers. He expected thousands of men and boys to respond, and was exasperated when only a few hundred did.

On August 30 Schuyler and Montgomery set off up the Richelieu. The main British post in their way was little Fort St. Jean, where Major Charles Preston had but five hundred British regulars and Canadian militia. He had orders from Carleton to hold his post for as long as possible. Meanwhile, another American force was moving toward Canada. Miffed at being left out of the invasion scheme after he had helped capture Ticonderoga, General Benedict Arnold—who would one day be vilified as the most infamous traitor in American history—had put together his own army of 1,200 in Massachusetts. He was going to march them through the wilderness, straight for Quebec. Arnold started from Cambridge on September 11, telling his men they would "dine in Quebec on Christmas Day—or in Hell!"

As the American army marched through the Richelieu valley it was joined by some Canadian sympathizers, and the campaign seemed destined for success. Then General Schuyler became ill and had to return home, leaving the command to Montgomery. When they reached Fort St. Jean on September 5, they found it a much tougher nut to crack than they had expected. The Americans attacked ferociously, and just as ferociously the defenders hurled them back. For almost two wet, frigid months, Major Preston stopped the American army in its tracks.

Then an American force went around Fort St. Jean and attacked Fort Chambly, nineteen kilometres (12 miles) to the north. Fort Chambly was Preston's supply base. It fell after only a day and a half. Cut off from Montreal, with food and ammunition running low, twenty of his men dead and many more sick, Preston was forced to surrender on November 3 after holding out for fifty-five days. However, Montgomery had lost almost half of his men to battle wounds, disease and desertion. Nonetheless, the way to Montreal was open.

Carleton was at Montreal when he learned that Forts Chambly and St. Jean had fallen. He decided that Montreal's garrison of ninety regulars could not hold the town, even with the help of a few militiamen. He sent the volunteers back to their farms. Then he spiked the big guns, burned any boats that were not in use, and loaded his men, powder and provisions into eleven boats for the trip to Quebec. Carleton left Montreal on November 11, and the Americans marched in the next day.

Contrary winds delayed the little fleet, and by the time they were off Sorel, the Americans had established a battery there. The fleet could not pass, and Carleton was in danger of being captured. If he fell into American hands, there would be no leadership in the St. Lawrence Valley, and the fight to keep it Canadian would be as good as lost.

A riverman named Jean-Baptiste Bouchette, known among his colleagues as "La Tourte" (the Wild Pigeon), agreed to take the governor through. Dressed in the plain clothing of a *habitant,* Carleton slipped over the side of the ship into Bouchette's whaleboat. As they rowed past the American post under cover of darkness and fog, they could hear the challenging calls of sentries only yards away. La Tourte and the governor shipped their oars, and quietly paddled with their hands until they were out of hearing range. They reached Trois Rivières just as American troops were arriving in that town. Carleton evaded detection thanks to his disguise. He boarded a ship, and made good his flight to Quebec, arriving on November 19. Back at Sorel his flotilla from Montreal was captured.

Benedict Arnold arrived at Point Levis, opposite Quebec, on November 9. His army's trek through the wilderness had been hell. Half of his troops had deserted, fallen sick or died. Stumbling through swamps and heavy brush, they'd been reduced to eating soap, hair grease and boiled moccasins. Arnold was now leading about six hundred starving, ragged men. As pitiful as his "army" was, Arnold crossed the river and advanced on Quebec across the Plains of Abraham. As though he had Wolfe's army behind him, he demanded immediate surrender. The fort's defenders replied with cannon fire. He retreated to Pointe-Aux-Trembles, thirty-five kilometres (22 miles) west, to await Montgomery.

The Americans found the Canadian civilians to be friendly and hospitable. They helped care for sick men, they willingly sold the invaders food (sometimes at greatly inflated prices) and they listened while the Americans explained the benefits of joining their union. But very few of them showed any desire to bear arms for the Americans.

General Montgomery left a garrison in Montreal and joined up with Arnold on December 3. Between them they had about 1,200 men. Montgomery had also brought artillery, which would be vital if they were to capture the stronghold. Now they just needed the right moment to strike.

Inside Quebec, Carleton had been preparing for the attack. Upon his arrival the man who'd been in command in his absence, Lieutenant-Colonel Alan Maclean—a Scot who had fought for Bonnie Prince Charlie—informed him there was a vocal pro-American faction in the city. Carlton ordered all American sympathizers to leave the city with their families within a week. After that, he said, any man refusing to serve in the militia would be treated as a rebel and a spy. Most of the Anglo American merchants left, to the disappointment of Montgomery and Arnold, who had counted on having "friends" inside the city. Carleton had a garrison of about 1,800 men, more than half of them French and English volunteers. He had made improvements to the fortifications, and had placed barricades at strategic locations in Lower Town, the city that lay in the shadow of the Citadel. Key houses had been evacuated and now held soldiers, and in some cases artillery. Carleton had enough supplies and ammunition to last for months. If he could hold out until spring, relief would come in the form of the Royal Navy.

The American army surrounded Quebec, but the commanders discovered that their artillery was ineffectual against the city's walls. As December wore on, Montgomery and Arnold were faced with several problems. They could not stay encamped outside the city indefinitely in the winter cold. Some of the men were down with smallpox. Many of their militiamen's enlistments would soon expire, and militiamen had a history of not serving a minute longer than the time for which they had signed up. Generals Arnold and Montgomery needed intervention from the hand of Providence, or they would have to pack up their tents and go home.

That intervention came on December 30, when a blizzard swept in. With visibility almost nil, and heavy snow muffling the sounds of troop movements, the Americans began their attack at about four o'clock on the morning of December 31. Montgomery led one column of troops south along the lower riverbank toward the town. Arnold took the other column in the opposite direction. They intended to meet in Lower Town, then charge the Citadel and take the defenders by surprise. Tucked into the bands of the men's hats were pieces of paper with "Liberty or Death" written on them. The men believed Quebec would be theirs by New Year's Day.

Guy Carleton had anticipated the attack. When the foul weather blew in, he knew the Americans would take advantage of it for what they hoped would be a surprise attack. He deployed his men and warned them to be on full alert. Then he went to his quarters and lay on his bed fully dressed to await the attack. The American approach was quiet enough, but they still had to use torches to find their way. Sentries saw the lights through the swirling snow. One British captain later reported:

"About 4 o'clock in the Morning Capt. Malcolm Fraser of the Royal Emigrants being on his rounds, saw many flashes of fire without hearing any reports (gunshots); the sentries inform'd him that they had perceived them for some time

on the heights of Abraham, the sentinels between Port
Louis and Cape Diamond had seen fix'd lights like lamps
on a street—the appearance being very uncommon and the
night favouring the designs of the enemy, Capt. Fraser
order'd the Guards and pickets on the ramparts to stand to
their arms. The drums beat, the bells rang the alarm, and in
a few minutes the whole Garrison was under arms—even
old men of seventy were forward to oppose the attackers."

The torches the sentries had seen were carried by Arnold's
men. Montgomery's column, moving in from another quarter,
had still not been spotted. But the element of surprise the
Americans had gambled on was lost the very moment the alarm
was raised. At the head of his troops, Montgomery barged into
Lower Town and swept past the first two barricades he encountered with little trouble. A third barricade lay before him. He
probably thought it would be no more of an obstacle than the
first two barriers. But in a small house off to the side Carleton
had hidden two three-pounders loaded with grapeshot, and a
squad of soldiers with muskets.

Shouting, "Push on, brave boys! Quebec is ours!", Montgomery
led his men right into the ambush. The night exploded in fire,
smoke and lead, and a minute later the stunned Americans were
staggering back the way they had come. Among the two dozen or
so dead left behind was General Richard Montgomery. His body
would be found frozen in the snow on New Year's Day.

Unaware that Montgomery was dead and his men put to flight,
Arnold was still advancing around the north edge of town. Musket
fire rained down on his men from the ramparts above. In the narrow *Sault-au-Matelot* they overcame the guards at a small

barricade, but Arnold was shot just below the knee. Two of his men helped him away, and Colonel Daniel Morgan took command.

A towering six-foot-four, Morgan was a backwoodsman from Virginia who had a searing hatred for the British. In 1755, while serving under the ill-fated General Edward Braddock, he had been sentenced to five hundred lashes for striking an officer. He was a hard drinking, brawling bull of a man who bore the scars of bullet wounds on his neck and face. Now he rallied his men and charged the next barricade. It was two and a half times the height of a man, and was the last obstacle they had to pass before joining with Montgomery's men.

The Americans dispatched the few defenders in front of the barricade. Then they brought up scaling ladders, thrust them into position against the barricades and began to climb. Others broke down the doors of houses on either side of the street and rushed inside. As the first men on the scaling ladders reached the top of the barricade, there was a sudden crash of gunfire. The Americans were flung back off the ladders like leaves in a strong wind. A company of British regulars had been waiting patiently on the other side, their muskets primed and loaded.

With their comrades crumpled in the bloody snow, wounded or dead, a second wave of Americans stormed up the ladders, hoping to get over before the redcoats could re-load. A Canadian militiaman named Charles Charland, who was as big as Morgan, hauled himself up to the top of the barricade where a ladder had been placed. With a blow that could have felled a horse, he slammed the American climbing the ladder back to the ground. Then he pulled the ladder up and hauled it over to his side.

Charland placed the ladder beneath the second floor window of a house adjacent to the barricade. Then he, some other militiamen and a few British regulars scurried up and into the house. In deadly hand-to-hand combat they killed the Americans who were in the house, or drove them out to the street. Now the Americans found themselves targets in a shooting gallery. Hemmed in between the rows of buildings, they were fired upon by British soldiers and Canadians at the second-floor windows. Before Morgan could bring his men into any sort of order, another force of soldiers appeared at the end of the street. They had a cannon mounted on a sleigh, and it was pointed directly at the Americans. Rather than see his men slaughtered, Morgan told them to throw down their arms. He would not, however, surrender his sword to a despised redcoat officer. Instead, he gave it to a priest who had been accidentally caught in the middle of the battle and was cringing in a doorway.

Carleton's men had seven dead and eleven wounded. The Americans had thirty dead, and many of the over four hundred taken prisoner were wounded. In the spring, however, another twenty bodies were found when the snow melted.

What was left of the American army stayed in camp on the Plains of Abraham, with the exception of Benedict Arnold, who was taken to Montreal to have his wound tended to. The only thing that kept them there was Arnold's promise of plunder once they captured the city. They spread the word around the countryside that they had killed over six hundred redcoats, had lost but fifteen men themselves, and would take Quebec as soon as General Arnold returned with reinforcements. But when some local riff-raff showed up, hoping to do a little looting, they learned the truth. In May a British warship sailed into harbour, and the Patriots fled so fast they left behind not only most of their belongings, but also a freshly cooked meal that had just been laid out for the officers.

The American Congress still wanted Canada as a fourteenth state, and they sent more soldiers to try to ensure that it became one. At the same time, however, more British troops were pouring into Canada. On one occasion a Canadian farmer cheerfully agreed to be a guide for two thousand American troops. He guided them right into a swamp, where they were immediately surrounded by British troops. Most of the Americans fled, but two hundred were taken prisoner. In Montreal, Benedict Arnold realized he could not hold the town, and so withdrew.

The American Congress made one last try at verbal persuasion to convince the Canadians to join their rebellion. In 1776 they sent Benjamin Franklin to Quebec to state the case for the American union. But not even Franklin's silver tongue could sway the Canadians. Franklin arrived on April 29, and left on May 11, convinced the situation was hopeless. Compared to some of the major battles that occurred in the Revolutionary War, the battle at Quebec was a mere scrap. Nonetheless, had the Americans won, the history of North America could have taken an entirely different course.

The War of 1812

A Mere Matter of Marching

Ill feelings between Great Britain and the newly formed United States of America continued after the Revolutionary War ended in 1783. Anti-British rhetoric was common in the American press, and American literature constantly presented Britain as an ogre whom the heroic and righteous Patriots had driven from their land. The British still looked down their noses at the Americans as "Yankee Doodle" bumpkins.

British troops continued to occupy western forts in what the Americans now considered United States territory. British agents and traders armed Native warriors who stubbornly resisted American expansion. Not until after General Anthony Wayne's crushing victory over the tribes at the Battle of Fallen Timbers in 1794 did the British pull out of Detroit and other western posts. On the other hand, the British complained that the Americans had never fully compensated United Empire Loyalists who had lost homes and property as a result of supporting the king during the war.

During the Napoleonic Wars, Britain blockaded all European ports controlled by the French. This was part of their strategy to deny Napoleon the materials he needed to sustain his armies. British warships turned back merchant vessels of neutral nations, including the United States. Moreover, because the Royal Navy was desperate for men, its officers took sailors they claimed were British deserters off American vessels by force, and pressed them into service. In 1807 when the USS *Chesapeake* refused to allow a British officer aboard to search for "deserters," H.M.S. *Leopard* opened fire on the American ship, killing four men and wounding eighteen more. The British then seized four men from the *Chesapeake,* identifying them as Royal Navy deserters. President Thomas Jefferson responded by placing an embargo on all American trade with Britain and British colonies. This actually caused much more financial distress to the United States than it did to Britain, and smugglers along the U.S.–Canadian border had a heyday.

After the Battle of Tippecanoe in 1811, in which American General William Henry Harrison defeated a confederacy of Native tribes who had obviously had British support, "Hawks" in Washington, D.C., most of them Southerners, clamoured for war with Britain. Great Britain had her hands full with the fight against Napoleon, and the sabre-rattlers in the American government saw an opportunity to capture Canada and throw the British out of North America. Land-hungry American settlers and speculators cast covetous eyes on the fertile and underpopulated colonies of Upper and Lower Canada. On June 18, 1812, the government of President James Madison declared war on Great Britain.

The military governor of Upper Canada and commander of the British forces in the colony was Major General Isaac Brock, a forty-two-year-old native of the Island of Guernsey who had been in the army since the age of fifteen, seen action in Europe, and had arrived in Canada in 1802 with the 49th Regiment of Foot. Brock was disappointed with his posting in a colonial backwater while other British officers were winning glory in the struggle against Napoleon. But he proved himself to be an above average officer. Soon after arriving in Canada, Brock quelled a mutiny and whipped a slovenly garrison into shape. Over six feet tall, athletic, and full of energy and self-confidence, Brock was a strict commander but a fair one. After a decade in Canada Brock had won more than the respect of the men who served under him; the soldiers loved him. In the spring of 1812 Brock turned down an opportunity to return to England. With the Americans threatening war, he felt it was his duty to remain in Canada until the crisis had passed.

Canada was not well prepared to fight off an American invasion. The Americans boasted that the conquest of Canada would be "a mere matter of marching," and many Canadians believed it. Brock had but 2,500 British regulars to defend the long border. He could call up militia, but was unsure of their loyalty. Many of the settlers in Upper Canada were Americans who had arrived well after the Revolutionary War to get cheap land; "Johnny-come-lately Loyalists," as their new neighbours called them. Could they be relied upon to fight for the king? Most Canadians didn't think so. A defeatist attitude settled over the colony before an American soldier even set foot on Canadian soil. Brock considered this apathy the greatest of his concerns. He acted quickly to do something about it.

First he authorized Captain Charles Roberts to seize the American fort at strategic Michilimackinac. Roberts accomplished this without firing a shot, before the garrison were even aware they were at war. This lightning move galvanized the

Canadians out of their lethargy. They suddenly saw Brock as a man of action who could well be a force to be reckoned with when the Americans attacked. The capture of Michilimackinac also impressed the Indians of the American western frontier, whose faith in the British had plunged after the disasters at Fallen Timbers and Tippecanoe. The legendary Shawnee Chief Tecumseh met Brock personally and liked him. He agreed to an alliance with the British.

Then Brock delivered the masterstroke that made his name legendary. The American General William Hull was at Detroit with an invasion force of 2,500 men. On August 16, with a force of three hundred British regulars, four hundred Canadian militiamen, and six hundred Native warriors, Brock bluffed the timid General Hull into an unconditional surrender, simply by telling him he would be unable to control his Indian allies once the fighting began. Few shots were fired and no blood was shed. In one bold move Isaac Brock had captured an American army—and all its weapons and supplies, badly needed in Upper Canada. He had thoroughly disrupted the Americans' grand strategy for the conquest of Canada, and he had delivered a severe blow to American morale. Two important American posts had fallen, and no American troops were marching on Canadian soil.

With Upper Canada's western frontier secure for the moment, Brock hurried back to his headquarters at Fort George, at present-day Niagara-on-the-Lake, on the Niagara Frontier. Brock wanted to continue taking the war to the Americans. He had plans to capture Fort Niagara, New York, and raid Sackets Harbor, a major American port on Lake Ontario. However, Sir George Prévost, Governor in Chief of British North America, and therefore Brock's superior, believed in a more defensive strategy. He forbade any more adventuring in American territory. Prévost proposed a truce, which the Americans happily accepted. It gave them a chance to reorganize and build up their forces.

Isaac Brock spent the month of September organizing Upper Canada's meagre defences. He established a communications system that would alert him to any major border crossing. He knew the American attack was coming. But where?

The Battle of Queenston Heights

A Hero's Death

Major General Isaac Brock could only watch in frustration as the Americans built up their forces on the other side of the Niagara River. The date was October 12, 1812, and the Americans had called off the truce that Governor General Sir George Prévost had arranged. On October 9 American raiders had successfully snatched two armed British vessels from Fort Erie and sailed them to Black Rock, New York. On October 11 American forces had gathered near Lewiston, apparently with the intention of crossing the river, but rain and an insufficient number of oars for their boats had forced them to abort the attack.

Now Brock had information that the Americans were going to attack at Queenston. He believed the gathering of troops at Lewiston, across the river from Queenston, had been a feint; that the real assault would be against Fort George. His problem was not having enough men to effectively garrison the entire Niagara Frontier. He had about nine hundred regulars and five hundred militia, with some six hundred militia in reserves. It would take that many just to man Fort George properly. On the other side of the river, Major General Stephen Van Rensselaer commanded 2,500 regulars and 2,700 militia. Brock was well aware of the enemy's numerical superiority. However, he was not aware of dissent in the American ranks.

Stephen Van Rensselaer was not an experienced soldier. He was a militia officer who had risen through the ranks in peacetime. The men in his command were, to a great degree, undisciplined. They were short on supplies and were threatening to go home because they hadn't been paid. Brigadier General Alexander Smyth, who commanded 1,650 of Van Rensselaer's regulars, refused to take orders from the Major General. Smyth was regular army, and was indignant that he should be subordinate to a militia officer. When Smyth, whose troops were encamped at Black Rock, received a message from Van Rensselaer requesting him to bring his men to Lewiston on the twelfth, the brigadier general replied that his men were doing their laundry.

Van Rensselaer was a reluctant commander. He had accepted the Niagara Frontier posting for political reasons and because the Secretary of War, William Eustis, could find no one else willing to lead the troops in the Niagara region. Van Rennselaer did not think his men were adequately prepared for an invasion of Canada. But the season was getting on and he was under pressure from Washington to capture the Canadian side of the Niagara Frontier before winter set in. His attempt to make a crossing on the eleventh had been farcical, and Van Rensselaer wanted to put the whole idea of campaigning off until spring.

Then on October 12 informants told Van Rensselaer that Brock had gone to Fort Erie to look into the theft of the two vessels. The American general decided this was the moment to strike. With the best British general in Canada temporarily out of the way, he might grab a foothold on the Canadian side before Brock could return to take command in the field. If the Americans could capture and hold the Heights above Queenston, they could effectively command the transportation routes along the Niagara River, thus cutting off the main link between the western part of Upper Canada and York (Toronto). Van Rensselaer did not know, however, that Brock had made a quick visit to Fort Erie, and on that night of October 12 was back in his headquarters in Fort George, fully expecting the Americans to attack there.

Captain James Dennis of the Forty-Ninth Foot was in command at Queenston. He had with him about eighty officers and regular troops, and about 150 Canadian militia. His artillery consisted of just three cannons, strategically positioned by Brock. In the village of Queenston itself Brock placed one gun—either a six-pounder or a nine-pounder (cannons were classified according to the weight of the balls they fired). At Vrooman's Point, about a mile downstream, the British had a twelve-pounder that could rain iron down on any attempted crossing. Halfway up the Heights was a "redan"—a crescent-shaped gun emplacement—with a big eighteen-pounder and a mortar. These weapons effectively covered the river and the village, but below the redan there was "dead ground"; terrain the cannon could not be lowered enough to sweep clear of attackers. Though Brock still thought the Americans would strike at Fort George, Captain Dennis told his men to stay alert for any sounds of enemy activity.

By midnight of October 12, about three thousand American troops were assembled near Lewiston. General Van Rensselaer was resolved to erase the humiliation American arms had suffered at Detroit. But dissension still plagued his army. The general had given command of the initial phase of the operation to his cousin,

Lieutenant Colonel Solomon Van Rensselaer, an officer who actually had some battle experience. This annoyed Lieutenant Colonel John Chrystie, commander of the Thirteenth Infantry, which was to be part of the first wave. The quarrel was settled only when the squabbling colonels agreed to share command.

By about 3:30 on the morning of October 13 the Americans were ready to embark. But already things were going wrong. It began to rain, which of course was good cover for the crossing, but did little for the spirits of the sodden troopers. Then the officers discovered there weren't as many boats as they had expected. The rowers would have to make numerous trips to ferry the men and supplies of ammunition across. A dispute arose over who should cross first, the regulars or the militia. When the boats did embark, the one in which Colonel Chrystie rode was swept downriver. It had to return to the American shore and try again.

That left Colonel Solomon Van Rensselaer in charge of the landing and the advance on the Canadian shore. He had about 270 men with him. A Canadian militiaman detected the enemy and ran to give the alarm. He had been instructed to fire his musket as a signal, but in the excitement of the moment he forgot. This gave Colonel Van Rensselaer a few minutes respite to form up his men. Then the quiet autumn morning was shattered as the British and Canadian defenders opened up with what witnesses later described as "a perfect sheet of fire."

As soon as Captain Dennis was told of the landing he rushed into action with fewer than fifty regulars and a handful of militia. The well-trained British soldiers poured volley after volley of .75 calibre musket balls into the Americans, while the Canadians did their best to keep up with the professionals. Colonel Van Rensselaer had already started to lead an advance, but the effect of the

British–Canadian fire was horrific. Smooth-bore muskets were not at all accurate weapons. A soldier could not use one to "pick off" an enemy unless he was at point-blank range. But when fired en masse by men drilled in their use, muskets inflicted frightful damage on opposing troop formations. The heavy lead balls tore through muscle, shattered bones and mangled internal organs. A musket ball made a marble-sized hole where it entered a man's body, and ripped out a hole the size of a fist if it exited the other side. This was the kind of carnage Solomon Van Rensselaer and his men now endured. Before the Americans could return a volley, almost fifty of their officers and men were dead or wounded. The colonel himself was hit several times in the legs and foot. He put on a greatcoat to hide the wounds from his men, and bravely tried to continue the advance. But his men were panicking in the face of enemy fire, and he was growing weak from loss of blood. Van Rensselaer knew he had no hope of success unless he was reinforced. He told his men to pick up their dead and wounded and retreat to the riverside where they could take cover under a high embankment. From there the Americans were finally able to shoot back at Captain Dennis's men. The British and Canadians took their first casualties of the battle; five men were hit. But the Americans were pinned down and going nowhere. Now they were taking not only musket fire, but bombardment from the eighteen-pounder in the redan. Van Rensselaer had been expecting Colonel Chrystie to follow right behind him with the next wave of soldiers. Now he wanted to know where the hell Chrystie was. He had no way of knowing that his co-commander had been swept downriver and even wounded in the hand by fire from the Canadian shore. It was all Van Rensselaer could do to remain conscious and cling to his toehold on Canadian soil. Meanwhile, the battle had become an artillery duel.

Brock's big guns were lobbing cannonballs at the Americans huddled along the riverbank and at the river itself, in hopes of hitting boats. The American artillery in Lewiston opened fire on the British redan. One British gunner was killed and two more were wounded. Then, as musket flashes in the dark revealed the position of Captain Dennis's men, the American batteries were turned on them. Several infantrymen were killed, and Captain Dennis and a dozen others were wounded. The captain ordered his men back to the cover of a stone guardhouse in Queenston. The American guns began to bombard the village.

The British guns concentrated on the river. Even though the gunners were blasting away at darkness, they were making the crossing difficult for the Americans. One ball scored a direct hit on a boat full of soldiers and sank it. Five other boats containing about a hundred men were badly damaged and drifted downstream. They washed ashore on the Canadian side where the occupants were killed or taken prisoner and marched off to Fort George. The men handling the boats were mostly local civilians who were familiar with the river. Many of them were unnerved by the roar of the guns and the plumes of water thrown up by falling cannonballs. As soon as they regained the American side they deserted, abandoning their boats to inexperienced soldiers. The scene at the American embarkation point was one of utter confusion. Nonetheless, boatloads of American soldiers were making it through the gauntlet of fire to the Canadian side where they bolstered the numbers and the wilting morale of Van Rensselaer's bloodied company.

Neither Chrystie nor any other senior officer had crossed the river to take over command from the ailing Van Rensselaer. The colonel turned to Captain John Wool of the Thirteenth Infantry.

Twenty-eight-year-old Wool was inexperienced, and had received an embarrassing wound in the buttocks. But he was a courageous and enthusiastic officer, and he had a plan that could turn the tide of a battle that, thus far, had not been going well for the Americans.

Wool saw the eighteen-pounder in the redan as the key. The big gun had the invaders pinned on the riverbank and was wreaking havoc with the boats. If it could be silenced, the Americans could advance and sweep the outnumbered defenders from the field. If it could be captured intact, the Americans could turn its lethal firepower on the enemy positions below. Wool had learned of a fisherman's path that wound up to the Heights, out of the view of the gun crew. If he could sneak some men up that path, he could take the gunners by surprise and capture the gun. Colonel Van Rensselaer approved of the plan. Using bushes growing along the riverbank as a screen, Wool set off with 150 men to outflank the redcoats at the redan. Van Rensselaer's last order to him was to shoot the first man in his company who tried to turn tail. The Americans did not know that one of the officers at the redan was General Isaac Brock.

Brock had been asleep in his residence in the village of Niagara, near Fort George, when a dispatch rider brought the news of the American landing at Queenston. A high wind was blowing off Lake Ontario, and the noise of the battle eleven kilometres (7 miles) away could barely be heard. Brock still suspected the Queenston landing was a diversion, and so was reluctant to commit troops from Fort George. He decided to look into the situation himself. As his horse was being saddled he told his second-in-command, Major General Roger Sheaffe, to make no decisive movements with the troops until the enemy's intentions were fully understood. Then Brock swung into the saddle and galloped off to Queenston and his appointment with destiny. His two aides,

Lieutenant Colonel John Macdonell of the York Militia and Captain John B. Glegg of the Forty-Ninth Foot hastily had their horses readied and dashed off to catch up with him.

Brock probably took an hour, riding in the pre-dawn darkness along the muddy trail that passed for a road, to reach Queenston. En route he passed a company of militia, the York volunteers, who were hurrying toward the sound of the guns. He also saw the first groups of American prisoners being escorted to Fort George. By the time he arrived in the village the first daylight of a dull, grey morning was breaking through an overcast sky. The general was covered with mud, but the sight of him brought a cheer from the British soldiers and Canadian militiamen.

Brock needed but a glance to realize this was no diversion. He quickly sent a messenger off to Fort George with orders for reinforcements. Then, seeing more boatloads of Americans on the river, either he or Captain Dennis gave an order for a company of the Forty-Ninth Foot who had been stationed on the Heights near the redan to move down into the village. This order, which left the redan exposed to assault from an unexpected flank, would have grave consequences.

For a few minutes Brock watched as the eighteen-pounder and mortar hurled shells at the batteries on the American side of the river. The balls were falling short of the target, so Brock rode up to the redan to direct the eight-man gun crew himself. He instructed the gunners to use more powder and longer fuses. Immediately the fire from the redan began to have greater effect on the American emplacements. But the advantage was to be short-lived.

Unseen by any of the defenders, Captain Wool and his men had clawed their way up the narrow path, hidden by trees and brush. Wool had expected to have to fight his way through the company of the Forty-Ninth they'd seen on the Heights earlier. He couldn't believe his good luck when his men reached the summit and found no redcoats there. He quickly deployed his men, and then advanced through the woods on the summit. Soon the Americans were above and behind the British redan.

Not until they heard the whoops of the American soldiers and the crack of gunfire did the men in the redan realize the danger. Brock knew the redan was lost. He ordered the crew to spike the gun (this was done by driving a rod into the touch-hole, rendering the cannon useless). Then he and the gunners beat a hasty retreat down the hill. Wool's men raised an American flag to signal their countrymen that the position had been taken. A cheer went up from the blue-coated soldiers dug in on the riverbank.

Captain Wool was disappointed that the British had been able to spike the big gun, but he had nonetheless turned the tables on the foe. Now the Americans held the high ground, and already more troops were moving to join his force on the heights. He began to consolidate his position as his men poured rifle and musket fire down on the British positions, forcing the redcoats and Canadian militia to withdraw to the north end of the village.

The American regulars, like the British, were armed with muskets rather than rifles. Muskets were cheaper to manufacture than rifles, and could be fitted with bayonets, which rifles could not. The musket could be reloaded much faster than a rifle, and fired a heavier bullet, giving it greater killing power. The rifle was the preferred weapon of snipers, however, because it was more accurate and had a longer range. Militiamen often carried their own weapons rather than army-issue muskets, and usually those were the same rifles the men used for hunting. Captain Wool quite possibly had snipers with him up on the Heights, and he certainly had militia.

The time was about 7:30 a.m. Brock quickly reorganized his startled forces. He knew reinforcements would be coming from Fort George, but he did not want to waste time waiting for them. He was going to attack the Americans on the Heights before they could dig themselves in. If they secured that position, the battle for Canada could well be lost.

First Brock sent a party of about seventy men to strike Wool's left flank. Then he personally led a band of about fifty regulars and militia in a charge up the slope. The men advanced at double quick time. The Americans on the Heights had the protection of forest cover, but the Canadians and British struggling up the hill had no cover. At a stone fence where there was some shelter from the lead balls pouring down from above, Brock halted his men. "Take a breath, boys," he said. "You will need it in a few moments."

Seeing his flanking party in position, Brock ordered his men forward again. Now the face of the Heights was shrouded in the thick smoke produced by black gunpowder as the Americans unleashed a withering fire on the attackers. Red-coated men dropped. Others began to retreat. Brock cried angrily, "This is the first time I have ever seen the Forty-Ninth turn their backs!"

This was a general who commanded not from the safety of a hilltop in the rear, but from the front line. For Brock to so place himself in harm's way may have been impetuous, even foolhardy, but it was the kind of gallantry soldiers admired. The troops rallied behind their leader and renewed the attack. They were reinforced now by Colonel Macdonell, who came charging up the hill with more men. The Americans still had the advantage in numbers, but they began to fall back.

Brock led the advance, waving his sword and urging his men on. Dressed in his scarlet uniform with gold braid, and the plumed, cocked hat that identified him as an officer of high rank, Brock easily stood out from the rank and file. Bullets whizzed around him and one even struck the wrist that held the sword. Brock ignored the wound. Then, as the general had his head turned slightly toward his troops, an American soldier stepped from behind a clump of trees and aimed his weapon directly at Brock. Some of Brock's men saw the soldier and fired at him while they shouted warnings to the general. Their shots all missed, and the warning came too late. The American soldier fired from about thirty paces and drilled a bullet into Brock's right breast. The lead ball knocked Brock off his feet. George Jarvis, a fifteen-year-old militiaman, was just a few feet away from the stricken general.

"Running up to him I enquired, 'Are you much hurt, Sir?' He placed his hand on his breast and made no reply, and slowly sunk down." The general was dead!

Isaac Brock's death became one of those moments in history around which legends grew. There are stories of him uttering stirring last words like, "Push on, brave York volunteers," and, "My fall must not be noticed or impede my brave companions from advancing to victory." He has even been quoted as saying in Latin, "*Surgite,*" which could be interpreted as "Press on." Quite likely he died without saying a word.

The American soldier who had shot Brock disappeared into the trees. His identity is uncertain. A soldier named Robert Walcot later claimed the honour of being the man who killed the famous English general. But Walcot, who was a gunner and not even an infantryman, said he took aim at Brock with a borrowed musket and shot him down. If so, it was a very lucky shot indeed, because muskets were not made to be "aimed." More than likely the soldier who was seen to take deliberate aim at Brock was armed with a rifle. The slain general never knew that he had been knighted for his capture of Detroit. On the very day Brock died, back in England church bells were ringing in honour of his bloodless victory. News travelled slowly in 1812.

On the bloody slope of Queenston Heights a group of shocked British soldiers gathered protectively around the fallen general, refusing to believe he was dead. A cannon shell exploded right by them and a soldier stricken by iron fragments collapsed across Brock's body. An officer ordered a party of men to remove the general from the field.

Command now fell to Colonel Macdonell. The twenty-eight-year-old officer had no experience in war, but he had idolized Brock and was enraged at his leader's death. He rallied a group of about seventy regulars and militiamen and renewed the assault on Wool's position. He cried to his men, "Charge them home and they cannot stand you!" The soldiers responded with shouts of, "Revenge for the general!"

Macdonell led on horseback, presenting an even more conspicuous target than Brock had done. Bullets ripped through his coat, miraculously not touching him. Captain Wool's original company had almost run out of ammunition, but was reinforced by more regulars and militia. Even so, the Americans fell back before the ferocity of the British–Canadian attack. They were driven to the very brink of the cliffs. An unidentified American officer tied a white handkerchief to the end of his sword and began to wave it. Captain Wool, the kind of man Brock would have liked had they not been foes, angrily knocked it away. He regrouped his shaken and bloodied force and American resistance stiffened. The redcoat advance faltered. Macdonell galloped up and down the line, exhorting his men to push forward. Then for the second time that day, disaster struck.

A bullet struck Macdonell's horse, causing the startled animal to make a sudden turn. Almost immediately another bullet smashed into Macdonell's back and tore through his abdomen. Macdonell tumbled from the saddle, mortally wounded. He was not the only officer on the British–Canadian side to go down. Captain Duncan Cameron, attempting to go to Macdonell's assistance, had his elbow shattered by a musket ball. Lieutenant Archibald McLean tried to help both officers get to cover, and was shot in the leg. Captain John Williams had the scalp practically ripped off his skull by a bullet and was stumbling about in dazed confusion. With their officers dropping around them, the British and Canadians wavered, and then fell back. Captain James Dennis, who had been fighting since the first American boat touched the Canadian shore, was the only officer still standing, and he was limping with a bullet in his thigh. He pulled the men back to the village in an orderly withdrawal, taking the wounded with them. Captain Wool, though he had received more reinforcements, did not attempt pursuit. He, too, had been wounded again. He turned to strengthening his position on the Heights. His men had taken several prisoners, including young George Jarvis, who had witnessed Brock's death. It was now sometime after eight o'clock, and the Americans seemed to have control of the field.

By now many of the Americans' boats had been destroyed or otherwise lost, but reinforcements continued to trickle across the river. Among them was Colonel Chrystie, who finally set foot on the Canadian side. He took over command of the invading force as Captain Wool and Solomon Van Rensselaer were evacuated to the American side with the rest of the wounded. Chrystie knew the British would be receiving reinforcements from Fort George and elsewhere, so he had his men throw up defensive works on the slope of the Heights facing Queenston. He led an assault on the village and managed to penetrate a short distance, but British troops under Captain William Holcroft made a determined stand behind the cover of a stone fence. Chrystie's attack on the village petered out, and some of his men turned to looting the few houses now in their hands. Holcroft had cannon, which he now turned on the American boats and on the dock from which they were embarking. His gunners quickly sank three boats, once again throwing the Americans still on their own shore into turmoil.

By now about 1,600 Americans (of whom five hundred were militia) were on Canadian soil. They commanded the Heights. They had the battered redcoats and Canadian militia hemmed into one end of the village. The senior British general was dead—though the Americans were probably unaware of this. When their fellows waiting on the New York shore crossed over and doubled their strength, they should have had little trouble carrying the day, even with the arrival of reinforcements from Fort George.

But their fellows on the other side of the river did not join them. General Alexander Smyth never did bring his 1,650 regulars from Black Rock. And 1,800 New York militiamen stood on their side of the river and did nothing but watch. They were under no obligation, their officers said, to fight outside their home state. Of those five hundred militiamen who *had* made the crossing, two hundred—unnerved by their first taste of war—refused to advance beyond the riverbank.

General Stephen Van Rensselaer, who had not made the crossing, now summoned Colonel Chrystie to return to Lewiston and report on the situation in Queenston. The general sent Brigadier General William Wadsworth of the New York Militia across the river to take command of the militia units. With him went twenty-six-year-old Lieutenant Colonel Winfield Scott, future commander-in-chief of the United States Army. Young Scott was to take command of the vital position on the Heights. He had a six-pounder field gun, but only a few rounds of ammunition. Van Rensselaer had promised him reinforcements and more ammunition. At the redan Scott put an engineer to work trying to unspike the eighteen-pounder, but the British gunners had done their job well. The big gun remained silent for the duration of the battle.

Back at Fort George, when General Shaeffe received Brock's message, he immediately sent a detachment of Royal Artillery with two field guns and a howitzer to Queenston. With them went a company of the Forty-First Regiment of Foot. Also heading for Queenston were three hundred warriors from the Six Nations Reserve on the Grand River. They were led by the colourful Captain John Norton, son of a Cherokee mother and a Scottish father. His second-in-command was Lieutenant John Brant, son of the great Chief Joseph Brant. More reinforcements would soon be on the road from Chippawa.

General Shaeffe did not immediately rush off to Queenston. Like Brock, he was concerned about an assault on Fort George. He became more convinced of this when the guns of Fort Niagara across the river opened fire on Fort George and the village of Niagara, setting several buildings ablaze. The Fort George gunners replied with stunning accuracy and soon silenced the American batteries. Then Shaeffe received the shattering news of Brock's death. He called out the rest of his garrison, and leaving only a handful of men in the fort, led his red-coated column down the road toward Queenston.

The arrival of reinforcements was greeted with cheers by the beleaguered defenders in Queenston. The Americans were quickly forced to withdraw from the part of the village they had occupied. Now Shaeffe knew he had to retake the Heights. He was under the mistaken belief it was held by five thousand American troops. He had nine hundred regulars. Not given to the kind of rash action that had sent Brock to his death, Shaeffe chose a more cautious strategy than a direct advance up the slope. With Norton's warriors in the vanguard, he took his men off in a wide, flanking circle that would take them up and around the entrenched Americans. Part of his army had to stay back and keep the Americans at the riverside in check.

Shaeffe's flanking movement called for a three-mile march over rough ground. As a precaution against the Americans countering this move by ambushing the column from the forest, Norton took his warriors into the woods. The Natives fanned out, but encountered only a few Canadian militiamen fleeing the battleground. These men greatly exaggerated the number of American soldiers dug in on the heights. When the Natives arrived at their predetermined rendezvous, Norton discovered to his disgust that he had a desertion problem of his own. All but eighty of the warriors who had started out with him had decided that five thousand Americans were simply too many to take on, and had turned around to head back for their homes. As Norton later put it, the men remaining with him "burned with indignation, and panted to come in contact with the insolent Invaders." Norton told his men, "Comrades and brothers, we have found what we came for…there they are. It remains only to fight." As events would show, those eighty men had a far greater impact on the outcome of the battle than their numbers would indicate.

Down below, General Van Rensselaer had finally crossed the river to oversee operations on the Canadian side. Messengers brought him repeated pleas from Scott for reinforcements and ammunition. With the arrival of Shaeffe and his regulars, Van Rensselaer knew he had to get more troops across the river to fight off the British counterattack that was surely coming. He got back into his boat to return and plead his case with the New York militia. Before the boat pushed off, several American militiamen piled into it, eager to escape the gunsmoke and the bloodshed. Van Rensselaer's arguments with his own men would fall on deaf ears.

At his position centred on the British redan, Winfield Scott felt victory slipping away. Not only was there no sign of the promised reinforcements, but desertion was shrinking his command. At one point he'd had nine hundred men on the Heights. Now his force had thinned to about seven hundred. Then, as he watched for the attack he expected to come up the slope, a racket like all hell breaking loose arose to the rear of his position.

Emerging from the trees behind Scott's lines, Norton and his warriors encountered American pickets who had been placed there to watch for a rear attack. Shrieking like demons and firing their guns, the warriors went straight at the Americans. The American soldiers discharged their weapons, then turned and ran, with the Natives howling and shooting at them as they did. Those soldiers piled into what was supposed to be Scott's secondary line of defence, frightening some of those men, too, into flight. It would have been bad enough had it been redcoats striking them from the rear, but these were *Indians!*

The average American infantryman or militiaman was no Davy Crockett or Daniel Boone. He was a young man from a farm or a small settlement who had grown up listening to stories about Indian savagery that went all the way back to the French and Indian Wars. He had a numbing fear of being tomahawked and scalped; or even worse, being dragged off alive by the "red demons."

The panic might have become general, and the Americans on the Heights may well have poured down the slope to seek the protection of the redcoats. But Winfield Scott was no ordinary officer. Barking orders and making liberal use of the flat of his sword, he put a halt to what could have become the disintegration of his command. He whipped his men back into formation, and ordered a bayonet charge. Norton's warriors melted back into the trees, and from there continued to snipe at the Americans and chill their nerves with bloodcurdling war cries. Scott called back the charge, having no idea how many warriors were in the woods. Norton's men had inflicted but a few casualties on the enemy, while taking a few themselves. But the psychological damage had been done, and it was considerable. Scott had steadied his men, but individuals still slipped off to make their way down the escarpment to the river. Moreover, those war-whoops could be heard on the other side of the river. Now, not an order from President Madison himself could have gotten those New York militiamen into the boats.

The British brought more artillery up from Fort George and began to shell Scott's position while at the same time hurling iron at the batteries on the American shore. Behind Scott's position, General Shaeffe's column linked up with the relief column from Chippawa and some fresh militia units. He decided on a three-pronged attack, with Norton's warriors joining on the extreme left.

Scott finally had a message from General Van Rensselaer. There would be no reinforcements. The general was pulling the army back to the American side. He advised Scott to take his men to the riverbank, where boats would be waiting to ferry them across. Some of his men would have to fight a rearguard action to keep the

British from capturing the whole army—or to prevent the Indians from slaughtering them.

Scott was in a quandary. Some of his officers wanted to stay and fight so they could erase "the disgrace of Hull's recent surrender." Scott knew, however, that the situation had become all but hopeless. He and his officers had not yet reached a decision when the British and Canadians attacked. It was now 3:00 p.m.

The attack began with blasts from a pair of small field pieces. Then the British regulars advanced with fixed bayonets, flanked by units of Canadian militia. The Americans fired a volley, then began to withdraw, one unit at a time. They would have to engage in a fighting retreat down the hill to the river. Scott and his officers tried to keep the withdrawal orderly, but the men were clearly on the verge of panic. Then Norton's warriors burst out of the trees on the Americans' right, and chaos ensued. This time not even Scott could stem the tide. A few of the more steady men tried to slow the British troops advancing from the American rear, but most of the soldiers dropped their weapons and ran for the river. Some headed the wrong way and ran right over the cliff to fall to their deaths three hundred feet below. Others managed to reach the riverbank, only to find the promised boats were not there. Some tried to swim across. A few made it, but several men drowned or were shot by red-coated soldiers in "revenge for the general." Some sought shelter among the rocks, where they prayed they would be found by redcoats and not Indians. Some unlucky ones were, in fact, tomahawked and scalped, to the utter fury of General Shaeffe.

Winfield Scott realized only a hasty surrender would save the lives of his remaining men. He tied a white cravat to the end of his sword and holding it aloft, started to walk toward the British lines, anxiously seeking out an officer. He was quickly seized by two

Natives, one of them young John Brant. Before they could do the American officer any harm, Lieutenant John Beverly Robinson of the York Militia took custody of Scott and escorted him to General Shaeffe, to whom Scott surrendered his sword.

A bugler sounded the call for cease-fire, but the Natives were bent on revenge of their own. Two of their chiefs had been killed, and the warriors wanted American blood. It took an explosive outburst of temper from Shaeffe—the sort of behaviour he might otherwise have considered unbecoming an officer and a gentleman—to put an end to the butchery. When the shooting finally stopped the dejected Scott had one more humiliation to endure. Scores of American militiamen who had taken no part in the fight emerged from the rocks where they had hidden themselves and surrendered.

The Battle of Queenston Heights was over, and once more an American invasion of Canada had been turned back. The British and Canadians had fourteen men killed, seventy-eight wounded and twenty-one taken prisoner. In the days and weeks to come several of those wounded men would die. Norton's warriors had five dead and nine wounded.

No one has ever been certain about the number of American casualties that day. The British counted 925 prisoners, more than half of whom were militia. Seventy-three of the captured Americans were officers. General Van Rensselaer, who would shoulder most of the blame for the humiliating defeat, and who would never command men again, said it was not possible to give a precise account of his losses. He estimated that sixty officers and men had been killed and 170 wounded. But no one seemed to know how many men had been lost in the river during the initial crossing and then the disastrous retreat. One estimate was as high as five hundred.

A truce was called after the battle, and the British buried Isaac Brock and John Macdonell at Fort George with full military honours. Across the river the guns of Fort Niagara boomed in a salute to a gallant foe. The British and Canadians had won a key battle, and the enemy was in disarray. But the cost of that victory had cast a pall of gloom over any notion of a celebration. General Brock was dead! Was there an officer in Canada who could replace him?

The Battle of
Beaver Dams

A Walk in the Woods

The great battles of history have always been the stuff of legends. Out of the smoke and carnage of earth-shattering collisions between mighty armies—bloodbaths such as Waterloo, Gettysburg, Normandy—arise tales of heroism, courage and sacrifice. Measured against these colossal military clashes, even the major battles of the War of 1812 appear to be minor affairs. The Battle of Waterloo produced more casualties in a single day than the War of 1812 did in its entire duration. By further comparison, the smaller engagements of that war might seem almost insignificant. Yet, one of those short, sharp border clashes wove a legend around a woman who would become a Canadian icon. General Isaac Brock, who died with his boots on while leading his troops up Queenston Heights, entered the pantheon of Canadian heroes as the "Saviour of Upper Canada." But a thirty-eight-year-old mother of five would have her name enshrined as the "Heroine of Upper Canada," because she took a walk in the woods.

The opening campaigns of the War of 1812 had gone very badly indeed for the United States. Not only had American armies failed to seize Canada, but their forts at Michilimackinac and Detroit were now in British hands. The defeats suffered by American arms had gone beyond being military reversals; they had been humiliating debacles that embarrassed the Madison government before the world. During the early months of 1813, as both sides waited for the snows to melt and the ice to go out of the Great Lakes so the fighting could be renewed, the American War Department reviewed its strategy for driving the British out of Canada. The first plan called for a three-pronged assault against Montreal, Kingston and Niagara. But the Americans overestimated the British strength at Kingston, and decided to strike first at York (Toronto), and then Fort George at Niagara. The American generals knew their forces outnumbered the British troops in those places, because the enemy had to commit the bulk of his forces to the defence of Montreal. By seizing York and Niagara, they reasoned, they could control Lake Ontario, shutting off the western part of Upper Canada from supplies and reinforcements. Then they could turn their attention to the stronghold at Kingston.

On April 27, 1813, an American fleet landed an attacking force at York and after a brief struggle forced General Roger Shaeffe, the victor at Queenston Heights, to retreat to Kingston. The Americans burned the town, then departed, the taking of York being of more political than military value. Shaeffe's withdrawal cost him his command, even though his troops were outnumbered three to one.

On May 25, an American army of seven thousand men, supported by sixteen gunboats on Lake Ontario, attacked Fort George. The commander was aged, ill and overweight Major General Henry Dearborn, a veteran of the Revolutionary War. The officer who actually led the assault was Colonel Winfield Scott. Colonel

Scott had been taken captive at Queenston, and then repatriated in a prisoner exchange. He was anxious to wipe out the humiliation of having to surrender his sword.

The British commander, Major General John Vincent, had 1,400 troops and only 300 supporting militia. Most of the Canadians had returned to their farms. Vincent's men tried to prevent an American landing, but the enemy were too many and the cannon fire from the ships was murderous. In no time Vincent had fifty-two killed and more than three hundred wounded or missing. When he realized the true size of the attacking force and understood that Scott could turn the British flank and kill or capture them all, Vincent wisely decided to withdraw.

"I could not consider myself justified in continuing so unequal a contest, the issue of which promised no advantage to the interests of His Majesty's Service," he later reported.

With Fort George in flames from the cannon barrage, Vincent had all the big guns spiked, and then set a charge to blow up the powder magazine. He then made an orderly evacuation, taking his men across the Niagara Peninsula to a place called Beaver Dams, near present day Thorold. There, Vincent had prudently made a supply depot. En route he was joined by companies from Fort Erie, who had also been forced to abandon their post by overwhelming American numbers. He now had about 1,600 regulars. Vincent sent his few militiamen home, and took his troops to Burlington Heights on Lake Ontario, where he could be supplied by British vessels. One of his officers was a lieutenant named James Fitzgibbon.

Thirty-two-year-old, Irish-born Fitzgibbon had been in the army since the age of seventeen. He had served as a sergeant and an adjutant under Isaac Brock, whom he practically worshipped. Brock had seen potential in young Fitzgibbon and had more or less made him a protegé. He helped the barely literate youth become self-educated, taught him social graces and correct pronunciation, and advised him on how to handle soldiers. Fitzgibbon was stationed in Kingston when he received the news of Brock's death. Years later he would write that Brock, "had been more than a father to me in that regiment which he ruled like a father." Now encamped with General Vincent's small army at Burlington Heights, Fitzgibbon was anxious to have a crack at the Americans.

As the retreating British column disappeared down the road, the Americans entered Fort George. Winfield Scott, the first man through the gates, suffered a broken collarbone when the fort's powder magazine exploded. The pain from this injury hardly slowed him down. He wanted to pursue the redcoats and "bag their whole force," but to his disgust his overcautious superior officers would not permit it. With battered, empty Fort George as the prize, the American victory was a hollow one. It had cost them forty dead and 120 wounded, and General Vincent had escaped.

Not until June 1 did the Americans set out to catch General Vincent's small force. Under brigadier generals William Winder and John Chandler, a pair of incompetents who had none of the zeal or professionalism of Winfield Scott, three thousand men, 150 cavalry and four field guns headed toward Burlington Heights. The column was disorganized and advanced slowly. When a local farm boy they encountered claimed to be sympathetic to the American side, the American officers believed him. One even gave him the password, so he could move about freely without being detained by American patrols. The boy promptly took this information to Burlington Heights.

On June 5 the American army camped at Stoney Creek, about 6.2 kilometres (10 miles) from Vincent's position. Winder and

Chandler were not sure just where the British were, but Vincent knew where *they* were, and had scouts under Lieutenant Colonel John Harvey reconnoitering their camp. There is a story (undocumented) that Lieutenant James Fitzgibbon, disguised as a butter seller, actually entered the American camp and had a good look around. Whether or not the butter seller story is true, Colonel Harvey reported back to General Vincent that the American camp was a poorly arranged, sprawling hodgepodge. The sentries were few and not very well-placed. The Americans, said Harvey, were over-confident, and ripe for a night attack. General Vincent agreed.

In the early hours of June 6 General Vincent led seven hundred hand-picked men, including Fitzgibbon, through the darkness to the American camp. They were under orders of absolute silence and had removed the flints from their muskets so there would be no accidental discharge to alert the enemy. When the advance parties approached the American pickets, the sentries called out in challenge. Voices from the darkness replied with the password. The sentries relaxed, and then were bayoneted before they knew what was happening.

The British now rushed into the meadow that was the centre of the American camp, where cooking fires were still glowing. Disregarding orders, some of the soldiers whooped, stuck flints into their firing mechanisms and discharged their muskets. Then they saw to their astonishment that the meadow was empty. The Americans had moved a short distance away to the safety of a ridge. Now it was the British who were in a trap as, illuminated by the campfires, they were easy targets for the aroused Americans. The Americans poured a volley into them. Then all became confusion.

In the darkness, and with thick clouds of gunsmoke enveloping all, it was difficult to tell friend from foe. Companies from both sides fired on their own men. Somewhere General Vincent fell off his horse and became lost in the woods, and command fell to Colonel Harvey (Vincent did not find his way back to his own camp until noon the next day). Fitzgibbon saw the men of the British left falling back, so he took charge of the line and ordered them forward. The five hundred Americans opposite them were soon retreating in disorder. At the other end of the field the bulk of the American army was on the verge of overwhelming the British. The Americans' field pieces were wreaking havoc. A company of some twenty British soldiers charged the gun positions, bayoneted the crews, and captured the cannons. Generals Winder and Chandler had neglected to provide their gunners with infantry protection. They had also encamped their cavalry so far back that by the time the horsemen reached the battleground they couldn't tell who was who.

Both American generals suffered the indignity of being captured by a mere sergeant, a young soldier named Alexander Fraser. General Chandler fell off his horse and wandered around in the darkness looking for his line. He blundered into the British soldiers who had just captured his big guns. When Chandler tried to hide under a gun carriage, Fraser dragged him out and took him prisoner. Winder also became lost in the confusion and stumbled into the same party of redcoats. When he realized he was among the enemy, Winder dramatically pulled his pistol from his belt. Before he could fire it, Sergeant Fraser called out, "If you stir, sir, you die!" General Winder sensibly tossed down his pistol and sword and surrendered.

Unable to locate General Vincent, and having taken heavy losses, Colonel Harvey decided to withdraw his men. He had over a hundred prisoners—including two generals—and the enemy's artillery, but he believed the attack had been a failure. Hours later he learned from a scout that the American camp was in a panic. They were smashing everything in that could not be carried off, and preparing to retreat to Fort George. They weren't even taking time to bury their dead.

That afternoon the British returned to the battlefield and found the camp abandoned. The ground was littered with cast-off provisions, blankets, munitions—and bodies. It would be up to the redcoats to bury the American dead. The British had twenty-three men dead, 134 wounded and five missing. Besides the one hundred or so taken captive, the Americans had fifty-eight casualties. But it was they who were beating a hasty retreat, leaving the British in possession of the battlefield at Stoney Creek.

At Fort George, General Dearborn ordered his second in command, Major General Morgan Lewis, to take a column of men immediately to attack Vincent's small army at Stoney Creek. Had Winfield Scott been given the assignment, the exhausted British troops might have been in a difficult spot. But General Lewis was another of those inexperienced, non-professionals who owed his rank to political connections. He was pompous, slow-moving, and very much attached to his personal comfort. Instead of dashing off to lock horns with the enemy, as Scott undoubtedly would have done, Lewis delayed his departure for half a day because of rain.

When Lewis did finally move out, he got only as far as Forty Mile Creek (present day Grimsby), when a British fleet commanded by Sir James Yeo hove into view and began shelling his camp. General Dearborn feared an attack on Fort George, so he sent a dispatch to Lewis, ordering him back to defend the fort. So great was General Lewis's haste to obey the order that he left behind his baggage train and all of his provisions and extra arms and munitions, which Yeo promptly seized.

Before the clash at Stoney Creek the Americans had a stranglehold on the Niagara Peninsula. Now Dearborn ordered Fort Erie burned, and all the troops stationed in posts along the Niagara Frontier called into Fort George. Only at Queenston did he leave a detachment of troops. He was preparing for a siege.

When the British found the abandoned American camp at Stoney Creek, General Vincent pursued the retreating Americans only as far as Forty Mile Creek. James Fitzgibbon, like Winfield Scott, was disappointed in his commanding officer. Like many another junior officer serving in Upper Canada, he compared his commander with Brock, and found him wanting. To Fitzgibbon, General Vincent was, "at all times a feeble man, both in mind and body."

Fitzgibbon was impatient with what he considered the tardiness of the British army in going after the Americans. He had a plan of action that he took to Colonel Harvey. It involved harassing the enemy with a form of guerrilla warfare.

The Americans had barricaded themselves inside Fort George, but they sent out patrols that foraged for food—which generally meant taking it from farmhouses. They also locked up men and boys they suspected of being in the Canadian militia or otherwise aiding the British. The local citizens also lived in fear of Doctor Cyrenius Chapin and his fifty mounted riflemen, and Joseph Willcocks and his "Canadian Volunteers." Chapin was an American who lived in Buffalo and knew the country on the Canadian side of the line well. Willcocks was an Irish-born Canadian settler who turned traitor and supported the American cause. Both these men led gangs that haunted the countryside, terrorizing settlers known to be staunch British Loyalists and plundering their homes.

Fitzgibbon wanted to lead a band of fifty personally selected men to counter the activities of Chapin and Willcocks, who were really little more than brigands. Fitzgibbon's partisans would also harry the American patrols out of Fort George. Colonel Harvey liked the idea, but warned Fitzgibbon not to allow "the excesses to which men removed from the wholesome restraint of discipline may be expected to give way." Any looting or incidents of conduct unbecoming an officer and gentleman would seriously harm his reputation and his chances for promotion.

For about a fortnight Fitzgibbon and his band of stalwarts roamed the Niagara country, annoying the Americans at every opportunity and making life difficult for the likes of Chapin and Willcocks. Because of their green tunics and tough, "Indian manner" of fighting, they were quickly nicknamed the Green Tigers. They used cowbells for signalling, since the sound would hardly raise suspicion in the countryside. Though these men were constantly on the move, their headquarters was a stone house at Beaver Dams known as the DeCew House. It was on Twelve Mile Creek, about twenty-seven kilometres (17 miles) from Fort George.

There were several clashes between Fitzgibbon's Green Tigers and Chapin's marauders, but one incident became part of local folklore. Fitzgibbon wanted to capture some of the brigands and traitors alive for questioning. Early on June 21 Fitzgibbon learned that Chapin was in the vicinity of Niagara Falls. He and his men mounted up and rode off in search of him. At the Falls they were told that Chapin had just passed through, accompanied by 150 American soldiers. Unfazed by the difference in numbers, Fitzgibbon galloped off in pursuit. A short way down the road, he spotted a horse he knew to belong to one of Chapin's men tied up in front of a tavern run by a man named Deffield. Not wishing to alarm his quarry by roaring up to the inn with a full company of armed men, Fitzgibbon left his men back in the trees while he went on alone.

Inside the tavern Fitzgibbon saw one of Chapin's riders. The man instantly levelled a rifle at him. Before he could fire, Fitzgibbon grabbed the gun barrel and ordered the man to surrender. Just then an American infantryman entered, saw the situation, and pointed his musket at Fitzgibbon. Fitzgibbon was a big man, of considerable physical strength. While still holding the other man's rifle, he grabbed the musket barrel, and then dragged both of his foes outside. As the three men struggled, one of the Americans managed to grab Fitzgibbon's sword and pull it from the scabbard. The innkeeper's wife, who had been anxiously watching the fight, ran up and grabbed the sword from him as he was about to run Fitzgibbon through. Now Deffield the innkeeper entered the fray, and with his help Fitzgibbon made both men his prisoners. He rejoined his men and made a getaway minutes before Chapin came riding through with his whole gang. When Chapin learned of the capture of his man and the American soldier, he decided something had to be done about those Green Tigers. He headed straight for Fort George to see General Dearborn.

Fitzgibbon's Green Tigers were not the only men causing the Americans in Fort George sleepless nights. Not far from Beaver Dams John Norton of Queenston Heights fame was encamped with his Mohawks. So was Captain Dominique Ducharme, a French Canadian who had lived all his life among the Natives. He had come from Lower Canada (Quebec) with 180 Caughnawaga warriors. General Dearborn knew the British had Indian allies in the woods. He just didn't know how many. He felt that if he could destroy the enemy base at Beaver Dams he could put an end to the harassment of his patrols and of "militia" like Chapin's bunch. This might also clear the way for his men to wipe out a few other small garrisons the British had re-established after the debacles at Stoney Creek and Forty Mile Creek. Dearborn believed the "fortified stone house" was defended by a company of regulars and sixty to a hundred Natives. In fact, there were closer to four hundred warriors in the vicinity.

General Dearborn sent Lieutenant Colonel Charles Boerstler to "capture or dislodge" the enemy at Beaver Dams. Colonel Boerstler left Fort George after dark on the evening of June 23 at the head of five hundred men. His column included a company of light artillery, and "Major" Chapin, along with forty of his riders. Boerstler believed he would have little trouble, with the element of surprise on his side. He was wrong.

Just how Laura Secord, a Massachusetts-born, Loyalist wife of a Canadian militiaman who was wounded at Queenston Heights, learned of the American advance on Beaver Dams is not certain. Many versions of the story would evolve and circulate. The most popular version had some American officers, possibly in the company of the notorious Doctor Cyrenius Chapin, entering the Secord house near Queenston and demanding a meal. As the intruders ate, Laura overheard them talking about the coming attack on Beaver Dams. (In another version her husband James overheard the Americans talking about the attack, but being incapacitated by his war injury passed the information to Laura.) She slipped away, intending to warn Lieutenant Fitzgibbon. The journey was not an easy one. She had 30.5 kilometres (19 miles) of rough country full of wolves and rattlesnakes to cover on foot, and at thirty-eight she was, by the standards of the time, middle-aged. There were American patrols on the roads, as well as the ruffians who rode for Chapin and Willcocks. Capture by regular American troops could mean detention in the guardhouse at Fort George. Capture by border bandits in the guise of militia could have much more frightful consequences for a woman alone on the road.

To avoid these dangers Laura stayed off the roads and hiked through a dreary area known as Black Swamp. There she was undoubtedly tormented by that bane of early Canadian summer, clouds of black flies and mosquitoes. It is not certain if she actually had to bluff her way past American sentries, but her destination was up on the Niagara Escarpment, which meant she must have scrambled up some very steep terrain. The cross-country ordeal took her nineteen hours in the June heat, and by the time she staggered into a Native camp her shoes were in tatters and her feet blistered and bleeding.

Laura was still not completely out of danger, because the Caughnawagas, into whose camp she stumbled, weren't sure if she was a Loyalist or an American spy. They finally agreed to take her to Lieutenant Fitzgibbon. Covered with mud and exhausted by her ordeal, Laura Secord told Fitzgibbon of the impending American attack on Beaver Dams. Thus, Fitzgibbon was ready for Boerstler's "surprise attack." That, at least, is the legend.

Quite likely Fitzgibbon's Native scouts would have told the lieutenant of the Americans' approach anyway. That does not take anything away from Secord's heroic act. She still risked her own safety, perhaps even her life, to deliver what she considered vital information.

Colonel Boerstler was yet another officer who had no business leading soldiers. He was petty-minded and took great offense when Winfield Scott, and not he, was chosen to lead the assault on Fort George. Cyrenius Chapin considered Boerstler a "broken-down Methodist preacher." Boerstler, in turn, described Chapin as "a vain and boastful liar." Chapin was with the expedition because he claimed to know the country like the back of his hand.

When the column reached Queenston, Boerstler called a halt so the men could rest. To prevent Fitzgibbon from being warned of his coming, he gave orders that no one was to leave the village. Laura Secord was already with Fitzgibbon.

The Americans moved out again at dawn. At the village of St. Davids two of Dominique Ducharme's Caughnawagas saw the Americans. One was shot and killed, but the other one ran off to carry the news to Beaver Dams. Fitzgibbon had more than enough time to prepare.

The American column moved up the Niagara escarpment. When they reached the top they continued on for about a mile until they reached a narrow path bordered by forest on either side. It was the perfect place for an ambush, but neither Boerstler nor Chapin realized it. Neither man seemed to think it odd that their advance scouts had not returned. Those men had, in fact, already been tomahawked and scalped. In the woods on one side of the path in front of the Americans were Ducharme's Caughnawagas. On the other side were Norton's Mohawks. The Americans marched straight into the trap.

Gunfire from both sides of the trail tore into the blue-coated ranks. Boerstler was almost immediately wounded in the leg. For the rest of the battle he commanded from the back of a wagon. Chapin—according to Boerstler—fled to the rear and took cover among the wagons in the baggage train, and did not participate in the fight at all. (Chapin would claim that he almost single-handedly drove four hundred Indians from the field, but Boerstler's incompetence cost him the battle).

Inexplicably, after the first volley the Mohawks withdrew. The Americans fought their way to a coulee where they could take defensive positions and make use of their two cannons. The Caughnawagas surrounded the Americans but were reluctant to charge in the face of cannon fire. The opposing sides blasted away at each other from behind the cover of trees. At this the Natives were more successful because they had rifles. The Americans were all armed with muskets. Boerstler could not take any riflemen with him, because it was their turn to do guard duty at the fort.

Fitzgibbon was present but neither he nor any of his fifty men fired a shot. Three hours after the first shots were fired in ambush, Fitzgibbon held a white flag aloft, stepped out where the Americans could see him, and demanded a surrender. Boerstler sent an artillery captain named McDowell to parley with him. Fitzgibbon said he had been sent by Major Peter DeHaran (who was actually several miles away with a small company of troops) to inform the American commander that he was surrounded by a superior British army, and must surrender. Boerstler replied that he would not surrender to an army he could not see.

Fitzgibbon pretended to go back to consult with his superior officer. Just then a British captain named John Hall arrived, leading only twelve dragoons. Captain Hall agreed to impersonate Major De Haran. At Fitzgibbon's invitation, Boerstler sent an officer to personally talk to the British "major." The officer reported back that he saw Major De Haran, but the Englishman would not allow him to see his troops.

Boerstler was still uncertain. He said he needed time to make a decision. Fitzgibbon told him he had five minutes. After that, he said, the British could not guarantee to control the Indians.

This was the same ruse Brock had used at Detroit, and it worked. Colonel Boerstler cried, "For God's sake, keep the Indians from us!" He agreed to surrender, but said his men would lay down their arms only in the presence of the British army. Fitzgibbon again pretended to consult with his superior. This time Boerstler was tricked into thinking that if the Americans did not disarm immediately, the Indians would massacre them. The soldiers dropped their weapons. Immediately the Mohawks, who had pulled out of the fight early, swooped down on the Americans, not to kill and scalp but to plunder. They carried away a bounty in guns, ammunition and other equipment. John Norton would later comment, "The Caughnawaga Indians fought the battle, the Mohawks got the plunder and Fitzgibbon got the credit."

Fifty-eight Americans were killed or wounded in the Battle of Beaver Dams. The rest became prisoners, including Doctor Cyrenius Chapin. He eventually escaped and returned to Buffalo where he was hailed as a hero. The Caughnawagas had five men killed and twenty wounded.

News of the defeat at Beaver Dams stunned the Americans in Fort George. Henceforth foraging details would rarely go farther than a mile beyond the protection of the fort's walls. After spending several miserable months as virtual prisoners within the captured post, the Americans abandoned Fort George on December 10 and returned to their side of the river. Before that happened, an exasperated War Department in Washington relieved General Dearborn of his command, diplomatically citing his poor health as the reason.

Beaver Dams made Fitzgibbon an overnight hero in Upper Canada, to the chagrin of many. The Caughnawagas were bitter over being ignored in published accounts of the battle. Dominique Ducharme believed he deserved the credit because he, not Fitzgibbon, set up the ambush. He said he would have called on the Americans to surrender, but could not because he spoke little English. Fitzgibbon did eventually give credit to the Caughnawagas. He wrote:

"With respect to the affair with Colonel Boerstler not a shot was fired on our side by any but the Indians. They beat the American Detachment into a state of terror and the only share I claim is the taking advantage of a favourable moment to offer them protection from the Tomahawk and the Scalping Knife. The Indian Department did all the rest."

However, Fitzgibbon did not make this admission until well after he had been promoted to captain as a reward for "his" victory.

It was a long time, too, before Laura Secord received any recognition for her brave action. Fitzgibbon did not mention her at all in his initial reports. Three times, however—in 1820, 1827 and 1837—when Laura asked him for testimonials to accompany applications she or her husband were submitting for government appointments or favours, Fitzgibbon wrote letters confirming that she had, indeed, made the hazardous journey to inform him of the American attack.

Still, relatively few people knew of Laura Secord's daring adventure. It did not become public until 1845 when her son Charles wrote about it in a letter to a Cobourg periodical. Laura herself wrote a narrative that appeared in a Toronto publication in 1853. But these accounts drew little attention.

Then in 1860 the Prince of Wales (later King Edward VII) was in Niagara Falls to participate in a memorial ceremony honouring

Sir Isaac Brock. Through Laura's own efforts, the Prince became aware of her perilous journey, and of the fact that her late husband had been wounded at Queenston Heights while serving under Brock. The Prince was fascinated by the story, and rewarded Laura with an honorarium of one hundred pounds in gold. Laura Secord was eighty-five at the time.

The fact that she had been personally rewarded by the very popular Prince of Wales brought Laura national attention. In 1864 a historian named William F. Coffin wrote a book about the War of 1812 in which he included an imaginative account of Laura's famous journey. In Coffin's tale, Laura bluffs her way past an American sentry by walking a cow. This story, which presents Laura as wily, as well as brave, became known to every schoolchild in Canada. Even after Laura's death at the age of ninety-three in 1868, her fame grew. A new nation in search of heroes could not resist the image of the courageous little woman outwitting the American invaders to deliver a warning to the gallant lieutenant. In recent years some revisionists have downplayed the Laura Secord story, and even questioned its authenticity. But if Americans can make an icon out of Betsy Ross, who merely stitched a flag, surely Canadians are entitled to do the same with Laura Secord and her daring walk in the woods.

The Battle of Moraviantown

In the Hands of the Great Spirit

On September 10, 1813, the American Commander Oliver Hazard Perry with a newly constructed fleet of nine ships, defeated the British Commander Robert Barclay with his undermanned fleet of six in the Battle of Lake Erie. The American capture of York the previous spring had deprived Barclay of badly needed provisions and guns, forcing him to go into battle under less than ideal conditions. Perry's victory was of vital strategic importance to the United States, because it gave the Americans absolute control of Lake Erie. Prior to that September day, Erie had belonged to the Royal Navy. Now the Americans could land men anywhere they pleased on the lake's Canadian shore. That meant they could cut communications and supply lines between Niagara and the western part of Upper Canada. British garrisons in that part of the colony, denied reinforcements and provisions, could be surrounded and forced to surrender. The British hold on Detroit, captured by General Isaac Brock a little over a year earlier, suddenly became tenuous. The American General William Henry Harrison was on his way with more than 4,500 men, many of them Kentucky militiamen who, unlike the New York militia at Queenston, were eager for battle and had no qualms about fighting outside their own state. In Detroit there were nine hundred British regulars and Canadian militia, and some 1,200 Native warriors. For Major General Henry Procter, the officer Brock himself had left in command at Detroit, there was only one sensible option: retreat! For Procter's ally, the Shawnee chief Tecumseh, who had helped Brock take Detroit, the word *retreat* did not exist. He wanted to fight.

Tecumseh, approximately forty-five years old, had been fighting the Americans for most of his adult life. But he was more than a war chief. Tecumseh was a visionary. He imagined a great Native Confederacy in the heart of what is now the United States; an alliance of tribes that could stand up to the land-hungry Americans and negotiate with them. He had spent years traveling amongst the various tribes trying to convince them to cast off their traditional rivalries and follow his dream. That dream had all but evaporated on November 11, 1811, when, in Tecumseh's absence and against his instructions, his brother Tenskwatawa—known as The Prophet—fought the army of this same William Henry Harrison at Tippecanoe, and lost. The defeat had seriously undermined Tecumseh's credibility amongst the tribes.

Then war had broken out between the British and the Americans, and General Brock had convinced Tecumseh to join him as an ally. Tecumseh had little reason to trust the British. They had a history of betraying Native allies. But he had liked and trusted Brock. Now Brock was dead, and Tecumseh did not think much of General Procter.

Like Brock, fifty-year-old Henry Procter was a lifelong soldier. His career, up to this point, had been commendable, if not spectacular. Following the capture of Detroit and Brock's return to the Niagara Frontier, Procter had, on January 22, 1813, defeated an American force made up largely of Kentucky militiamen led by General James Winchester at Frenchtown, forty-eight kilometres (30 miles) south of Detroit. The battle had thwarted an American attempt to retake Detroit, but it was a tarnished victory. Procter had unwisely left eighty sick and wounded American prisoners in the custody of his Native allies while he hurried back to Detroit. In his absence (and Tecumseh's) the warriors massacred the helpless men on the banks of the Raisin River. Henry Procter was now a hated man in Kentucky.

Following his victory at Frenchtown, Procter had tried, and failed, to capture the American stronghold of Fort Meigs on the Maumee River. The fort was on the verge of capitulating when a relief column of Kentucky militiamen managed to fight through the besiegers. Procter blamed the failure on his Canadian militia, who had to return to their farms, and the Natives, who took the scalps and plunder they'd gained in early skirmishes and went home. Left with just four hundred British regulars against a garrison four times that many, Procter had no choice but to withdraw.

Proctor was not a general who inspired his men. He was corpulent. He was indecisive. He was secretive, not telling even his subordinate officers what his plans were. He did not like to take risks.

With the loss of the British fleet on Lake Erie, Procter had sound reasons for a strategic withdrawal. He had given Lieutenant Robert Barclay men and guns to beef up the naval commander's fighting strength. Now those men and guns were gone, and there was little chance of replacing them. His provisions were running low, and without new supplies from the east, he could not hope to feed his troops and the Natives camped outside his walls. Even while Lake Erie had been controlled by the British, provisions had come through at such a trickle that his soldiers' uniforms looked ragged.

Instead of telling Tecumseh the truth about the disaster on Lake Erie, Procter told the chief that the British ships had defeated the Americans. He was afraid the Natives would vanish overnight if they knew what had really happened. Tecumseh soon learned the truth. He was not a fool, and he didn't like being treated like one. Then Tecumseh received more infuriating news. British soldiers were demolishing Fort Malden, the main post on the Canadian side of the Detroit River, downriver from Detroit. That could mean only one thing. The redcoats were leaving! This was in the face of promises made by Brock, and then Procter, that the British would stand by their allies and help them protect their homes from the Americans. He had a wampum belt—a sacred treaty as far as his people were concerned—that symbolized the alliance he had forged with the King of England. Tecumseh sent word to Procter that he was prepared to cut that wampum belt in two and throw it at the general's feet.

Procter did not want a confrontation with Tecumseh. But he knew Britain needed the Shawnee leader as an ally. He was afraid, too, that once the redcoat soldiers were gone, the angry Natives might turn on the Canadian settlers. Procter reluctantly agreed to meet Tecumseh in a council. The meeting was held on September 18 at Malden. The Natives sat in the centre of the room, and the British officers and other whites around the walls. Tecumseh, who knew little English, spoke through an interpreter. Fifteen-year-old John Richardson, a volunteer who would one day be Canada's first novelist, was present. He left a vivid impression of the Shawnee chief.

"Habited in a close leather dress, his athletic proportions
were admirably delineated, while a large plume of white
ostrich feathers, by which he was generally distinguished,
overshadowing his brow, and contrasting with the darkness
of his complexion and the brilliancy of his black and piercing eye, gave a singularly wild and terrific expression to his
features. It was evident that he could be terrible."

Tecumseh had a reputation as a gifted orator. As the interpreter
repeated his words in English, Procter began to understand why.
The chief wasted no time with protocol, but leveled his verbal
attack straight at the British, and Procter in particular:

"Listen! When war was declared, our Father (Procter) stood
up and gave us the tomahawk, and told us he was now
ready to strike the Americans; that he wanted our assistance; and that he certainly would get us our lands back
which the Americans had taken from us. Listen! You told us
at that time to bring forward our families to this place. We
did so, and you promised to take care of them, and that they
should want for nothing while the men would go to fight
the enemy.... Father, listen! Our fleet has gone out. We
know they have fought. We have heard the great guns, but
know nothing of what has happened to Our Father With
One Arm (Barclay). Our ships have gone one way, and we
are much astonished to see our Father tying up everything
and preparing to run the other, without letting his red children know what his intentions are. You always told us to
remain here and take care of our lands. It made our hearts
glad to hear that was your wish. You always told us you

would never draw your foot off British ground. But now, Father, we see you are drawing back, and we are sorry to see our Father doing so without seeing the enemy. We must compare our Father's conduct to a fat animal that carries its tail upon its back, but when affrighted, it drops it between its legs and runs off."

Tecumseh had insinuated that Procter was a coward. The other British officers in the room took great satisfaction at seeing the major general squirm, because he hadn't told them anymore about what his actual plans were than he had told Tecumseh. Now Tecumseh let Procter and the rest of the British officers know what kind of men his warriors were.

"Listen, Father! The Americans have not yet defeated us by land; neither are we sure they have done so by water. We, therefore, wish to remain here, and fight our enemy should they make their appearance. If they defeat us, we will then retreat with our Father...Father! You have got the arms and ammunition which our Great Father (the king) sent for his red children. If you have an idea of going away, give them to us, and you may go and welcome for us. Our lives are in the hands of the Great Spirit. We are determined to defend our lands, and if it is his will, we wish to leave our bones upon them."

When Tecumseh had finished speaking the other Natives in the room rose to their feet, shouting their approval and waving their tomahawks. It was an ordeal for Procter, who had been humiliated and insulted in front of his own officers. Now, over a week after the battle on the lake, he had to openly admit what everyone knew; that Barclay had been defeated. But he still would not say what his intentions were. He said he would have answers for Tecumseh in two days. Then Procter hurried off to Sandwich (Windsor), leaving instructions for Lieutenant Colonel Augustus Warburton, his second-in-command, to sort out any problems with Tecumseh and the other Natives. This Warburton could not do, since he did not know what promises had been made to the Indians and he had been told nothing of the general's plans.

For two more days Tecumseh and the other Native leaders were kept in the dark. But they saw provisions and ordnance being packed up and transported toward the Thames River, which cuts through the southwestern peninsula of what is now Ontario and empties into Lake St. Clair. Clearly, Procter still intended to retreat, but chose to tell the Natives nothing. Discontent hung over the Native camps like a pall. Some of the chiefs were packing up their own gear and leaving. They were going to seek terms with Harrison. Others presented Tecumseh with the argument that the British had broken the treaty, and therefore it would not be dishonourable for the warriors to turn on the redcoats and kill them. Tecumseh would not agree to such a thing. But he went to Colonel Matthew Elliot, a long-time agent with the British Indian Department who spoke several native dialects fluently. Tecumseh warned Elliot that the situation was dangerous and could soon be beyond his control.

On September 20 Procter returned to Malden and Elliot repeated Tecumseh's warning to him. Procter asked to have Tecumseh and other Native leaders meet him in the council room. There, Tecumseh proposed a plan. Let Harrison land at Amherstburg, he said, and march on the British in Malden. He and his warriors will strike the Americans' flank and cut them to pieces. It was a tactic he had successfully used in the past. But Procter rejected the plan. Tecumseh angrily called him "a miserable old squaw."

Then Procter unfurled a map and, with Colonel Elliot interpreting, explained the implications of American naval control of Lake Erie. He showed how, if the outnumbered British and Native army remained at Malden, the Americans could land men on the Erie shore, along the Detroit River and on the shore of Lake St. Clair and totally surround them. Procter's plan was to march to Lake St. Clair, and then up the valley of the Thames River, which would put them well out of the reach of Perry's gunboats. It also meant that if Harrison pursued them, he would have to have an extended supply line, being inland where he could not easily be provisioned by water. At the forks of the Thames (present-day Chatham), Procter said, he would fortify a position and make a stand against the Americans. There, he would have a better chance of being reinforced and resupplied from the east.

Tecumseh listened carefully, asked many questions and, according to officers who were present, made several shrewd remarks. The prospect of fortifying the forks of the Thames and making a fight there seemed to reassure him. He asked Procter for time to discuss the plan with the other chiefs. Within two hours, he had won them over.

General Procter's plan was a good one. But he executed it with a degree of incompetence that was mind-boggling. He had lost precious days by not sharing his plan with his officers and Tecumseh. This cost Tecumseh part of his fighting force, and Procter the trust of the chiefs who remained. More time was lost packing up nonessential baggage. Canadian civilians who accom-

panied the army out of fear of the wild backwoodsmen of the
Kentucky militia insisted on taking along useless household items.
Much of the packing was badly done. Entrenching tools, for example, to which men should have had easy access, were placed in the
bottoms of boats and wagons, with loads of cargo on top. The procession of goods, people, and livestock included the warriors'
families—some ten thousand men, women, and children. Such a
migration should have been handled with top-notch efficiency. It
was not. Everything moved ponderously, and for this Procter's
superiors to the east shared at least part of the blame. They told
him to take his time in his withdrawal to the forks of the Thames.

When Fort Malden had been emptied of everything that could be
carried away, the British burned it. They also destroyed the public
buildings in Amherstburg. Then those who were not already on the
road began the trek to Sandwich. Tecumseh was among the last to
leave. He began to have uncharacteristic doubts about his decision
to follow a general he did not trust into a country that was strange
to him. He said to a companion, "We are going to follow the British,
and I feel that I shall never return." The date was September 27.

That night in Sandwich, Procter, his senior officers, and
Tecumseh had supper in the home of François Baby, a colonel in
the militia and one of the community's most prosperous citizens.
Tecumseh appeared in a sullen mood. His pistols and hunting
knife were on the table beside his plate. The meal was interrupted
by a sergeant who reported that American boats had been seen on
the river near Amherstburg. When Elliot translated the news,
Tecumseh said to Procter:

"Father, we must go to meet the enemy... we must not
retreat... If you take us from this post you will lead us far,

135

far away...tell us goodbye forever and leave us to the mercy of the Long Knives (Americans). I tell you, I am sorry I have listened to you thus far, for if we had remained at the town...we could have kept the enemy from landing and have held our hunting grounds for our children.

"Now they tell me you want to withdraw to the river Thames... I am tired of it all. Every word you say evaporates like the smoke from our pipes. Father, you are like the crawfish that does not know how to walk straight ahead."

For all his eloquence, Tecumseh knew it was too late to go back. He and the thousand warriors still with him had no choice but to follow the British. That very night they moved out of Sandwich. Rain had turned the road into a quagmire that the wagons struggled through at an agonizingly slow nine miles a day. It took the column three days just to go from Sandwich to the mouth of the Thames River.

General William Henry Harrison, former governor of the Indiana Territory, future President of the United States and the hero of Tippecanoe, was surprised to find that the British had withdrawn from Detroit and Malden. He was even more surprised that his old foe Tecumseh had withdrawn. He had met Tecumseh on several occasions during highly charged treaty negotiations in which the Shawnee leader had demanded the Americans withdraw from Indian lands, and Harrison had steadfastly refused. In one confrontation tempers had flared when Tecumseh called Harrison a liar, and the two men stood facing each other on the brink of violence, Tecumseh with his hand on his tomahawk, Harrison with his sword drawn. Now, with Detroit back in American hands and American troops landing unopposed on Canadian soil, Harrison was determined to not repeat the mistakes made by American generals earlier in the war and allow a British army to escape. He left behind enough men to garrison Detroit and Malden in case the British or Indians doubled back. Then he and three thousand regulars and Kentucky militia set off on the clearly marked trail. Harrison was going after Procter—and Tecumseh!

Procter's long column trudged slowly up the valley of the Thames. The general spent most of his time well out in front, claiming to look for a good place to make a stand against the pursuing Americans. The Natives, who followed the British as a rearguard in case the Americans caught up, took this as cowardice. One wanted to rip the epaulets from Procter's shoulders. Procter still did not confide in his subordinate officers, leaving Warburton wondering what he was to do if the enemy attacked while the general was absent. As the mass of people crossed rivers, Procter did not even bother to burn bridges behind them, which would at least have slowed the Americans.

On October 1 Tecumseh was at a place about eight kilometres (5 miles) downstream from the forks of the Thames. He and his warriors were south of the river. Warburton and a rearguard of redcoats were to the northeast. Procter was nowhere to be seen. Supposedly, he was at the defences the British were establishing at the forks. Scouts who had been watching the rapidly approaching Americans reported to Warburton that the Americans were right behind them. Warburton sent Matthew Elliot across the river in a scow to tell Tecumseh he wanted to stop and fight the bluecoats right there, and he needed Tecumseh's warriors to protect his south flank. Tecumseh sent back a refusal. He had promised Procter he would stand with him at the forks. The general had built fortifications there because it was a good place to fight. He would keep his word to Procter. The redcoats and Natives withdrew to the forks.

Procter was not there, and there were no fortifications. A few dismounted guns lay uselessly on the grass. Procter, it turned out, had decided this wasn't such a good defensive position after all. He'd gone on ahead to inspect a better location at a Delaware mission called Moraviantown, and hadn't bothered to inform Tecumseh or Warburton. Then the scouts brought more news. The American army had not crossed the river to pursue the redcoats. It was coming straight for Tecumseh's warriors. Now it was Tecumseh who sent a message to Warburton, asking him to bring the redcoats over to fight beside his men. Warburton replied that he had no boats. The colonel was, in fact, in the midst of a near mutiny. The troops were so disgruntled over Procter's continued absence they wanted Warburton to assume command of the army. Warburton refused. In the British army mutineers were shot.

Tecumseh was furious. All around him his warriors were raging. Some wanted Procter's blood. Many deserted. Not far away Harrison's army was approaching cautiously. They had captured a British patrol.

That night in camp by a creek, Tecumseh and his remaining chiefs held a council. They decided that the next day they would withdraw to Moraviantown where Tecumseh would try to convince Procter to stand and fight. Warburton, after waiting for hours for orders from Procter and receiving none, also moved his men upstream.

The following day, after burning one bridge and partially dismantling another to slow the Americans, Tecumseh and his men fought a two-hour rearguard action with the Kentuckians. These backwoodsmen were led by Colonel Richard Mentor Johnson, Harrison's close friend and a future vice-president of the United

States. Three of them were killed in the skirmish, as well as a few warriors. Tecumseh was slightly wounded in the arm. The Indians were forced to burn a British ammunition depot, and the Americans captured two boatloads of British soldiers and arms. Tecumseh spent the next night at a mill owned by a man named Christopher Arnold. His angry warriors had burned down another mill, and Tecumseh decided to protect this one. He deplored useless destruction. When he saw a boy playing along the riverbank, he told him, "Boy, run away home at once. The soldiers are coming. There is war and you might get hurt."

The next day, October 5, General Procter finally made his stand. A mile below Moraviantown his remaining regulars—not many more than 450 men—were strung out in two lines on the north side of the river, facing southeast, the direction from which the enemy would come. The men were ragged, hungry, exhausted and dispirited. The only ammunition they had was what was in their shot pouches. They had one cannon loaded with case shot. They could get only one shot out of it, because there was no more ammunition. Their other big guns and spare ammunition were on a ridge above Moraviantown where Procter had moved them in anticipation of making his stand there (and it would actually have been a better place) before changing his mind yet again. The men had no faith in their general. He had sent his own family on to the safety of Burlington Heights. The troops did not believe he cared for his soldiers. One might almost think that was so, for even though a plentiful supply of dead wood and brush was available, Procter had given no orders to construct breastworks or impediments to slow enemy infantry or horsemen.

In a thick, swampy wood to the right of the British, Tecumseh waited with his men. Only about five hundred were with him now.

He had told them that morning, "Brother warriors, we are about to enter an engagement from which I shall not return. My body will remain on the field of battle."

Tecumseh had also gone down the line of British troops, trying to encourage the men, shaking hands with a few old friends. Young John Richardson, who was in the British line, later remembered that Tecumseh was wearing a fringed deerskin decorated with porcupine quills and ostrich feathers. He was riding a white pony. Tecumseh stopped in front of General Procter and said, "Father, have a big heart."

The outcome of the Battle of Moraviantown was never in doubt. When Harrison saw that Procter had decided to make a stand, he carefully studied the British position. He knew Tecumseh was in the woods, waiting to strike his flank. His original plan was to send his infantry on a bayonet charge, but Colonel Richard Johnson suggested a cavalry charge by his mounted Kentucky volunteers. Harrison considered the idea. The Kentucky horsemen were one thousand strong, and they were not typical militia. Johnson had drilled them as though they were regular cavalry. They were expert riders and skilled marksmen. They were veterans of Indian warfare. These men would not turn and run at the sound of a war whoop or the first whiff of gunsmoke. To attack an infantry position with a frontal cavalry charge was a tactic most commanders of the time would have considered suicidal. But Harrison turned to Johnson and said, "Damn them! Charge them!"

With the battle cry, "Remember the Raisin!" (where the American prisoners had been massacred) the Kentuckians thundered across the field toward the British line. A cavalry charge was the last thing the demoralized redcoats expected. They fired a single, ragged volley that killed one enemy and wounded three more.

Then, as the horsemen slammed into their formation, the British soldiers turned and ran. Their cannon had not even been fired. Procter cried, "Why do you not form? What are you about? For shame! For shame on you!" Then, fearing for his own life should the Kentuckians lay hold of him, Procter fled to the ridge above Moraviantown. He tarried there but a moment, and then dashed all the way to Ancaster, near the western end of Lake Ontario.

With the British lines shattered within a matter of minutes, the Kentuckians wheeled to the right to take on Tecumseh's warriors. The Shawnee chief had no intention of retreating. American soldiers would later say they could hear his voice above the din of battle, urging his warriors to fight.

Johnson sent a screen of twenty men ahead of his main body to draw the Indians' fire. He could then charge the woods while the warriors were reloading. The tactic was not uncommon, and was called "Forlorn Hope," on the assumption that the men in the screen were doomed. The twenty men in Johnson's screen were all volunteers. The Natives opened fire on them, and fifteen of the Kentuckians went down. Johnson then led the main charge, only to have the horses bog down belly deep in the swamp. Many of the riders sprang to the ground and rushed forward on foot to close with the enemy in hand-to-hand combat. To the crackle of gunfire was added the ring of hunting knife against tomahawk. John Richardson, disoriented after the collapse of the British lines, saw a warrior cleave open the head of a wounded Kentuckian with his tomahawk, then calmly scalp him while all around the battle raged.

Richard Johnson, who had already been wounded several times, was trying to extricate his horse when a musket ball struck his left hand. (It would be withered and useless for the rest of his life.) He looked around and saw a warrior advancing on him with a raised tomahawk. Johnson pulled his pistol and fired, and the warrior fell to the ground. By that time Johnson was so weak from loss of blood, he had to be carried from the field.

At one point the warriors were actually pushing the Kentuckians back. But then Harrison threw the bulk of his army into the fray, and the Natives were forced back to their original positions. Except for William Henry Harrison, no American present had ever seen Tecumseh, nor knew what he looked like. Many of the men fighting that day would later report having seen an Indian wearing deerskins, with a large medal hanging from his neck (Tecumseh had been presented with such a medal by the English), and a bandage on one arm (Tecumseh had been wounded in the arm during the earlier skirmish). They claimed to have seen this man firing his weapon while shouting encouragement to his men.

Not quite an hour after Harrison had first ordered the charge, a great cry of many voices arose from the woods. Then suddenly the shrill battle screams of the warriors stopped. The surviving Natives were retreating deeper into the forest. Tecumseh was dead!

The Battle of Moraviantown was a humiliating rout for the British; "shameful in the highest degree," Matthew Elliot would say later. They had eighteen dead and twenty-five wounded. About six hundred, including those who had been captured before the battle, were prisoners, including young John Richardson. They were taken to the United States, and eventually allowed to return to Canada. General Procter faced a court martial in Montreal, and was found guilty of negligence and poor judgment. He was suspended from active duty without pay for six months.

The Americans had fifteen men dead or mortally wounded, and about the same number injured. They burned the village of Moraviantown so it could not be used as a British base, and looted the homes of settlers. Then they returned to Detroit. The Kentucky militiamen wanted to go home, and General Harrison felt his supply line was too far extended for him to remain so deep in Canadian territory. A battle had been lost, but Canada remained unconquered.

Perry's victory on Lake Erie and Harrison's victory at Moraviantown, which Americans called the Battle of the Thames, were widely celebrated in the United States. The death of Tecumseh was practically viewed as more important than the defeat of Procter. It certainly ended any hopes the Natives of the Midwest had of a nation of their own. Many Americans who were present at Moraviantown claimed the "honour" of having killed Tecumseh. One even said he had taken a silverplated pistol— Brock was known to have given Tecumseh such a gun—from the dead chief's body. Undoubtedly the most famous story was that the warrior Richard Mentor Johnson shot was Tecumseh.

For many years Johnson made no claim to being the man who shot Tecumseh. But as he advanced his political career, he allowed friends and supporters to spread the tale that he had. His political opponents ridiculed him with a bit of doggerel: "Rumpsey-dumpsey, he shot Tecumseh," but popular paintings and illustrations that show the colonel shooting Tecumseh down as the Shawnee attacks him with a tomahawk convinced the public that he had. In 1843 Johnson finally stated that he had in fact killed the great chief. However, none of the claims as to who killed Tecumseh, including Johnson's, could be satisfactorily proven.

Nor is it certain what became of Tecumseh's body. Usually the Natives carried off their dead to prevent mutilation by the enemy. At Moraviantown the leaderless Natives left behind about thirty of their slain. How many they took away is not known. One story says they took Tecumseh's body away and secretly buried it, and that the location is known only to a few Native people to whom the secret has been passed down.

Other stories say Tecumseh's body was found on the battlefield, and had been shot several times. This body was shown to General Harrison, but by the time Harrison saw it the face was so swollen he could not positively identify it as Tecumseh. Another story says the vengeful Kentucky militiamen skinned Tecumseh's body, and used the skin to make razor strops. Such atrocities were not uncommon. American frontiersmen often scalped fallen warriors, and were known to remove the scrotums and breasts of dead Native men and women for use as tobacco pouches. A Canadian farm boy who had seen Tecumseh the day before the battle did see a group of Kentuckians flaying the corpse of a Native, but said the dead man was not Tecumseh.

In death Tecumseh became a Canadian hero, and to Native people everywhere he became a martyr. Among the many legends that grew was one that said one day the spirit of Tecumseh would return to deliver the Native peoples from white oppression. Yet another legend has it that Tecumseh reached from beyond the grave to strike down his nemesis, William Henry Harrison, in his greatest moment of triumph. In 1840 Harrison was elected President of the United States. After only a month in office, Harrison died. The cause of death was said to be pneumonia. The Native people believed otherwise. Following Harrison's victory at Tippecanoe, they said, Tecumseh had put a curse on him.

The Battle of Crysler's Farm

A Tremendous Roll of Thunder

Americans rejoiced that the Stars and Stripes once again flew over Detroit, and the battles on Lake Erie and at Moraviantown had given them victories that would be embellished in song and story, while the defeats at places like Queenston Heights and Beaver Dams were forgotten. But in the autumn of 1813 the armies of the United States were no closer to seizing Canada than they had been a year earlier. John Armstrong, who had replaced William Eustis as Secretary of War, decided that instead of the Niagara Frontier, the key to final victory lay farther east. The United States would have to capture Kingston or Montreal. They could thus starve all garrisons to the west of supplies and reinforcements and force a surrender. Armstrong had written in August of that year:

"Operations westward of Kingston, if successful, leave the strength of the enemy unbroken. It is the great depot of his resources. So long as he retains this, and keeps open his communication with the sea, he will not want the means of

multiplying his naval and other defences, and of reinforcing
or renewing the war in the West.... in conducting the present campaign, you will make Kingston your primary object,
and you will choose (as circumstances may warrant)
between a direct and indirect attack upon that post."

That letter had been sent to Major General James Wilkinson,
General Dearborn's replacement as the senior commander of the
American forces, who had made his headquarters at Fort George
(still in American hands at the time). General Wilkinson, fifty-six,
was a veteran of the Revolutionary War, and had a background that
was, to say the least, colourful. He was despised by almost every
other officer in the regular army. Winfield Scott referred to him as
"an unprincipled imbecile." Wilkinson had been involved in scan-
dals and conspiracies that involved misappropriated funds, neglect
in military matters, and downright treason. He had quarrelled with
superior officers. He had been brought before a court martial—
which, amazingly, cleared him of all charges. Now, in an army in
which political connections carried more weight than actual ability to command, he was the senior officer, answerable only to the
Secretary of War and the President of the United States.

Armstrong's instructions to Wilkinson to make Kingston his
primary object, and to choose "between a direct and indirect
attack" meant, in effect, that Wilkinson could strike Kingston
itself, or cut it off from the outside world by striking at Montreal.
Whatever plan of action he decided upon, it was imperative that he
move quickly, before winter set in.

Wilkinson did not move quickly. He dallied at Fort George for
weeks, laid low by a fever. He was also plagued with indecision.
He couldn't decide if he should attack Kingston or Montreal. John

Armstrong travelled to Fort George, and the general and the Secretary of War argued over the issue several times. Not until the first week of October did General Wilkinson go to Sackets Harbor with the main body of troops from Fort George, to join the companies already assembling there for the next invasion of Canada. Wilkinson's most dependable officer was Winfield Scott, but the general didn't like young Scott, so he left him at Fort George with a handful of soldiers in case the British tried to recapture the fort. Scott eventually got permission from the Secretary of War to join the forces at Sackets Harbor. He rode for thirty hours through driving rain and sleet to get there.

General Wilkinson had about eight thousand men at Sackets Harbor, but hundreds of the soldiers were sick. Because of bad food and sanitary conditions that were appalling even by the standards of the early nineteenth century, the army camp was ravaged by dysentery. Army doctors complained about the rotten meat, the filthy bread and the placement of latrines right by the shore where the cooks fetched water for the camp kitchens, but nothing was done. The number of names on the sick list grew steadily.

On October 17 Wilkinson's army left Sackets Harbor, the commander-in-chief still sick and still undecided as to his target. His men and supplies were loaded onto boats that would carry them down the St. Lawrence River. Preparing the boats and provisions for the journey should have taken about five days. The job took more than two weeks. The army's first destination was Grenadier Island, where Lake Ontario drains into the St. Lawrence. There, three hundred *bateaux* and other craft were to rendezvous, along with twenty gunboats to protect the flotilla. Bad weather held things up for days. The Americans were unaware that the British were being told of almost every move they made.

The war was never popular with the people of the border states. Vermont even considered withdrawing from the Union. People on the Canadian and American sides of the international line conducted business as usual, in spite of the efforts of the United States Army to crack down on smuggling. American farmers cheerfully sold their vegetables and meat to the British. There were even instances of British officers crossing the St. Lawrence River to do some shopping in American towns. Many of the citizens in those towns were related to United Empire Loyalists on the Canadian side. They heard all the gossip about the big military build-up around Sackets Harbor, and they happily passed the news on to their Canadian kinfolk. The British officers knew that General Wilkinson's army was on the move. They just didn't know if he was going to attack Kingston or Montreal. But neither did General Wilkinson.

Meanwhile, another American army was on the move 320 kilometres (200 miles) farther east. General Wade Hampton, leading four thousand regulars and 1,500 militia, had been ordered to support General Wilkinson's invasion. General Hampton, sixty, hated Wilkinson to the extent that he would not communicate directly with him. All correspondence between the two American commanders had to go through John Armstrong, which cost valuable time. Hampton himself was not popular with other senior officers. He was known to be impatient, bad-tempered, pompous, and to have "too free use of spirituous liquors." Hampton rose from being a poor Virginia farm boy to one of the wealthiest planters in the state, with armies of slaves labouring on his plantations. It did not sit well with his men, mostly Northerners, that he was waited upon hand and foot by black slaves. Hampton had served a term in Congress, and like so many American officers of the time freely mixed military affairs with political matters.

Hampton had been ordered to move his army into Lower Canada (Quebec) from his base on the New York shore of Lake Champlain. This was intended to confuse the British. If Wilkinson attacked Kingston, Hampton's army would appear to be threatening Montreal. This might cause the British to hesitate in sending reinforcements from Montreal to Kingston. Should Wilkinson choose to attack Montreal, Hampton could link up with him, and their combined armies should be strong enough to take the city.

General Hampton's first foray into Canadian territory was along the Richelieu River from the head of Lake Champlain. He had to turn back at Odelltown, barely inside the border, because the summer had been so dry, he could not find enough clean well water for his men and horses. The local Canadians had also slowed his advance by felling trees across the primitive road and manning barricades from which they fought brief but brisk delaying engagements. The general from Virginia, moreover, was not impressed with his men, whom he considered green, undisciplined and insubordinate.

Rather than try to fight his way through the Richelieu Valley, where it seemed that any tree not toppled in his path hid a Canadian with a musket, Hampton withdrew from Lower Canada and moved his army about sixty-four kilometres (40 miles) west to the Chateauguay River. That river's valley had plenty of good water and it reached into Lower Canada just west of Montreal. The Chateauguay would suit the American grand plan just as well as would the Richelieu. General Hampton camped his army at a place called Chateauguay Four Corners, only a few miles from the Canadian border. There he waited for orders from Armstrong. In the meantime he put his disgruntled men to work improving roads. In his reports he praised their efforts, but other American observers called the roads the worst they had ever seen. The Southerners in Hampton's ranks were starting to feel the bite of the northern autumn, and the army had not provided the men with enough coats. This was certainly not a good beginning for a winter campaign. To make matters worse, Canadian spies were watching and reporting everything the Americans did. When General Hampton moved his army north on October 19, the British knew about it. But they were still watching General Wilkinson's army at the headwaters of the St. Lawrence, and didn't know yet if the target was Kingston or Montreal. No doubt they would have been amazed had they known that the Americans had still not decided which city to attack.

Hampton's army moved slowly along a cart path that followed the course of the river. It was burdened with heavy freight wagons, and the Canadians had destroyed every bridge across every creek. When at last they reached the border, the New York militia refused to cross. Nonetheless, an advance column under Brigadier General George Izard surprised a picket of Canadian militia and Natives at a farm belonging to a man named Spears at the junction of the Chateauguay and Outard rivers. The Americans opened fire, killing two warriors, wounding several others and putting the rest to flight. Then they waited for the rest of the army to catch up.

Over the next two days Hampton's scouts brought back reports that the enemy was building an abattis (defensive work made of fallen trees) and blockhouse at a bend of the river about eleven kilometres (7 miles) from his position. They were also throwing up breastworks. To Hampton's delight, the scouts said the defenders were not British regulars, but about three hundred Canadian militiamen supported by a few Indians. They were commanded, the scouts said, by a "militia colonel" named de Salaberry.

Hampton did not think a handful of militia would pose any serious threat to his army of four thousand. But he decided to march on and brush them out of the way before they could build up strength. He was not aware that this "militia colonel" named de Salaberry was the very man whose militiamen had harassed him during the abortive invasion through the Richelieu Valley.

Far from being a militia officer, Lieutenant Colonel Charles de Salaberry was regular British army, and from a family with a long military history. His grandfather had fought for New France in the Seven Years War. His father had fought for the British in the Revolutionary War, and was a personal friend (as was Charles) of Prince Edward Augustus, the Duke of Kent, the father of Queen Victoria. All three of Charles' brothers had commissions in the British army. Two had died in the East Indies and another was killed in action while serving under the Duke of Wellington in Spain. Charles de Salaberry, thirty-five, had been in the army since the age of sixteen, and had combat experience. He had fought and won a duel over an affair of honour. As an officer he was a strict disciplinarian, but well-respected by his men because he was tough but fair. His friend and superior officer, Major General Francis De Rottenburg, called de Salaberry "my dear Marquis of cannon powder." De Salaberry was fiercely proud, and was not about to let an American army brush him aside, even if it did have four thousand men to throw against his tiny force.

De Salaberry chose his defensive position well. Several ravines cut through the terrain at right angles to the river. He made these his lines of defense. To these natural defenses he added an abattis, blockhouse, and breastworks of fallen trees and branches. He had the river's gorge on his left and a swampy forest to the right. Manning the barricades were 350 Voltigeurs and Fencibles,

French-Canadian militiamen whom de Salaberry had drilled as though they were regulars. They were supported by a small detachment of Caughnawaga, Abenaki and Nipissing warriors. De Salaberry had about six hundred men, the "Select Embodied Militia," held in reserve under the command of Lieutenant Colonel "Red George" Macdonell. Red George was a Scot in his early thirties who had been in the army since the age of sixteen. His men would play an important part in the battle that was shaping up on the banks of the Chateauguay River.

Thus far in this war, most of the fighting and the bloodshed had been in English-speaking Upper Canada. French-speaking Lower Canada had been virtually untouched. English generals had doubts about the loyalty of the *habitants* just as they did about that of the American-born settlers in Upper Canada. American generals believed the *Canadiens* would be anxious to throw off the British yoke. But if the people of Lower Canada disliked the English, they liked the Americans even less. They were happy to do business with them, but they had no wish to be absorbed into the American union. They answered the call for volunteers, and they marched off to war singing *voyageur* songs and shouting *"Vive le roi!"*

On the morning of October 24 General Hampton's army came within sight of de Salaberry's defenses. Hampton was surprised to see how well dug-in the French Canadians were, and realized he would suffer a lot of casualties if his men simply stormed the position. In a flanking manoeuvre intended to surprise the Canadians from the rear and cut them off from reinforcements, Hampton sent Colonel Robert Purdy and 1,500 men across the river under cover of darkness. Purdy was to advance through the woods to a ford the scouts had reported was to the rear of the Canadian position. There his men would re-cross the river and attack de Salaberry from behind. At the same time Hampton would launch a frontal attack. The Canadians would have to surrender or die.

There was in fact a fording place several miles to the rear of de Salaberry's lines, but the guides with Colonel Purdy's column couldn't find it. The Americans were soon lost in a heavily forested area with thick underbrush. Struggling through such country in the daylight would have been difficult. In the dark of night it was almost impossible. A heavy, cold rain made the night all the more miserable for the soldiers. Back in the American camp, General Hampton received instructions from John Armstrong telling him to prepare his army to winter at Four Corners. Hampton was confused. If he was to winter at Four Corners, what had become of the invasion plans? What was he doing here, about to assault an enemy position, if he was supposed to winter on American soil? He wanted to recall Purdy, but the scouts couldn't find the colonel. Hampton decided half-heartedly to go ahead with the attack.

At about ten o'clock on the morning of October 25 the fighting began when General Izard, commanding the frontal attack, sent in his advance skirmishers. These soldiers surprised some Canadian woodsmen cutting timber for the abattis and opened fire on them, thus alerting de Salaberry that an attack was imminent. He hurried to the front line and climbed up on a stump at the very centre of the barricade. A captain named Joseph-Marie Longtin led the men in a brief prayer, and then told them they had done their duty to God; now he expected them to do their duty to their king. Then the Canadians saw the blue uniforms of infantry advancing on them from the south. There was a brief exchange of musket fire and the Americans withdrew. The sound of the guns helped Colonel Purdy get his bearings, and he moved into position to cross the river and attack the Canadian rear.

De Salaberry had anticipated such a move. He had deployed his reserves under Red George Macdonell to serve as a rearguard should there be an attack from that quarter. They were positioned on both sides of the river. An advance unit of about a hundred of Purdy's men stumbled upon a picket of Canadians and a few Natives. The two sides exchanged volleys. Some of the Canadians and Indians turned and ran away, but the others stood their ground. The Americans fled, too, in the direction of Purdy's main body. Their countrymen heard them coming through the trees and thought they were Canadians. They fired on them, and killed several of their own men before they realized the error. Purdy now believed the woods were full of Indians. He pulled his men back to regroup, and sent a messenger to Hampton to ask for reinforcements. But Hampton had moved his headquarters, and the messenger couldn't find him. General Hampton thus had no communication with Colonel Purdy.

At about two o'clock in the afternoon General Hampton gave General Izard the order to attack. A mounted American soldier rode up to de Salaberry's defensive works and called out in French for the Canadians to surrender. De Salaberry aimed his pistol and shot the man out of the saddle. Then he told his bugler to blow the call to commence firing.

De Salaberry was aware that even if he called his reserves to the front line, he was greatly outnumbered. He had to create the illusion that he had many more men than he actually did. He had placed a small number of Caughnawagas in the woods to the right of the Canadian line. At the sound of the bugle, the warriors filled the woods with their battle cries and began firing at the Americans. Thinking the woods concealed large numbers of the enemy, the Americans sent volley after volley of musket balls into the forest.

The bullets hit nothing but trees. Then buglers de Salaberry had placed in locations to the left, right and rear of his position took up the call, giving the impression that many companies of troops were advancing to the fight. A few militiamen de Salaberry had sent into the trees appeared at the edge of the forest wearing red coats. They fired their muskets, withdrew into the woods, reversed their coats so the white lining showed, then re-appeared and fired again. To the Americans it looked as though they were being flanked by two different companies. A group of about twenty Natives added to the effect by stepping out of the trees, shrieking war cries and waving tomahawks, then ducking back into cover and repeating the performance at another place.

At the same time the Americans were taking heavy fire from the Canadians right in front of them. De Salaberry could be heard above the din of battle, "Defy, my damned ones! Defy! If you do not dare, you are not men!" The American attack lost its momentum, and the blue coated soldiers did not attempt to storm the abattis.

Meanwhile, on the other side of the river Colonel Purdy, thinking he was badly outnumbered, was withdrawing toward the main American army. The Canadian reserves were also on the move. On one side of the river the units with Red George were joining de Salaberry's men. On the other side, units under Captain Charles Daly were engaged in a running fight with Purdy's men. If Purdy were to realize the extent to which his force outnumbered the Canadians, he could easily have annihilated them.

De Salaberry became aware of the situation on the other side of the river. With the frontal American assault stalled, he hurried to the riverbank with a large number of militiamen and a few Natives. He shouted across the river, telling Captain Daly to speak French so the Americans wouldn't understand.

Acting on de Salaberry's instructions, Daly ordered his men to kneel and fire. When the Americans returned fire, the bullets went right over the Canadians' heads. Then the Canadians raced toward Purdy's startled line in a bayonet charge. One American sergeant would later write that Purdy's men repelled a bayonet attack by three hundred to four hundred Canadians. In fact, there were about eighty men in that charge.

The bayonet charge was audacious, but could not succeed against such numerical odds. Captain Daly was wounded, and the Canadians began to fall back to the river. With cries of triumph the Americans pursued them. But when the American soldiers burst out of the trees into the opening along the riverbank, they were right under the guns of de Salaberry's men on the opposite bank. At the order of "Fire!" the muskets boomed and a volley of lead tore into the Americans with shattering effect. The Americans hastily ran back for the cover of the trees. To Purdy's disgust, some of his officers raced to the riverbank that was opposite the main American army and plunged into the water, abandoning their men in their desperation to gain the safety of their own lines. Purdy's men by this time were cold, hungry, exhausted, and had no fight left in them.

General Hampton had still not committed all of his men to the battle. Nor had he used his cannon, which could have blown de Salaberry's wooden defensive works to splinters. But he now believed he faced three to four thousand enemy troops. He told his bugler to sound retreat, and sent a messenger to find Purdy and tell him to withdraw.

When Purdy and his surviving men reached the place where they expected to cross the river under the protection of the main army, the colonel was furious to discover that Hampton had retreated without them. He had to construct rafts to float his wounded across, and throw together a jerry-built bridge to get the rest of his men over. All this was done under sniper fire from Natives in the woods.

When Purdy and his men finally staggered into the American camp, Purdy attempted to arrest the officers who had fled on charges of desertion and cowardice. General Hampton cancelled the arrest order. Purdy tried to confront Hampton over the complete mishandling of the attack on the Canadian position, but could get nowhere with him. The colonel was convinced the general was drunk.

The Americans endured a miserable retreat back to Four Corners, leaving a trail of discarded guns, knapsacks and other equipment. They were drenched by almost constant rain, and were in fear of the Indians they knew to be watching them from the woods. No room was made in the baggage wagons for the wounded who could not walk. They were simply left behind. Shortly after reaching Four Corners, General Wade Hampton resigned from the army. John Wool, the captain (by this time promoted to major) who had led his men up Queenston Heights the previous year, would write that the Battle of Chateauguay was "from its inception to its termination a disgrace to the United States Army... no officer who had any regard for his own reputation, would voluntarily acknowledge himself as being engaged in it." The number of American casualties at Chateauguay is not certain. Hampton reported a total of fifty dead and wounded, but the number was undoubtedly higher. The Canadians buried more than forty American bodies that had been left behind.

De Salaberry had five men killed, sixteen wounded and four missing. He was surprised when the Americans withdrew. He sent Native scouts to watch them, but did not send his small force in pursuit because he was sure the American general was pulling back only to regroup his men and attack again. He would write to his father that the whole thing was "a most extraordinary affair."

Just as the fighting was dying down, two British officers, Lieutenant General George Prévost and Major General Louis de Watteville arrived on the scene, having heard that the Canadians under de Salaberry had engaged the enemy. To de Salaberry's chagrin, the redcoat generals claimed a portion of the credit for the victory, though he had been in command throughout the engagement. He quite correctly credited Red George Macdonell for his role in the fight, but later wrote, "It grieves me to the heart" that he had to share the glory with two superior officers who'd played no part in the battle.

The French Canadians, meanwhile, were ecstatic. A few hundred of them had turned back an army of thousands. They had put to rest any doubts the British high command had about their loyalty. Though the Canadians were not yet aware of it, they had thwarted any chance of two American armies linking up for an attack on Montreal. For that one fact, the Battle of Chateauguay, though not much more than a skirmish, was very significant indeed.

General Wilkinson was not having an easy time on Grenadier Island. He was still sick with dysentery, as were many of his men. A considerable number of those who were not sick were drunk, the expedition's supplies of medicinal port wine and brandy having been pilfered. Food was in short supply. It rained incessantly, and storms scattered the convoys bringing more troops and supplies from Sackets Harbor. Discipline was almost non-existent. Even though there was a standing order that soldiers were to respect the private property of the island's farmers, the men raided farms for food—which the farmers, though American, preferred to sell to the better-paying British. Wilkinson still had not told his officers if their target was Kingston or Montreal. Two days after the Battle of Chateauguay, he was not aware that Hampton had been defeated and was in retreat. He did not know that Armstrong had told Hampton to winter at Four Corners. Armstrong had made no mention of it in a letter in which he advised Wilkinson to avoid engaging with General George Prévost until he could join forces with Hampton. Wilkinson's letters to Armstrong were full of whining complaints about the "pretender" (Hampton).

Finally, on November 3 a flotilla of small craft of every description—schooners, scows, skiffs, *bateaux*—began to transport Wilkinson's army to the next gathering point at French Creek (now Clayton, New York). Many of the boats were overloaded and piloted by inexperienced soldiers. It took two days for all of them to get under way. A naval blockade across the entrance to the St. Lawrence River was supposed to prevent British warships on Lake Ontario from entering the great river, but a squadron of four ships and four gunboats commanded by Captain William Howe Mulcaster of the Royal Navy slipped through. Mulcaster caught up with the Americans, fought a brief engagement at French Creek, and then hurried to Kingston to report: the Americans were heading for Montreal!

Though it was very late in the season to be starting such a campaign, General Wilkinson had at last made up his mind. Kingston, he decided, was too strongly garrisoned. Far better to hook up with General Hampton and attack Montreal, and then starve the British out of Kingston. On November 5 his flotilla of 350 boats carrying six thousand men began the trip downstream toward Montreal. Captain Mulcaster was soon following close behind. As Wilkinson neared Prescott, he worried about the guns at Fort Wellington. He decided to put his men ashore at Ogdensburg and march them past that dangerous stretch, hauling most of the supplies and armaments in freight wagons. With only enough men on them to navigate, he slipped the empty boats past Fort Wellington during the night. When they were out of range of the fort's big guns, the men re-embarked. All this was costing Wilkinson precious time.

Wilkinson issued a proclamation to the citizens along the Canadian shore. It stated that the American army was not making war on them, but on the King of England. If they remained in their homes and did not fight with the redcoats, they and their properties would be safe. But if they took up arms against the Americans, they would suffer the consequences. The Canadians' response was predictable, considering so many of them were of United Empire Loyalist stock. At places where the river narrowed and the American boats came within rifle range, the men waited with their guns primed and took potshots at the Americans as their boats passed by. The promise to protect private property turned out to be an empty one; American soldiers pillaged Canadian homes of food and valuables at every opportunity.

While he was still at French Creek General Wilkinson learned of General Hampton's defeat at Chateauguay. "Damn such an army!" he cried. "A man might as well be in hell as command it!" But he thought the two armies might yet join forces and sweep down upon Montreal.

That night and during the small hours of the following morning, the Americans set out downriver again under a cover of fog. By this time Winfield Scott had joined them. He had met with General Wilkinson, and was sure the general was drunk. Quite likely, because of his illness, Wilkinson had been well dosed with laudanum, a mixture of opium and alcohol that could be found in every doctor's medical bag at that time. Wilkinson embarked with the others, but soon his condition was so bad his aides had to take him ashore and find a bed for him in the nearest farmhouse.

Over the next two days the American flotilla moved but a few miles. It was fired upon frequently, but with little damage done. Wilkinson sank deeper into the grip of fever and the delirium brought on by his doctor's medicine. On November 8 Wilkinson was lucid enough to call a council of war. His officers agreed, some of them reluctantly, to push on for Montreal. Wilkinson wrote to General Hampton, ordering him to bring his army to a rendezvous point and join the attack on Montreal. Hampton replied that he could not, being low on provisions. Then he took his army in the opposite direction, to Plattsburg. His letter—an outright refusal to obey orders—did not reach Wilkinson in time for that general to adjust his plans accordingly.

By now the Americans were at the start of the long series of rapids upriver from Montreal. Wilkinson had to worry about British and Canadian guns on land firing on his boats as they tried to negotiate the dangerous white water, and he had Captain Mulcaster's squadron closing in from behind. His troops were jittery. Canadians they had questioned had told them wild stories about thousands of British regulars waiting for them in Montreal, and woods full of bloodthirsty warriors.

Wilkinson sent Brigadier General Jacob Brown ashore with 2,500 men to clear away the British soldiers and Canadian militiamen so the American boats could descend the rapids without being fired upon. Brown saw his mission through, but only after facing tough opposition. While his troops were slugging it out on land, Mulcaster had moved in with his gunboats and was harassing the rear of the American flotilla. Then the pilots for the

American boats refused to go any farther. Ahead of them stretched torturous miles of wild water hell. These rapids (now vanished because of the St. Lawrence Seaway) had swept even the most daring and experienced of French Canadian voyageurs to their doom. The flotilla put ashore a mile or two above one of the most fearsome of the rapids, the twelve-and-a-half kilometre (8-mile) monster called the Long Sault, at a spot on the Canadian side called Cook's Point. It was a little more than three kilometres (about 2 miles) downriver from the farm of a Canadian militia officer named John Crysler.

By this time General Wilkinson was not the only senior American officer incapacitated by illness. His second-in-command, Major General Morgan Lewis, was also down with dysentery. General Jacob Brown was anxiously trying to learn just who was in charge. The senior American officer on Canadian soil was now Brigadier General John Boyd, a former mercenary whom Brown detested.

American progress down the river had been slow, giving the British ample time to respond, once they realized the target was Montreal and not Kingston. Lieutenant Colonel Joseph Wanton Morrison, leading about nine hundred British regulars and Canadian militiamen from Kingston, and some thirty Native scouts, made his headquarters in John Crysler's farmhouse while his men camped in the fields. Morrison was an American-born son of Loyalists. He had been in the British army since the age of eleven. Now thirty years old, he had seen action and been wounded in Holland, and had been stationed in such places as Minorca, Ireland and Trinidad. This would be his first battle command. His second officer was Lieutenant Colonel John Harvey, a veteran of the Battle of Stoney Creek.

Morrison had been on Wilkinson's tail for several days, following the American flotilla in one of Mulcaster's gunboats. Now that the Americans had been obliged to go ashore, Morrison had to decide if he should take on such a large force with his vest pocket army. His corps was augmented somewhat with the arrival of Lieutenant Colonel Thomas Pearson with 240 men from Prescott. And he could count on support from Captain Mulcaster, who had managed to bring down two of his gunboats. That still left the British–Canadian lines stretched thin.

Colonel Morrison knew that if the American generals wanted to get him off their backs, they would have to come after him. That gave Morrison the option of choosing the ground upon which the battle would be fought. He positioned the main part of his army in a field where, unencumbered by trees and brush, they could carry out the manoeuvres that had been drilled into them until they responded to orders instantaneously and with the precision of Spartans. They were protected by a heavy log fence one-and-a-half metres (5 feet) high that did not impede their own ability to deliver lethal volleys of musket fire. To Morrison's right was the river, with Mulcaster's gunboats just offshore. To his left was an impassable swamp which would prevent him from being flanked on that quarter. In front of his position was an open, muddy field cut by several ravines.

Morrison put his own company, the Eighty-Ninth Regiment of Foot on the left. On the right was the Forty-Ninth, Brock's old regiment. This was the Eighty-Ninth's first taste of battle, and they stood out in their scarlet coats. The experienced men of the Forty-Ninth hid their red uniforms under grey greatcoats. Spread out in front of this main position were militia and skirmishers. some in formation, others crouched behind rocks or stumps. Morrison knew the American troops who would come at him across that field were regulars. He was putting his trust in the superior training and discipline of the British regulars to make up for the vast difference in numbers. By drawing the Americans into a European-style set battle at which the British excelled, he was depriving the Americans of the type of individualistic type of forest fighting they preferred. Early in the morning on November 11 a dragoon galloped in, shouting that the enemy was advancing.

General Wilkinson gave the order to attack Morrison's position at Crysler's farm. He could not risk going downriver with a British army, however small, snarling at his heels. He wanted the siege of Montreal to be a brief one because the bitter cold of the Canadian winter would soon be upon them, and his men needed the provisions that would be in the city. But the order to attack was the only one the commander-in-chief would give that day. He was laid up in a boat at Cook's Point, too ravaged with illness to direct a battle. Not until midafternoon did General Boyd receive the command. By that time his men had already endured a chilling rainstorm.

On Boyd's command Lieutenant-Colonel Eleazar Ripley led his Twenty-First U.S. Infantry across the field toward the British left. They were halfway across the field when a line of French-Canadian Voltigeurs suddenly sprang up and fired two volleys at them. The American infantrymen immediately broke ranks and dove for the cover of rocks and stumps, from which they blasted away at the Canadians, firing at will, and with no effect. Ripley and his officers screamed at them to return to formation, but were ignored. When the troopers were out of ammunition, they withdrew to their own lines. An infuriated Ripley resumed the attack with reinforcements. This time the Americans advanced in proper order, and the Voltigeurs were driven back.

Now the Twelfth and Thirteenth U.S. Infantry joined the Twenty-First in an attack on the British left. If, through sheer weight of numbers they could break through the Eighty-Ninth, they could strike the Forty-Ninth from behind, and the battle would be over. But it was here that the training of the British infantryman and the manoeuvres practised over and over again made the difference. When an officer barked an order, the regiment responded as one man in movement, whether told to close up or wheel about. When the order "Fire" was given, the muskets roared all at the same time, with frightful effect on the enemy. Women and children hiding in the cellar of the Crysler house said later they could tell the sound of an American volley from a British one. The American guns made a series of distinctive pops as they fired independently of each other. The British guns resounded together at regular intervals, "like a tremendous roll of thunder." Morrison stopped the charge against his left by swinging the Eighty-Ninth around almost ninety degrees with machine precision, and meeting the U.S. Infantry with a wall of lead.

Boyd was not an imaginative commander. Having failed to crack the British left, he now hurled a direct assault at its right. This assignment fell to Brigadier General Leonard Covington and his Third Brigade. Seeing the grey-coated line across the field, Covington mistook the men for militia. He shouted to his troops, "Come, lads, let me see how you deal with these militia men."

But these were not militia. Beneath the grey coats were the red tunics of the Forty-Ninth, the men who had trained and fought under Brock. Formed up in staggered platoons, they held their positions and poured rolling volleys into the oncoming Americans. Three six-pounder field guns added to the carnage. General

165

Covington was killed. Then his second-in-command fell dead. The Third Brigade retreated in disorder.

General Boyd had six field guns of his own, but he was late in having them brought up from the boats and deployed for action. When the big guns did finally open fire, the barrage of roundshot and canister was effective against the British ranks. Morrison sent Major Charles Plenderleath and some of the Forty-Ninth to take the guns at bayonet point. As the Forty-Ninth raced across the muddy field, a company of American cavalry dashed in to strike the British flank. Plenderleath saw this and executed another manoeuvre straight out of the British drill book. He stopped his advance, wheeled his men around, and unleashed a wicked volley into the American horsemen. Riders spilled from saddles, horses screamed in pain and terror, and the cavalry charge was shattered. A company of the Eighty-Ninth rushed forward and seized one of the American field guns. American artillerymen managed to haul the others to safety.

All this time, Captain Mulcaster's gunboats had been hurling shells at the Americans. Now Morrison's field guns joined in the bombardment, and shrapnel slashed through the blue-coated ranks as iron balls burst amongst them. Looking across the field, General Boyd saw the British advancing with fixed bayonets. In all his years as a soldier of fortune, Boyd had never been in such a situation. He ordered a withdrawal. The British officers were astonished, because Boyd had divisions he had not yet even thrown into the fight. For that reason, and because night was falling and the weather once again turning foul, they did not attempt to turn the American retreat into a rout.

Ailing General Wilkinson wanted to keep his army on the Canadian side of the river overnight, but Boyd argued that was impossible. He said the men were exhausted and famished, and needed rest. The soldiers piled into their boats and made a disorderly crossing to the American side of the river. The following day General Wilkinson received General Hampton's letter bearing his refusal to join forces with him. Now Wilkinson had a scapegoat for the failure of his expedition. He wrote to John Armstrong that his attack on Montreal was only postponed, but he was soon removed from command.

Colonel Morrison, who was awarded a gold medal for his victory, had twenty-two men killed, 148 wounded and nine missing. General Boyd reported 102 men killed and 237 wounded, with over a hundred taken prisoner. Boyd claimed that the enemy had superior numbers, seven or eight gunboats (Mulcaster had two), and that he had, in fact "added some reputation to the American arms." Boyd held no more important commands during the war, and with the end of hostilities he was cashiered from the army.

There were no subsequent attempts to attack Montreal, and the Americans never did try to take Kingston. But the war continued for over a year. Back on the Niagara Frontier there was a bloody clash at Lundy's Lane in which the Americans were once again turned back, and Colonel Joseph Morrison distinguished himself yet again and was seriously wounded. The British razed the town of Buffalo, New York, in retaliation for the burning of York, but the British attempt to invade the United States via Lake Champlain was a dismal failure. In a raid on Washington, D.C., British troops put the garrison to flight and set fire to the Capitol Building. The Americans extinguished the fire and whitewashed over the scorch marks. The seat of the American federal government has been called the White House ever since.

On December 24, 1814, the war officially came to an end when British and American diplomats signed the Treaty of Ghent in Belgium. But in those days news could travel across oceans only as fast as the wind could carry a swift sailing ship, and a British invasion force was already on its way to New Orleans. On January 8, 1815, General Andrew Jackson won a resounding victory over the British. Based largely on the outcome of that battle, the United States claimed to be the victor of the War of 1812. The British, to whom the conflict was but a sideshow compared to the colossal struggle with Napoleon, were content to call it a draw. The fact remained, however, that attempts by American armies to invade Canada had failed utterly. For Canadians, the winner was obvious.

The Battle of Seven Oaks

Blood on the Prairie

I f the violence that occurred on June 19, 1816, at Seven Oaks, in what is now Manitoba, had taken place on American soil, it would quite possibly have become the subject of novels and films. The event and the principal characters would be as familiar to the general public as the story of the gunfight at the OK Corral, Wyatt Earp, Doc Holliday and the Clanton boys. Seven Oaks, however, was not an American tragedy, but a Canadian one. Thus, it is a story that is generally unknown to the public, even in Canada. While characters like Earp and Holliday have been portrayed on film many times, it's not likely that an actor on Hollywood's "A-list" will be stepping before the cameras in the role of Cuthbert Grant or Robert Semple.

Ironically, the series of events that climaxed in gunfire and bloodshed at Seven Oaks were set in motion by a philanthropist. A Scottish nobleman, Thomas Douglas, the Fifth Earl of Selkirk, was moved by the plight of Scottish crofters (tenant farmers) who were being evicted from their farms in the tens of thousands to make room for more profitable cattle and sheep. These victims of the Industrial Revolution had two choices: go to the already over-crowded slums of Britain's cities and look for jobs in the sweatshops that were called factories, or emigrate. Selkirk under-took, at his own expense, to give some of his unfortunate countrymen a new start in life by settling them in Britain's North American colonies. He started a successful colony in Prince Edward Island, and a not-so-successful one in Upper Canada. For his third humanitarian venture, Selkirk chose the junction of the Red and Assiniboine rivers in what was then called Rupert's Land, the domain of the Hudson's Bay Company. He intended to put set-tlers there, people who would till soil that at the time grew nothing but prairie grass, and who would build a permanent community. The Hudson's Bay Company liked the idea, and sold Selkirk a vast territory twice the size of England for a nominal ten shillings. Selkirk became a major Company shareholder. The idealistic Selkirk did not fully understand that he had chosen a very dan-gerous location.

In 1670 England's King Charles II granted the Hudson's Bay Company a charter that gave it sole trading rights in Rupert's land. The English traders set up posts, but found themselves in competi-tion with French traders based in Montreal, who had no regard whatsoever for the Hudson' Bay Company charter. After the fall of New France in the Seven Years War, the rivalry continued. The old French posts were taken over by Montreal's North West Company, many of whose directors were Scots. They had no more respect for the charter than the French had. The Hudson's Bay men and the Nor'westers competed for trade, but within an uneasy peace. There were no outstanding incidents of violence. By putting settlers at The Forks, as the junction of the two rivers was called, the Hudson's Bay Company was antagonizing a lot of people.

The Red River Valley, which was to be the centre of Selkirk's colony, was a major transportation route for the Natives and the Métis—the people of mixed white and Native blood. Through the valley passed bales of pelts and cargoes of pemmican, a food made from dried buffalo meat that was the staple diet of the *voyageurs* who paddled the big trade canoes from Montreal. With a settlement there, the Hudson's Bay Company could shut the Nor'westers off from the pemmican supply, or charge exorbitant tolls for taking it through. The Nor'westers also suspected the Hudson's Bay men planned to muscle in on the fur-rich Athabasca country, the source of a huge portion of the North West Company's profits. Moreover, the settlement would be too close to the traditional hunting grounds of the Saulteaux, Cree and Sioux nations. Even the Hudson's Bay men in Canada believed the company directors in England were fools to support Selkirk's scheme. The Nor'westers swore that the colony would not survive.

On July 26, 1811, the first shipload of seventy colonists, along with thirty-five Hudson's Bay Company employees, sailed from Scotland with dreams of a new life in Assiniboia, the name Selkirk had given the colony. Their leader was Captain Miles Macdonell, a Scot who had immigrated to Canada as a child. He'd had a varied career as a soldier, farmer and politician. Selkirk had met him in Upper Canada, and was impressed by what he considered to be Macdonell's leadership qualities. He failed to note that Macdonell could also be vain and arrogant. It did not go over well with Macdonell's family that he took a position with Selkirk and the Hudson's Bay Company, because several of them worked for the North West Company, including his cousin Alexander Macdonell, who was in the Red River Valley.

The colonists had a rough, stormy crossing, and by the time they reached York Factory, the company post on the coast of Hudson Bay, it was too late in the year for them to travel inland. They spent a miserable winter on that bleak shore and then made the grueling, fifty-five-day journey up the Hayes River to the Forks. When they arrived there late in August of 1812, they were greeted by Métis wearing war paint. The buffalo hunters had been sent by Alex Macdonell to scare the settlers away. The newcomers were not intimidated, and they began to build Fort Douglas, named for their patron. They had a cow, a bull, a few sacks of seeds, and no horses. In spite of the odds against them, they ploughed the ground and planted winter wheat. In the nearby North West Company post, Fort Gibraltar, the Nor'westers fumed. Their anger increased when more colonists arrived: families with children.

The settlers would have starved had they not been provided with buffalo meat and pemmican by friendly Saulteaux Natives. By 1814 their situation was beginning to improve. They had comfortable log cabins, and their numbers were growing. But food was still a problem. Early that year, acting on his authority as the Hudson's Bay Company governor and the representative of Lord Selkirk—the man who legally owned the land upon which both Fort Douglas and Fort Gibraltar stood—Miles Macdonell stepped over the line with the Nor'westers. He issued a proclamation forbidding the exportation of food from Assiniboia for one year. That meant pemmican could not be taken to the *voyageurs*. That was a threat to the Nor'westers, as well as to the Métis who hunted the buffalo from which the pemmican was made. The situation grew even more volatile when John Spencer, the colony's sheriff, confiscated several hundred hidden bags of North West

Company pemmican. Macdonell had a cannon manned by special constables placed at a strategic location on the Red River to enforce his "Pemmican Proclamation."

Miles Macdonell followed this up with yet another high-handed law. He declared it illegal to hunt buffalo from horseback on Lord Selkirk's land. The idea behind this was to give his Scots, who had no horses, a better chance of competing for the buffalo with the Métis, who were expert riders and professional hunters. Of course, Macdonell's rule infuriated the Métis. They simply used their horses to drive the herds out of sight of the Red River colony, and then hunted from horseback anyway. But there was a growing concern that these farmers would destroy the traditional Métis way of life.

The Nor'westers took note of Métis resentment, and began a campaign deliberately designed to fan the flames of anger. They stirred up Métis feelings of pride and nationalism. The Métis, the Nor'westers said, were a new and separate nation. The land they lived and hunted on was *theirs*. By what right did the Hudson's Bay Company dictate to them? By what right did an aristocrat in distant Scotland dump a load of unwanted settlers in the middle of buffalo country? Those settlers had to go!

Among the leaders of the Métis community was a man named Cuthbert Grant. Like his countrymen, Grant was a buffalo hunter. But he was also bilingual and well-educated, having been sent to school in Montreal under the supervision of William McGillivray of the North West Company. Grant was fiercely loyal to the North West Company, and he listened intently to what the Nor'westers had to say about Métis nationalism. He became outspoken on the matter in the Métis community, and soon he was rousing his people against the settlers.

Métis riders began to terrorize the farmers. They would encircle a farmhouse at night, firing their guns and uttering war whoops. Crops were trampled under horses' hoofs. Barns and cabins were put to the torch. Cuthbert Grant, whom the North West Company had made "Captain General of all the Half-Breeds" led many of the raids. Then, while Miles Macdonell was in Upper Canada on business, Nor'wester Duncan Cameron made an offer to the settlers. The North West Company would provide free transportation for any of them who wanted to re-settle on good land in Upper Canada. Unnerved by the Métis' night visits, 133 settlers accepted the offer. Pleased with his own efforts, Cameron then seized a cannon in Fort Douglas and took it to Fort Gibraltar.

When Miles Macdonell returned and found only thirteen families remaining in the settlement, he issued yet another proclamation. He ordered all Nor'westers out of Assiniboia. Of course, he had no way of enforcing the order. His cousin, Alexander Macdonell, rolled out the stolen cannon, pointed it at the gates of Fort Douglas, and told Miles to surrender.

For the next week Métis riders again terrorized the remaining settlers. They drove off their stock, shot at them from ambush, and forced them out of their homes. Fearful that there might be wholesale bloodshed, Miles Macdonell agreed to surrender if the Nor'westers promised no more harm would come to the settlers. On June 17, 1815, he gave himself up to North West Company officials and was sent to Lower Canada to stand trial for what the Nor'westers claimed was the illegal seizure of pemmican. The charges were eventually dropped.

The unlucky settlers, meanwhile, were forced to flee by boat to Jack River House, a Hudson's Bay Company post at the north end of Lake Winnipeg. Jubilant Métis burned down their mill, Fort

Douglas, and any cabins and barns that had not already been razed. From all appearances the Red River settlement was finished. Then the refugee settlers met Colin Robertson.

Born in Perth, Scotland, Robertson had apprenticed to be a weaver, but when the Industrial Revolution made that trade obsolete he travelled to Canada and joined the North West Company. Robertson was a big man, flamboyant, generous, and extravagant. He liked to drink Madeira and quote Shakespeare. Accused of being a braggart, he replied, "When you are among wolves, howl!" Robertson spent several years in the west, during which time he learned the fur trade business and even fought a duel. Disappointed at not getting a promotion, he returned to Britain and went over to the Hudson's Bay Company. Robertson was on his way to the Forks when he encountered the uprooted settlers.

Robertson convinced sixty of the people to return with him and start over again. They were back in the Red River Valley by mid-August. The farmers were able to harvest five hundred bushels of oats, four hundred bushels of wheat and two hundred bushels of barley. While the settlers rebuilt their homes, Robertson took over as their leader while awaiting the arrival of a new Hudson's Bay Company governor, Robert Semple.

Colin Robertson was made of tougher stuff than Miles Macdonell. He rebuilt Fort Douglas and pursued an aggressive trading policy that eventually undermined the Nor'westers' monopoly in the Athabasca country. He arrested Duncan Cameron and seized Fort Gibraltar. He would not release it to the Nor'westers until he had Cameron's promise that depredations against the settlers would stop. Robertson had always been popular with the Métis, and now he entertained them with food and drink, and told them the settlers would be a market for their pemmican. He soon had most of the buffalo hunters won over, though not Cuthbert Grant and his followers. Had Robertson remained in Assiniboia after Robert Semple's arrival, tragedy might have been averted for the simple reason that Robertson knew how to talk to the Métis and Semple did not.

Robert Semple was a strange choice for governor of the Red River colony. He was the Boston-born son of Loyalists and had at one time been a merchant. He was best known, however, as a novelist and author of several books about his travels in Europe, Africa, the Near East and South America. It is uncertain how he met Lord Selkirk, or why Selkirk believed he was qualified to govern a colony on a raw frontier that always seemed on the brink of explosive violence.

Semple arrived in Assiniboia in November 1815 with a new party of Scottish settlers. Early in 1816 he made a tour of the company trading posts on the upper Assiniboine and Qu'Appelle Rivers, and was back in Red River by the end of March. At first he respected Colin Robertson because of the man's knowledge of the country. But it soon became evident that the two were not going to get along. Robertson was outgoing, charismatic, and treated the Métis with dignity and respect. He would, in fact, one day marry a Métis woman, to the shock of some of his more bigoted white associates. Semple had a cold manner, was indecisive, and held the Métis in contempt. Robertson said later that Semple was, "a proud Englishman, rather too conscious of his abilities." It did not take Semple long to alienate the Métis. It angered them, too, that Semple kept the ban on the export of pemmican.

Though Robertson and Semple disagreed on many things, they did agree that keeping the supply of pemmican from reaching the *voyageurs* would be a severe blow to the Nor'westers. Robertson seized a storehouse full of it at Fort Gibraltar, and then dismantled the fort. Such was his good standing with the Métis that they didn't lift a finger to stop him. Semple agreed with the seizure as a necessary measure. Then Robertson wanted to blockade the rivers to prevent the transportation of pemmican, but Semple was afraid that might antagonize the Métis. When Robertson arrested some Nor'westers as troublemakers, Semple released them on parole. Such vacillating disgusted Robertson.

In June Robertson received instructions to return to England. Robertson warned Semple to be alert and not let the Nor'westers take the offensive. Cuthbert Grant and some of his followers who supported the Nor'westers had raided Brandon House, the Hudson's Bay post on the Assiniboine River, and made off with a large supply of pemmican. Robertson thought they might hit the Grand Rapids post on the Qu'Appelle or even Fort Douglas itself. Semple wasn't worried, because he had cannon at Fort Douglas. Robertson left on June 11, saying he would return. Semple told Robertson he had no need of him.

There are many conflicting accounts about what happened next. One story says some Saulteaux warriors rode into Fort Douglas on June 17 and warned Semple that a large band of Métis were on their way to attack the fort. They allegedly offered Semple their help, but he refused it. A group of Métis was indeed on the move, but in all likelihood they had no plans to attack Fort Douglas.

Cuthbert Grant and about sixty others were transporting the pemmican they had seized in their earlier raid. They could not move it by canoe because of the cannon at Fort Douglas, so they were moving it overland in three Red River carts. They intended to make a wide detour around Fort Douglas and avoid a confrontation, but as they crossed a place the Métis called the Frog

Plain, about three quarters of a mile north of the fort, a lookout spotted them. The Métis were all mounted and armed with their hunting rifles.

Semple gathered two dozen or so men, mostly Scottish settlers, and led them on foot out of the fort. Why he did so is not certain. Did he intend to intercept the pemmican? If so, he was at a clear disadvantage, outnumbered by more than two-to-one by horsemen. Not all of the men with him were armed, though some carried muskets and even bayonets. Someone allegedly suggested he take along the cannon, a three-pounder that could have been mounted on a cart, but Semple said he wasn't going out to fight. One report has Semple only saying that he wanted to "see what these fellows want."

When Grant and his followers saw the men from the fort advancing toward them, they stopped at a grove of oak and willow trees called Seven Oaks. Many of the riders with Grant wore Native dress, paint and feathers. Some carried spears and tomahawks in addition to their guns. Again the question arises: why were they dressed and armed this way if they wished to avoid trouble? Did they want any observers in the fort to think they were Indians, and therefore not interfere with them?

These men were exceptionally skilled horsemen. Not only could they shoot from the saddle, but because of the requirements of the buffalo hunt they could move together with the precision of trained cavalry. They divided into two divisions and began to draw away from Semple's men.

A gun in the hands of one of the Scots went off, probably by accident. Semple turned and angrily told his men to be careful. Perhaps then he realized the precarious situation in which he had placed himself and the others, because according to one story they began to move back toward the fort, only to have the Métis gallop up and form in a crescent alongside them. Whether that actually happened, or Semple boldly strode right up to the Métis, the confrontation began with heated words.

Semple stood abreast of a Métis named François Firmin Boucher. As much as the testimony of the survivors can be relied upon, Boucher asked, "What do you want?" Semple responded, "What do *you* want?" Shouting followed. Semple supposedly told one of his men to go back to the fort and get the cannon. Boucher called Semple "a damned rascal." Semple replied, "Scoundrel, do you tell me so!" He grabbed either for Boucher's bridle or the butt of his gun. Then there was a shot. Which side fired it, no one knows. Boucher swung his leg over his saddle and slid to the ground. That was the signal for the riders to open fire. Semple went down with a bullet in his thigh or hip. He shouted for his men to run to the fort, and then was shot again, by Cuthbert Grant according to one account. But another version says Grant tried to save the wounded Semple and restrain the Métis.

The explosion of violence that followed was so one-sided, it scarcely deserves to be called a battle. The Semple men were either grouped closely together, or were so stunned by the sudden murder of their leader they were unable to react. They were shot or otherwise dispatched before most of those who had guns even had a chance to fire them. Whooping and shouting, the Métis fell upon the wounded and slaughtered them. Three or four men escaped into the woods or the river. One was spared when he sought the protection of a Métis he had previously befriended. The victors stripped, scalped and mutilated the victims, and left the naked bodies for the wolves and coyotes. Robert Semple and nineteen or twenty others were dead. The Métis had one man dead and one wounded. Cuthbert Grant rode into Fort Douglas and demanded its immediate surrender, which he got. The numbed occupants were permitted to leave by boat for the Hudson's Bay Company post at Norway House.

There is no evidence whatsoever that this attack was planned, or that the Nor'westers had any foreknowledge of it. But they certainly took advantage of the situation. They occupied Fort Douglas and confiscated its contents. They also rewarded Grant and his Métis followers. The massacre at Seven Oaks, however, was the beginning of the end for the North West Company.

Lord Selkirk was at Sault Ste. Marie when he heard of the tragedy, on his way west with more settlers. The men in this group were former Swiss and German mercenaries who had fought for the British in the War of 1812. Now they were ready to fight again, for Selkirk. Moving in advance of the main body of settlers, they captured the Nor'wester stronghold of Fort William. Then, with two small cannon for artillery and with the help of Native allies, they captured one Nor'wester post after another. Miles Macdonell was with them when they quietly scaled the walls of Fort Douglas at night and caught the ten men inside sleeping. The Hudson's Bay men even put an armed schooner on Lake Winnipeg and used it to capture Nor'wester canoes loaded with furs.

Selkirk himself arrived at Red River for the first time in June 1817. He stayed four months, helping to rebuild yet again. He consolidated a good relationship with Chief Peguis of the Saulteaux, spent his own money to build roads and bridges, and brought in even more settlers, including a group of French Canadians. Then he went back to England to fight the legal battles that now raged between the North West Company and the Hudson's Bay Company. These involved over two hundred charges and counter-charges. It was all too much for Selkirk's health, and he died in 1820 at age forty-eight.

The British government was fed up with the warfare between the two fur companies. They were pressured into finding a solution. In 1821 the North West Company capitulated and agreed to be taken over by the Hudson's Bay Company. Many of the old Nor'westers and their Métis allies went on to become prominent Hudson's Bay men, including Cuthbert Grant, who was made "Warden of the Plains." Grant actually was charged with murder and placed in jail, but he escaped and hid in the woods until the charges were dropped.

Today the city of Winnipeg occupies the ground where those dramatic events of early Manitoba history occurred. In a park near the site of the Seven Oaks Massacre, a stone monument stands in memory of those who died on that bloody June day.

Prelude to
Rebellion

In the decades following the War of 1812, government in
Upper Canada was firmly in the hands of a small group of
social aristocrats called the Family Compact. A list of just a
few of their names reads like a list of names for Ontario streets,
communities and institutions: Allan Napier MacNab, William
Jarvis, Henry John Boulton, Thomas Talbot, John Beverley
Robinson, and the undisputed leader, John Strachan. These men
were not aristocrats in the hereditary sense of the word, and had
not necessarily been born to money. Some came from middle-
class or even poor backgrounds, and they were often self-educated.
They or their families had arrived in Upper Canada early, and
through hard work and connections they had scrambled to the top.
It did not hurt if one could point to a good War of 1812 military
record, as MacNab could, having fought in several engagements
as a member of General Isaac Brock's old regiment, the Forty-
Ninth Foot. They were staunch supporters of the Church of
England (Anglican), and many of them were of Loyalist stock.
They served as justices of the peace and as members of the

Executive and Legislative councils, and as the years passed they became the most influential men in their communities. Once they were in control of political and financial power in Upper Canada, the Family Compact held onto it tightly and saw to it that their own relatives and cronies benefited.

Former army officer William Jarvis, for example, was appointed provincial secretary by John Graves Simcoe, the founder of York (Toronto) and the first governor of Upper Canada. One of Jarvis' sons was made sheriff of the Home District, the territory between York and Lake Simcoe. Another of his sons was a court clerk and superintendent of Indian affairs. One of his cousins was registrar of deeds—an official who determined who got title deeds to prized Crown land. During the reign of the Family Compact, nepotism was rampant.

The Compact members enriched themselves at the colony's expense by various means, but especially through land speculation. They gained control of huge tracts of land, then sold or rented lots at great profit. The profits were invested in other enterprises that generated still more money. The squires of the Family Compact lived in magnificent houses like English gentry. MacNab built Dundurn Castle at Burlington Heights. Strachan had the Palace in York. In their opulent mansions the robber barons of the Compact held lavish dinner parties at tables graced with imported silverware and china, and toasted their good fortune with imported wine and brandy. Guests arrived and left in the finest of carriages.

The Family Compact could hold to this ostentatious lifestyle because the families presented themselves as firm bastions of all that was British. They were fiercely loyal to the Crown, and just as fiercely opposed to anything that (to them) smacked of "republicanism." That generally meant any sort of social reform that might undermine their privileges. They would point disdainfully to the "republic to the south" where the slogan "Life, Liberty and the Pursuit of Happiness" had led to nothing but demagoguery and anarchy. The men of the Compact stood, they said, for the British ideals of "Peace, Order and Good Government." When the Americans called themselves "Sons of Liberty," the Compact responded with "Sons of Sedition."

The elite of Upper Canada cringed at words like "reform" and warned the citizens against the evils of republicanism, in somewhat the same manner that opponents of social reforms in a later age would warn against the evils of socialism. To ensure that "radical" ideas were suppressed, the Family Compact usually had the ear and the co-operation of whomever was sent by London to govern the colony. If a governor naïve enough to have ideas of his own arrived, the Family Compact soon set him straight. John Strachan said of one such administrator: "He arrived here with some ideas on the Executive not founded on sufficient evidence, but now sees things more clearly."

The Family Compact also had the power to control elections to the Legislative Assembly. At that time a relatively small percentage of the adult male population had the right to vote. Elections were done by public ballot. Voters could be swayed by money, drink, promises of favours, or intimidation. Elections were frequently marked by violence as gangs of thugs turned out to ensure the "right" candidate won.

While the Family Compact enjoyed money, prestige and power, life was not so easy for the average citizen of Upper Canada. The testimony of one farmer provides a stark contrast to life in the gilded halls of Dundurn Castle:

"The author has been in Canada since he was a little boy, and he has not had the advantage of a classical education at a District School. The greater part of his time has been spent watching over and providing for an increasing and tender family. He had in most instances to make his own roads and bridges, clear his own land, educate himself and his children, be his own mechanic, and except now and then, he has had no society but his own family. He had his bones broken by the fall of trees, his feet lacerated by the axe, and suffered almost everything except death. He waited year after year in hope of better days, expecting that the government would care less for themselves and more for the people. But every year he has been disappointed."

Of course, there was widespread discontent. Ordinary people wondered why, in this land of "Good Government," the average citizen was not as well off as his counterpart in "the republic to the south." In 1817 a Scot named Robert Gourlay wanted to encourage immigration to Upper Canada, which lagged far behind the United States in attracting new people. In order to collect information he could send to Britain, he circulated a pamphlet of thirty-one questions. That last question was: "What, in your opinion, retards the improvement of your township in particular, or the province in general?"

The greatest number of replies complained of the huge tracts of land owned by absentee landlords and speculators. These uncleared, undeveloped blocks of land kept communities scattered, so they could not support such things as roads and bridges. Most of this land was owned by the Family Compact, or by the

Church of England—for whom John Strachan was an ordained minister and would one day be Toronto's first bishop.

To Gourlay this was "paltry patronage and ruinous favoritism." He vigorously denounced the governor's practice of dispensing land, public offices and other commodities to "supplicants and sycophants." In 1818 Gourlay organized a convention at York with the intention of petitioning reforms from the newly appointed governor, Sir Peregrine Maitland. Only fourteen men attended the convention, and it was a quiet affair. But the Family Compact saw in it the seeds of republican revolution. John Strachan and John Beverley Robinson easily persuaded Maitland to ban future conventions. The governor went a step further and refused land grants to all those who had co-operated with Gourlay. Robert Gourlay was arrested, and eventually banished from Upper Canada. Ten years later his name was a rallying cry for a new Reform party created to oppose the Family Compact.

In 1829 and 1834 the Reformers won majorities in the assembly, but the Compact still held the important appointed positions. In 1836 Sir Francis Bond Head arrived as the new governor. He detested the Reformers and was solidly behind the Family Compact. In the 1836 election Bond Head personally appealed to voters as the representative of the Crown to elect men loyal to the Family Compact and throw out the "Yankee rabble-rousers." He also sent agents to bribe voters with gifts of land grants. The Family Compact won a landslide. As far as the likes of MacNab, Strachan and Robinson were concerned, all was right with the universe again. But off in the wings a bitterly disappointed Reformer was thinking of rebellion. This firebrand's name was William Lyon Mackenzie.

The situation was no better in Lower Canada. There, politics and the economy were dominated by the *Parti bureaucrate* (the

Bureaucratic Party, also called the British or Tory Party), but known to those who despised it as the Chateau Clique. The Chateau Clique was to Lower Canada what the Family Compact was to Upper Canada. It was composed mostly of British businessmen—though there were a few self-serving French Canadian *seigneurs* in its ranks—who clustered about the governor (always an appointed British nobleman) and looked after their own interests and those of the province's English-speaking minority. The Clique included such prominent men as beer tycoon John Molson, and James McGill, founder of McGill University, and John Richardson, member of both the executive and legislative councils, and the power behind the founding of the Bank of Montreal—an institution many French Canadians considered a tool of the Chateau Clique.

Lower Canada's only elected body was the Legislative Assembly. The *Parti canadien*, which represented most French-speaking voters, always had a majority in the Assembly. But the Chateau Clique dominated the Executive Council and the Legislative Council. Members of those bodies were appointed and were answerable only to the governor, who in turn represented the Crown through the Colonial Office in London. Either of these unelected bodies could overturn legislation passed by the Assembly. The Assembly could raise taxes, but the governor controlled the disposal of Crown lands. The Clique controlled government appointments, the hiring and firing of civil servants, and government spending. This was a situation that was fertile ground for corruption. In 1823 it was discovered that Receiver General John Caldwell had made personal use of about one hundred thousand pounds from the treasury. He declared bankruptcy and was fired.

It angered the French majority that top government posts and the best civil service jobs almost always went to friends (usually English) of the Chateau Clique. It exasperated them that Lower Canada's government was compared to Britain's, because in Parliament *elected* members controlled all government revenues and spending. And they became fighting mad when they realized the goals of the Clique: to assimilate the French Canadians into British culture, to abolish the seigneurial system, to replace French civil law with British common law, and to gradually replace the Catholic Church with the Anglican Church.

Lower Canada's equivalent of Upper Canada's Reformers were *Les Patriotes*. They demanded reform, and had the support of some English-speaking citizens. London did grant a few concessions. But when the *Patriotes* insisted on having an elected legislative council, objections came all the way from the top. The idea was obviously inspired by American republicanism. King William IV refused to even let his ministers consider it. English supporters of the *Patriotes* began to fall away when the demands for reform became heated to the point of violence. The most demanding of all the voices was that of Louis Joseph Papineau.

The Battle for Lower Canada

"Them Fellers Fought Well"

T rouble had been simmering in Lower Canada for years. The English-dominated Chateau Clique, representing a minority of the population, had economic and political control of the province. The *Patriotes,* formerly the *Parti canadien*, held the majority in the Legislative Assembly, but that body had no control over the Executive Council or the Legislative Council, who held the purse strings and made key government appointments. Governors representing the Crown more often than not were tools of the Chateau Clique. The *Patriotes* demanded reform, and the most outspoken and eloquent of them was the leader, Louis Joseph Papineau.

Born in Montreal in 1786, Papineau owned the seigneury of La Petite Nation on the Ottawa River near Montebello. He had fought for the British in the War of 1812, and studied law. He was a pacifist at heart and abhorred violence. He probably would have preferred, more than anything else, to live in the country and read his books. But Papineau was devoted to the people of Canada, and entered politics as a member of the *Parti canadien*, first winning a seat in the Assembly in 1809. He quickly became the party spokesman, and from the very start he argued for reform. He had initially admired the British system of government, but became disenchanted when the parliamentary system that governed Britain was not implemented in Lower Canada. Papineau was a compelling orator, and was soon the most popular public figure in the province.

In 1822 when a bill was introduced in the British House of Commons to unite Upper and Lower Canada, Papineau was furious. He believed the French people of Lower Canada would then be dominated by the English in both provinces. With his friend and ally John Neilson, Scottish editor of the *Quebec Gazette,* Papineau travelled to London in 1823 to speak against the bill. By the time they arrived there, Parliament had already decided not to move forward with the idea, but Papineau had seen what he perceived to be a threat to his people, and agitated more vigorously for reform. His English friends, fearing that his speeches were becoming too radical, began to fall away. His popularity among French Canadians was stronger than ever.

When the *Parti canadien* became the *Patriotes,* Papineau was calling for a government more along the lines of the American republican system. His fiery oratory stirred those who heard him, as well as many to whom his words were repeated. Not all of those who cheered Papineau were French. His message appealed to liberal-minded English, the many Irish immigrants, as well as American farmers who were settling in the Eastern Townships of Lower Canada. But for all the passion he put into his speeches, Papineau quite likely never thought his words would inspire violence. He wanted peaceful reform, not the gunfire and bloodshed of the Revolutionary War. But violence did come.

A by-election was held in Montreal in the spring of 1832. An Irish journalist named Daniel Tracey was the *Patriote* candidate. He had been highly critical of the government and had even been jailed, which made him a hero to the French Canadians. His opponent was Stanley Bagg, an English merchant. The election was hotly contested, and there was fighting in the streets everyday. One journalist reported, "While there was a man in the city who could be bought, no pains were spared to buy him."

The election office was in Place d'Armes, in front of Notre-Dame Church. On May 21, with the square packed, an elections official announced that Tracey had won. His cheering supporters were forming up the traditional victory procession, when "whackers"— the club-swinging hired goons hired by both sides—collided. Others joined in with sticks and stones, and a full-fledged riot ensued. British troops had been posted on the church steps. They advanced on the mob, but the fighting increased. Four magistrates who were present gave the order to fire. The soldiers fired a volley, and three Canadians were killed. The crowd dispersed, but one witness claimed that Stanley Bagg's supporters laughed at the sight of Canadian blood on the street. Two of the magistrates who had told the soldiers to fire on the crowd were arrested. They were tried and acquitted by an all-English jury.

In 1834 the *Patriotes* presented their Ninety-Two Resolutions to the Assembly. Among other things, this document denounced partisan judges and government corruption, demanded representative government, and called for the impeachment of the current governor, Matthew Whitworth Aylmer. The Assembly voted in favour of the Resolutions fifty-six to twenty-three. All twenty-three men who opposed the Resolutions were defeated in a general election later that year. The Resolutions were forwarded to London, and

Archibald Acheson, the Earl of Gosford, was sent to replace Aylmer and to head a Royal Commission looking into problems in Lower Canada.

At *Patriote* meetings during the summer of 1836, the members adopted resolutions inspired by the American Declaration of Independence. They proposed a boycott of British goods. Instead of wearing clothing imported from Britain, they began wearing the colourful, homespun, traditional garb of the *habitant,* including the woven sash. In March of 1837 the British government turned down the Ninety-Two Resolutions and presented Ten Resolutions of its own, few of which satisfied the *Patriotes.*

The *Patriote* movement picked up steam as it rolled across Lower Canada in the summer of 1837. The *Patriotes* erected Liberty Poles, tall white posts topped with the red hats that symbolized revolution. They had their own flag, a red, white and green tricolour. And they had their own hero, Louis Joseph Papineau.

Papineau was at the peak of his popularity. But he was concerned about the increase in the incidents of violence. They were breaking out sporadically all across Lower Canada. Supporters of the *Patriotes* were attacking French Canadians suspected of supporting the Chateau Clique. They called these people *vendus* (people who had sold out) and *Chouayens* (after French militiamen who deserted during the Battle of Chougen in 1756). The *Patriotes* were boycotting the businesses of known or suspected *vendus,* and even destroying their houses. Some *vendus* were volunteering to fight alongside British troops if things boiled over. Opposing militant groups arose: the Doric Club, which supported the Bureaucratic Party, and the *Fils de la Liberté* for the *Patriotes.* Members of both groups were itching for a fight. Papineau felt the situation was getting out of his control.

On October 23 Papineau spoke to a crowd of about five thousand at the small town of Saint-Charles on the Richelieu River. Many of those in attendance had guns. Alarmed by this, Papineau spoke against violence. But another *Patriote* leader, Dr. Wolfred Nelson, exclaimed, "I say the time has come to melt down our tin spoons and plates into bullets."

Wolfred Nelson was an odd man to be championing French rights. His mother was a Loyalist and his father a teacher who was well-connected with Montreal's English community. Young Wolfred grew up among British soldiers, and was a hospital mate with the militia during the War of 1812. It was there that he met *habitants,* developed a fondness for them and became sympathetic to their cause. Nelson also hated bureaucracy, and if there was one thing that was a hallmark of British administration, it was bureaucracy. Nelson was passionate and temperamental, and he was all for fighting.

So was Thomas Storrow Brown. Born in New Brunswick in 1803, Brown was also of Loyalist stock. But this former hardware store owner sympathized with the *Patriotes* and with the Irish. He wrote letters and articles for the *Vindicator and Canadian Advertiser,* a publication that expressed radical views.

After Nelson had spoken another *Patriote* leader, Dr. Cyrille-Hector Coté stood up and said, "We must direct not words but lead against our enemies." Others spoke in a similar vein. The crowd cheered, and some discharged their guns. They erected a Liberty Pole in Papineau's honour, placed their hands on it and swore to fight to the death for liberty and for Papineau, the man who advocated reform without violence.

On November 6 a riot broke out again in the streets of Montreal when the Doric Club and the *Fils de la Liberté* clashed in a bloody confrontation, wielding clubs and hurling rocks. The Dorics broke into the office of the *Vindicator,* where they smashed the presses and threw the type into the street. Thomas Storrow Brown was on the premises, and was badly beaten up. A head wound left him permanently blinded in one eye. Other Dorics pelted Papineau's house with stones. A city magistrate read the Riot Act and Governor Gosford sent troops into the street. The redcoats put the rioters to flight, and arrived at Papineau's house just as the mob was about to storm it. The soldiers chased the attackers away, and then put a cordon around the house.

By November 8 General John Colborne, commander of the British forces in Lower Canada was recruiting and arming volunteers in anticipation of escalating violence. He sent requests to Halifax and to Upper Canada for reinforcements—all the regular troops they could spare. Within days Governor Gosford had warrants made out for the arrest of twenty-six *Patriote* leaders. Papineau's name was at the top of the list. Gosford was reluctant to issue the warrants, but on November 16 he did. Six of the *Patriotes'* lesser leaders were quickly picked up in Montreal, but the whereabouts of Papineau and the more senior members of the party were not known.

Then the government learned that two other minor *Patriotes,* Pierre-Paul Demaray and Dr. Joseph-Francois Davignon were in St-Jean d'Iberville. These two were not especially important, but they were close by. A troop of Montreal mounted volunteers, accompanied by a magistrate, set out to make the arrest. Davignon and Demaray were taken without resistance and placed in a wagon for the trip back to Montreal. Night had fallen, and they were passing a low stone fence near Longueil, when they were ambushed.

Thirty or forty men suddenly jumped up from behind the wall, opened fire on the volunteers, and then rushed them. One volunteer had his face peppered with buckshot. Two more had bullets in their legs, and another was slashed across the thigh with a knife or sabre. The volunteers galloped off into the fields, leaving behind a dead horse, and the overturned wagon with the two prisoners sprawled on the ground. When the volunteers limped into Montreal the next morning, taunting *Patriote* youths pelted them with eggs and snowballs.

The Montreal *Courier,* an anti-*Patriote* publication, carried this comment the next day:

"Blood has been shed at last, by rebels who now stand unmasked and fairly subject to the worst penalties of the laws they have insulted." When Thomas Storrow Brown heard of the incident, he said, "The ball is commenced; we must all take our place in the dance."

Papineau had fled Montreal when he was warned of his impending arrest. He met Dr. Edmund Bailey O'Callaghan, editor of the *Vindicator,* and the two went on to St-Denis, where they found Wolfred Nelson. By this time Papineau knew he had unleashed a whirlwind that he could not stop. A violent rebellion had begun. He and the other *Patriote* leaders made arrangements to raise funds for the purchase of weapons. They planned to recruit help from the United States. They would hold a convention the first Monday in December and declare independence. Their military headquarters would be St-Denis. *Patriote* militia seized the stone manor house of Pierre-Dominique Debartzch, a member of the Chateau Clique, and transformed it into a fort. Papineau said he believed a revolution could succeed in Lower Canada, and recommended that Brown be made a general.

At Fort Chambly on the Richelieu, reinforcements had barely entered the gates after a forced march in miserable weather, when they were ordered out again. Led by Lieutenant Colonel George Augustus Wetherall, the 350 troops were to be part of a two-pronged attack designed to trap the *Patriotes*, who were now being called rebels. Wetherall would move north toward St-Charles and St-Denis, where the rebels were known to be gathering, while Colonel Charles Gore moved south toward the same objectives with three hundred men.

On the night of November 22 a young Scottish lieutenant, George "Jock" Weir, became lost while carrying dispatches to Colonel Gore. He was captured by a *Patriote* patrol near St-Denis, and promised fair treatment if he did not try to escape. Weir did try to escape, though he had given his word he would not. His attempt failed. He was shot twice, and then stabbed repeatedly. Witnesses later said that the man in charge of Weir's guards, Captain François Jalbert, cried, "Finish him! Finish him!", and ran Weir through with his sword. Others would deny Jalbert's part in Weir's death. Whatever actually happened, Weir's brutal death meant there was no turning back for the *Patriotes*. They had killed a British officer! It would also result in tragic consequences for men who had nothing to do with the murder.

Papineau and O'Callaghan knew nothing of Weir's death, and Nelson would not know of it until the redcoats were in sight. Early in the morning of November 23 the three *Patriote* leaders were in an emergency conference. They had received warning of Colonel Gore's advance, and were alarmed. They had expected a force of volunteers, not the British army. Just what was said between Papineau and Nelson would be the subject of debate for decades to come. Each would contradict the other's statements to his dying day.

In Papineau's version, it was agreed that Nelson should lead the fighting men. Papineau was the statesman, and should not be made "repugnant" to the British by having blood on his hands. Nelson wanted him to leave. According to some accounts, Nelson told Papineau, "I demand that you go. You should not expose yourself unnecessessarily. We shall have more need of you later."

Papineau allegedly replied, "I might, perhaps, leave the village; but it does not seem right…to go at such a time is to expose myself later, perhaps, to severe reproach."

According to Nelson, he agreed to fight the battle, but expected Papineau would remain in the safety of the stone house. If he (Nelson) fell, then Papineau would take command. Whichever version is true, the men burned documents that could be incriminating, including the declaration of independence they had just drawn up. Then Papineau and O'Callaghan got into a carriage and joined the stream of refugees hurrying south. About that time Nelson was informed of the killing of a captured British officer. Nelson allegedly said to Jalbert, "You old fool! You don't know what you've done." By then Gore's troops were in sight.

Nelson had about two hundred men at the beginning of the Battle of St-Denis. Some were veterans of the War of 1812, but many were armed with nothing but pitchforks and stakes. They had one cannon, with only scrap iron for ammunition. The men were well entrenched in the stone house, a distillery, some other houses, and behind defensive works along the road.

Colonel Gore had hoped to take the rebels in St-Denis by surprise, but any chance of that was dashed when Nelson's forward skirmishers began firing at his troops from the trees. The skirmishers fell back to the village, leaving the redcoats to struggle across streams where bridges had been destroyed. When at last they reached the edge of the village, Gore had a shot fired from his single cannon to get the range. The iron ball rang off the stone wall of the main house, doing no damage at all.

The village was strung out along the river, so it could not be encircled. Houses and other buildings, trees and brush offered defenders many protected places from which to shoot. The large stone house was obviously the key to the village, so Gore made that his first objective. His infantry chased some rebels from a nearby barn, which Gore intended to use as a shelter from which to bombard the enemy with his cannon. But as they were unlimbering the big gun, three of his soldiers were picked off by gunfire from the stone house.

When the cannon was finally in a firing position, its first shot crashed through a window and killed four of Nelson's men. The next three iron balls rang harmlessly off the stone wall. Gore decided the house would have to be taken by storm. He assigned that dirty but necessary task to Captain Markham of the Thirty-Second Regiment.

With his two hundred men Captain Markham cleared the rebels out of houses that blocked the approach to the barricade. Then they managed to take a house across from the stone manor. Markham tried three times to rush that little fortress, and three times rebel fire blew his men back. He had suffered casualties, and had been wounded himself in the neck and leg. Whenever his men tried to move, they were caught in a crossfire between the house and the distillery. Now it seemed they were being fired upon from all directions. From across the river and the surrounding countryside, reinforcements were hurrying to the aid of Nelson's rebels. Captain Markham had no choice but to order a withdrawal. He was carried off the field on a stretcher.

Colonel Gore had been hammering the stone house with his cannon, and seemed to have driven the defenders from the upper floor. But it would take much heavier artillery than he had available to put a dent in the ground floor walls. He had fired sixty iron balls and had but six left. Moreover, enemy reinforcements were now threatening his position, as well as Captain Markham's. Colonel Gore believed he now faced 1,500 rebels. In fact, there were about eight hundred. All Gore could see was that his troops were being increasingly outnumbered. He had to retreat before his men were encircled, but could not go the way he had come. He would have to take his men to Sorel. There was only one bridge over the Richelieu still intact.

Colonel Gore had to leave behind some wagons and several of his wounded. But he was determined not to leave the enemy his cannon. His infantry crossed the bridge, leaving only a rearguard to cover the men struggling with the cannon. The gun was stuck in the mud, and the troops trying to move it were being harried by enemy snipers. The draught horses strained in their harness, and then quit. They were replaced with officers' horses, and those animals, too, collapsed from the effort. Then men tried to do what horses couldn't. Infantrymen hauling on long ropes pulled until their arms and backs ached and their hearts were about to burst. The medical officer told Gore that gun would be the deaths of all of them. Gore reluctantly ordered the gun spiked and abandoned.

The cold, wet, tired and hungry troops marched until sometime after midnight, when Gore called a halt at an abandoned farm. They found a cache of potatoes in a root cellar; enough to distribute three or four to each man. The soldiers roasted them over campfires, and then fell into exhausted sleep on the open ground. Gore had six dead, eighteen wounded and six men missing. He thought the rebel losses must have been at least a hundred. Actually, Nelson's losses were twelve dead and seven wounded. The following morning as Gore's men continued along the road to Sorel, they met a relief column that had been sent to join them at St-Denis. Too late, Gore told the commanding officer, and all marched to Sorel. Along the way ninety-two men deserted and fled across the American border.

In St-Denis the rebels were jubilant! They had beaten British regulars! Soon Papineau would return with American volunteers, and American money to buy guns and ammunition. They would take Montreal, and then Quebec City itself. Then they would banish the English, as well as any French Canadians who sided with them. There had been rumours of rebellion in Upper Canada, too. Perhaps more help would come from there! As word of the victory spread across the countryside, more men and boys set out for St-Denis. Some had guns; others expected Nelson to arm them. In spite of his incredible victory, Nelson was in a sombre mood. He knew there would be many more redcoats to fight. He was distressed, too, at the sight of the dead and wounded men, men who had been his friends and neighbours.

A further pall fell over the joyous atmosphere on Saturday November 25, the day for the burial of the dead. The Church in Lower Canada had opposed the *Patriotes* from the beginning. The clergy certainly did not condone armed insurrection. When the rebels took the bodies of their slain to the local church, the pastor stopped them at the door. The dead men, he said, had stepped outside the faith when they took up arms. He would not give them the last rites of the Church, and he would not permit them to be buried in consecrated ground. Amidst cries of anger and grief, he and the other priests walked down to the river and were rowed away from the village, taking with them all hope of spiritual comfort. As silent men buried the dead, unshriven, in unblessed ground before a sullen crowd, the people heard the sound of gunfire coming from St-Charles.

Colonel Wetherall had been held up by bad weather and a lack of communications from Montreal. He was sure General Colborne had sent messengers, and the messengers had been captured by the rebels. With no other orders to act on, he decided that his original orders stood: march on St-Charles as soon as possible.

On November 22 the rain eased to a drizzle, so Wetherall crossed the Richelieu at the Chambly ferry at dusk and began his march north. The road was a bog, which slowed the column to about a kilometre an hour. The two cannon kept sinking in the muck. Wagons tumbled over and men knee-deep in goo had to set them upright. Wetherall knew there were eyes in the woods watching every move the soldiers made.

At 3:00 a.m. Wetherall called a halt to give the men a rest. At dawn they moved out again, but went only as far as St-Hilaire, the halfway point. There Wetherall decided to wait for news from Gore. He bivouacked his men on the farm of Hertel de Rouville, a seigneur who was loyal to the British side.

Wetherall didn't learn of Gore's defeat until November 24. He considered retiring to Montreal, but had received no orders to do so. He did not know Colborne had dispatched two riders with orders for him to return to the city, but both couriers had been captured. Wetherall decided he would continue on to St-Charles, but first he wanted a reserve company he had left at Fort Chambly. He needed the strongest fighting force he could muster, or he would be trapped in the middle of very hostile country. He sent a courier to Chambly, and the following morning the rider returned, hotly pursued, the man said, by a rebel patrol. Wetherall's reinforcements were coming by river, he said, because they dare not use the roads. The man also reported that ice was starting to form on the river. Soon the Chambly ferry would be out of commission. If Wetherall did not defeat the enemy, he would be caught on the wrong side of the river and out of communication with Montreal. Reinforced by his reserve troops, Wetherall moved out early on November 25.

Wetherall's troops were fed and well rested, and morale was high. But the commander was worried about the odds. St-Charles was said to be even better defended than St-Denis, with about three thousand men. His advance was slowed by fallen trees and wrecked bridges. Rebel skirmishers fired at his men from barns and from the forest. Several times Wetherall halted the column so his troops could clear the barns of snipers and then burn them down. But he could not clear the woods, and rebel guerillas harried his men all the way.

When Wetherall at last emerged from the woods and came within sight of St-Charles, he was stunned. The defences that had been thrown up by "General" Thomas Storrow Brown were about as ramshackle as could be. There was a rampart of logs and branches covered with frozen mud. His guns could blast that to pieces easily. But even that would be unnecessary. The low wall curved up from the river and crossed the road, leaving a manor house isolated on its right flank. Neither structure offered the other any protection. A high and apparently undefended hill rose behind both of them. On the left flank the rampart straggled into some clumps of bushes. Beyond that was open ground. Wetherall had but to put his guns on that hill, and the village would be his.

But what of those three thousand rebel fighters? Wetherall could see a hundred or so. With his two cannon front and centre, Wetherall deployed his men so the enemy could clearly see his strength. Then he called for a prisoner who had been picked up along the road, and sent him into the village with a message. He was to tell the man in command that the British were on their way to St-Denis. If they were allowed to pass through St-Charles peacefully, no one would be hurt and no damage would be done.

The messenger had a hard time finding Brown because the general had been rushing about, giving orders and trying to prepare his defences. For several days he had been in St-Charles, sending out men to forage for grain and cattle, arresting locals suspected of being loyalists, and building fortifications, such as they were. Men had swarmed into the village, and then left to join the garrison at St-Denis. In pain from his injured eye and dislocated jaw, Brown was scurrying around with no real idea of what to do. He'd been told Wetherall was retreating to Montreal. That was good, he thought. The British would have to sit out the winter in the city, while he built up a real army. Now here Wetherall was, right on his doorstep, and requesting safe passage. Brown considered the request, and then said the British could pass through if first they laid down their arms in the road.

The messenger started back with this reply, Brown close behind him, shouting at some villagers to join the men on the rampart. But in the time it had taken for the messenger to find Brown, Wetherall had grown impatient. He moved his troops forward. His centre and left closed on the rampart, and his right flank swung around it. Then he stopped. He hoped he would see a white flag, or perhaps his messenger returning. He saw neither. Then there were shouts of defiance from the ramparts and the rebels opened fire.

The well-trained and disciplined British troops in the centre and left dropped to the ground, fixed bayonets, and awaited the order. The soldiers on the right swept forward to clear a way to the hill for the guns. In fifteen minutes the cannon were on the hill, firing iron balls and grapeshot into the rebels trapped below. The barricade was smashed to splinters and men were torn to shreds. Then the big guns fell silent and Wetherall ordered the bayonet charge.

The redcoats poured through the gaps the guns had blasted in the rampart, and the rebels fought fiercely, often hand-to-hand. Some fell back to the village, where the fighting became house-to-house. But one by one the houses were taken and the defenders killed. Within an hour the shooting was over and St-Charles was in flames. At the first sound of gunfire Brown had jumped on his horse and fled to St-Denis. Of the rebel fighters, one British soldier said later, "Them fellers fought well; they waited too long to run."

Wetherall had three men dead and eighteen wounded. He and two other officers had their horses shot out from under them. In his report to General Colborne he said he had counted fifty-six enemy dead, but did not know how many had died in the flaming houses or had drowned trying to escape in the river. That night the smell of roasted flesh was everywhere in St-Charles.

The pastor from St-Denis arrived in St-Charles. Wetherall sent him back to St-Denis to tell the people to return to their homes or their village would be destroyed. On November 27 he began the march back to Montreal. He encountered rebels at the Chambly ferry and needed but a few shots to drive them off. Three days later his men entered Montreal with thirty prisoners in tow, carrying the St-Charles Liberty Pole with its red cap on top.

On the same day a triumphant Lieutenant Colonel Wetherall entered Montreal, a somewhat shamefaced Colonel Gore was back on the road to St-Denis. When he arrived there he found the place almost abandoned. His spiked cannon was where he had left it. A few local residents approached under a white flag and said all the fighters had gone. The people still in the town, they said, were loyal. They would have to prove that loyalty. Troops had orders to burn the homes of rebels. As the soldiers searched the area for Papineau and other rebel leaders, they found the body of Lieutenant George "Jock" Weir. It was plain to see that in addition to being shot twice, the young officer had been pounded with gun butts and slashed and stabbed many times with knives, sabres and bayonets. Three fingers had been cut off one hand. The people the soldiers had thought of as the "poor, deluded habitans [sic]" now became the "murdering French." The soldiers would have their revenge.

Papineau, O'Callaghan and Brown escaped to the United States. Neilson was caught as he was about to cross the border, and taken to Montreal where crowds jeered him as he was taken to jail. The rebellion in the Richelieu Valley was finished. But it was still alive elsewhere.

Northwest of Montreal lay the county of Two Mountains and in it the communities of Saint-Eustache and Saint-Benoit. In the years following the fall of New France many English, Scottish and Irish settlers moved into the region, and they got along reasonably well with their French-Canadian neighbours. Things changed, however, with the rise of the *Patriotes*. Sharp divisions were created as the French Canadians began to fear they would be crowded out by the English speakers in their midst and in Upper Canada, just across the Ottawa River. People sympathetic to the *Patriote* cause boycotted English-speaking merchants and tradesmen, and threatened other French Canadians who did not follow their example. Feelings ran high, and soon there were clashes in the woods between the opposing sides. In the weeks before the battles at St-Denis and St-Charles, a steady stream of refugees from Two Mountains poured into Montreal. Both French- and English-speaking people brought stories about *Patriotes* requisitioning food and livestock, forcing French-Canadian men to take up arms with them, and running loyalists out of the county.

One of the *Patriote* leaders was Jean-Olivier Chénier, a physician and politician who had become a follower of Papineau. He and his colleagues knew of the forces that were being raised to the south in the Richelieu Valley. They were determined to raise an army in the north. The two armies could then descend upon Montreal from opposite directions.

Late in November Chénier received a message at Saint-Eustache that the *Patriotes* had won a resounding victory at St-Denis. The British dead lay in heaps, and many had been taken prisoner. The *Patriotes* had captured three cannon. The retreating British were throwing away their guns in their haste to reach the safety of Montreal. Chénier was elated. He began to make plans for his attack on Montreal.

Over the next few days, however, more sobering reports came in. The revolt in the Richelieu Valley had been crushed at St-Charles. Papineau and other leaders had fled. Chenier would not believe them. These were lies, he said, made up by the British and the loyalists to deceive the people about their defeat. He continued to send out his foraging parties and requests to communities to send him men. Chénier had once told an audience, "What I say to you, I believe and I will do. Follow me, and you may kill me if you see me run away." He would hold to that conviction to the bitter end.

Other people did not believe the reports of defeat were lies. Chénier's chief lieutenants pleaded with him to send his men home and get away himself. The local priest told him it was hope-less to try to fight the British. Communities that had promised to send him men now sent messages saying they could not. Foragers were coming in empty-handed. Men who had volunteered or had been "conscripted" began to desert. Chénier's army of 1,500 dwindled to a few hundred.

On December 13 General John Colborne left Montreal for Two Mountains with a force of two thousand regular troops and civilian volunteers. Among the latter were men who had recently been driven from their homes by the *Patriotes*. Colborne had infantry, cavalry, and six cannon. Somewhere along the way he expected to be joined by a Major Townshend with a company of regulars and a thousand or more volunteers from English communities on both sides of the Ottawa River. With Colborne's army was Lieutenant Colonel Wetherall, the hero of St-Charles. That officer's son, Lieutenant Wetherall was also with the column. So was Colonel John Maitland, senior officer of the Thirty-Second, Jock Weir's regiment.

British troops appeared on the frozen Rivière des Mille Iles within sight of Saint-Eustache at about 11:30 on the morning of December 14. Chénier still had about two hundred fighting men with him. They dashed out to snipe at the British from the cover of islands. But they were flanked by mounted volunteers on the other side of the river. Then Colborne's artillery fired a couple of rounds and Saint-Eustache became bedlam.

Chénier's skirmishers abandoned their posts on the river and ran. Some ran back to the town, but most only sought escape. Seeing people fleeing along the road leading north from the town, Colborne sent Maitland and Wetherall to encircle Saint-Eustache. Meanwhile, the cannon continued to roar. As the heavy shot smashed into houses, the surviving rebels in them tumbled out. A few took up new firing positions and blasted away at the British. The majority ran for their lives to escape the net that was closing around them. By one o'clock Saint-Eustache was surrounded.

Maitland and Wetherall's infantry now entered the town. Wetherall, who advanced down the main street toward the church, had two cannon. Soldiers swept through shattered houses, but they were empty. As he approached the stone church, Wetherall could see that the doors were barred and the glass knocked out of the windows. Wood had been nailed across, with slits left open for firing. The same had been done with the presbytery on one side of the town square, and the convent on the other. Chénier and the surviving rebels, perhaps eighty of them, had holed up in three solidly constructed stone buildings. Wetherall told his men to fire a warning round.

Instantly the windows of the buildings exploded with gunfire as muskets, rifles and shotguns raked the square. Infantrymen dove for cover and the gunners hauled the two cannon around a corner. Colborne heard the noise and soon his big guns were hurling iron at the church.

The British poured musket fire at the windows, and for an hour they hammered the church with roundshot. But all they did was make pockmarks in the stone. The huge oaken doors were battered, but still in place. Behind them were two iron stoves and a pile of wooden benches. Any movement in the square still drew a barrage of gunfire.

Inside the church the men choked on gunsmoke and their ears rang every time iron struck the walls. Some of them screamed at Chénier that they had no guns. "There will be dead soon," he answered, "you will be able to use theirs," Some of the British musket fire at the windows had found marks, and now defenders were using guns taken from the dead.

Outside, some of the volunteers had worked their way toward the presbytery, which had only a few defenders and was connected by a covered walkway to the church. The volunteers attacked from the rear and drove the rebels out. Regular troops led by young Lieutenant Wetherall burst through the front door. He saw a large iron stove that heated the room. He kicked it over, spilling a pile of red hot coals. Then he piled on mattresses and blankets. In a minute the building was ablaze and smoke was billowing across the square.

Colonel Wetherall quickly sent men under the cover of the smokescreen to attack the convent, which they set on fire. The rebels who weren't killed dashed out and made a run for the river, pursued by the volunteers. Now only the church remained.

Under the protection of the covered walkway, Lieutenant Wetherall and two other officers rushed to the back door of the church. They broke it down, and found themselves in the sacristy. They could hear the sound of gunfire coming from the main body of the church, as well as the ringing of axes. The rebels had retreated to the choir loft and upstairs galleries, and were chopping the stairs away.

The three officers and a group of infantrymen went around behind the altar. They could see almost nothing because of the smoke and the interior gloom. As they moved out from behind the altar, they were shot at from above. The soldiers ducked back behind the altar, then began tearing down the woodwork and smashing it to kindling. They dragged out the priests' vestments from the sacristy and added them to the pile. Then they poured gunpowder over it and set it alight. Once the fire was burning well, they ran outside.

The church was entirely surrounded by soldiers. Some had their muskets primed and loaded. Others waited with fixed bayonets. The word was passing through the ranks: "Remember Jock Weir!"

Screams came from the church as the interior became an inferno. Some of the victims would have fallen from the galleries into the flames. Those who leapt out the windows were shot or impaled on bayonets. One was Jean-Olivier Chénier. He had squeezed out through a narrow window but was shot through the heart as he touched the ground. A few men managed to escape through the smoke, but for most of them there was no mercy. Even when the officers finally tried to put a stop to the murder, men on their knees with their hands in the air were bayoneted.

No one was certain how many French Canadians died that day, but the number was probably over one hundred. About 120 prisoners were rounded up. The British had only three casualties. The rebellion in the north had been effectively crushed, but the victors weren't finished.

The following day Colborne's army moved on to the town of Saint-Benoit. When they reached that community a deputation of fourteen people came out to meet them. They carried a white flag. Indeed, a white flag fluttered from almost every house. The townspeople said they would offer no resistance. They wanted only peace. Colborne asked about rebel leaders who were still at large. He was told they had gone.

Colborne sent the delegation back to town with instructions for the residents. They were to turn over every firearm in town. They must help the soldiers search for wanted men. If a single shot was fired, he would burn the town to the ground.

The soldiers found a few guns and some rebels hiding in cellars. The houses of men known to be *Patriotes* were put to the torch. That might have been the worst the town suffered had it not been for the arrival of Major Townshend with about two thousand volunteers. These men were Protestant English and Scots, many of them Orangemen, with a venomous hatred of all things Catholic. The following morning General Colborne led his regular troops out of town and left Saint-Benoit in the hands of a drunken mob. The redcoats were still within sight of the town when the first house was pillaged and put to the torch, but Colborne did not look back.

The volunteers rampaged through Saint-Benoit like a barbarian horde. They stole everything they could carry away, and burned what they couldn't. Horses and cattle were rounded up to be taken away. Drunken louts befouled and desecrated the church before setting it on fire, and staggered through the streets wearing the priests' vestments. Three days later General Colborne expressed regrets that such "acts of violence" had happened, and ordered reprisals to be stopped.

There were a few more minor incidents, but with the destruction of Saint-Eustache and Saint-Benoit the rebellion in Lower Canada was finished. About eight hundred *Patriotes* were in prison. Ninety-nine of them were condemned to death, but only twelve were hanged. Fifty-eight were transported to a penal colony in Australia, two were banished and twenty-seven were released. Wolfred Nelson was exiled to Bermuda, but eventually returned and became mayor of Montreal. Thomas Storrow Brown fled all the way to Florida, but returned to Canada and by the 1860s was well-established as a businessman in Montreal. Edmund O'Callaghan did not return to Canada. He became an archivist for the state of New York. François Jalbert was tried for the murder of Jock Weir and acquitted.

Louis Joseph Papineau lived in exile in the United States and France until he was granted amnesty. He returned to Canada in 1845. Papineau continued to be politically active, serving in the Assembly until his retirement in 1854. Many of his former *Patriote* colleagues blamed him for the failure of their rebellion because he did not agree with the very concept of armed insurrection. Papineau died in 1871, still a firm believer in the American republican system of government.

The Battle for Upper Canada

"Up Then, Brave Canadians"

"**R**eptile" was the word Solicitor General John Beverley Robinson of Upper Canada used to describe William Lyon Mackenzie. Robinson and the rest of the Family Compact, the tightly knit oligarchy that ruled Upper Canada, had good reason to detest the pugnacious little Scot. He had been a thorn in their side for years. In his newspaper, the *Colonial Advocate* (shortened to the *Advocate* when Mackenzie became disenchanted with the British government), Mackenzie had made scathing attacks on the Compact and had been relentless in his demands for government reform. In a typical editorial he called the Family Compact, "...a few shrewd, crafty, covetous men under whose management one of the most lovely and desirable sections of America remained a comparative desert." As an elected member of the Assembly he had verbally attacked leading Tories (all members of the Family Compact were staunch Conservatives), the Church of England, and the Bank of Upper Canada. He collected twenty-five thousand signatures on a petition demanding reform. The Compact had done everything short of murder to silence Mackenzie. On five occasions they had him

213

thrown out of the Assembly. One day a gang of youths, sons of well-known Family Compact members, disguised themselves as Indians and broke into Mackenzie's newspaper office in York. They smashed his printing press and threw his type into Lake Ontario. Mackenzie had even been waylaid by thugs and beaten up.

But no matter how many times the Tories knocked Mackenzie down, he got back up, ready for another scrap. His supporters kept re-electing him to the Assembly. When York was incorporated as the City of Toronto in 1834, Mackenzie became the first mayor. To the common people Mackenzie was a hero. He was certainly a champion to Upper Canadians of American descent—about half the population—whose rights he had battled for in the Assembly. On one occasion his constituents presented him with a gold medal and chain worth 250 pounds, after he had won an election in which his Tory opponent received only one vote.

Mackenzie was understandably bitter then, when in 1836 he lost an election for the first time. The Family Compact and the new governor, Sir Francis Bond Head, had effectively denounced Mackenzie and other reformers as "republicans" whose ideas of "home rule" would lead to Upper Canada's separation from Mother England; a notion that was completely unacceptable in a strongly Loyalist province. One of their election broadsides said, "Victory or Death! The Rebels shall be defeated!!!" The Tories even convinced more moderate Reformers to withdraw their support from Mackenzie.

Mackenzie had sold the *Advocate,* so he started a new publication, the *Constitution,* in which he escalated his editorial attacks on the Family Compact, as in this passage in which he names some of the families in question:

"The backwoodsman, while he lays the axe to the root of the oak in the forests of Canada, should never forget that a base basswood is growing in this, his native land, which, if not speedily girdled, will throw its dark shadows over the country and blast its best exertions. Look up, reader, and you will see the branches—the Robinson branch, the Powell branch, the Jones branch, the Strachan branch, the Boulton twig, etc. The farmer toils, the merchant toils, the labourer toils, and the Family Compact reap the fruit of their exertions."

Nor did Mackenzie spare the governor. When a Tory newspaper asked, "Who is Wm. Lyon Mackenzie?", and then answered the question with a series of personal and ethnic insults which included the insinuation that he was a rebel, Mackenzie replied:

"I am proud of my descent from a rebel race; who held borrowed chieftains, a scrip nobility, rag money, and national debt in abomination...this rebel blood of mine will always be uppermost. Words cannot express my contempt at witnessing the servile, crouching attitude of the country of my choice. If the people feel as I feel, there is never a Grant or Glenelg who crossed the Tay and Tweed to exchange highborn Highland poverty for substantial Lowland wealth, who would dare to insult Upper Canada with the official presence, as its ruler, of such an equivocal character as this Mr. what do they call him _____ Francis Bond Head."

Bond Head dismissed Mackenzie as a lunatic, but the Family Compact considered him dangerous, especially now that his speeches and editorials began to truly smack of Yankee republicanism. Like

Papineau, Mackenzie had lost his faith in the British system. He felt a whole new government, modelled after the one in the United States, was necessary for Upper Canada. Now when he travelled, Mackenzie needed a bodyguard. Tory supporters threatened him with physical violence and even assassination.

Bond Head believed he had "saved Canada" with his unprecedented interference in the election of 1836. He had, among other things, warned the voters not to interfere with their "bread and butter" by voting Reform. But as the year progressed, the despotic manner in which Bond Head behaved alienated many people. Though they were a minority, there were enough of them that Bond Head should have had concern. Rumours were starting to circulate that farmers were moulding supplies of bullets, and that men who didn't have guns were making pikes. Some reports even said rebels were drilling and preparing to form an army. Bond Head brushed these stories aside. So great was his contempt for them, that when a request came from Lower Canada for troops to help put down the *Patriote* rebellion, Bond Head sent every redcoat soldier in Upper Canada. In the armoury in Toronto only two constables were left to guard thousands of muskets and the stores of gunpowder and ammunition.

Bond Head has often been accused of causing the Upper Canada Rebellion. While his autocratic method of governing certainly helped bring matters to the boiling point, trouble had been simmering for a long time. The abuses of the Family Compact were becoming offensive to more and more people, even those who did not agree with the radical ideas of William Lyon Mackenzie. A period of economic depression followed by poor harvests was also a factor in pushing some people over the edge.

Meetings of the discontented began in June and continued through the summer. They were not always secret, and sometimes bloody brawls erupted between Tory and Reform factions. Mackenzie received a letter from the *Patriotes* urging him to join their cause. On October 9 Mackenzie and several Reform leaders had a secret meeting in the back room of a Toronto brewery. Mackenzie spoke of their failure to effect change by constitutional means. He said they had a choice between gradually building up an organization for armed insurrection, or an immediate *coup d'etat*. As his own words show, Mackenzie was in favour of swift action:

"I said that the troops had left; that those who had persuaded Head to place four thousand stand of arms in the midst of an unarmed people seemed evidently not opposed to their being used; that Fort Henry was open and empty, and a steamer had only to sail down to the wharf and take possession; . . . and that my judgment was that we should instantly send for Dutcher's foundrymen and Armstrong's axe makers, all of whom could be depended on, and with them go promptly to the Government House, seize Sir Francis, carry him to the City Hall, a fortress in itself, seize the arms and ammunition there and the artillery, etc., in the old garrison, rouse our innumerable friends in town and country, proclaim a provisional government, send off the steamer that evening to secure Fort Henry, and either induce Sir Francis to give the country an executive council responsible to a new and fairly chosen assembly to be forthwith elected after packing off the usurpers in the 'Bread and Butter Parliament', or, if he refused to comply, go at once for Independence and take the proper steps to obtain and secure it."

The others were reluctant to go to such extreme lengths as kidnapping the governor. They first wanted to find out if there was enough support among the population for such an action. Mackenzie said he would speak to the Reform units throughout the province and learn their feelings on the matter. All agreed to another meeting on December 7. But when Mackenzie met with other Reformers, he spoke of revolt. On December 7, he said, five thousand men would assemble at Montgomery's Tavern on Yonge Street, six-and-a-half kilometres (4 miles) north of Toronto. They would then march on Toronto, led by a blacksmith named Samuel Lount and Captain Anthony Anderson, a young man who allegedly had some military experience. Mackenzie led his followers to believe two important Reformers, Dr. John Rolph and Thomas Morrison, approved of the plot. Rolph and Morrison were angry when they learned of Mackenzie's deception, but in the end agreed to the plan. They did ask for a more experienced military man to lead the march on Toronto, so Mackenzie sent for Colonel Anthony Van Egmond, an old Dutch soldier who had served in Napoleon's army and now had land in Upper Canada.

Colonel James Fitzgibbon, the War of 1812 hero, knew insurrection was in the air. He pleaded with Bond Head to take action. Bond Head obstinately refused. "I do not apprehend rebellion," he said. When Fitzgibbon requested permission to call out volunteers, Bond Head denied it.

On November 24 Mackenzie rode through the country north of Toronto, spreading the word that the Lower Canadians had arisen and defeated a British army. The St. Lawrence would be closed to reinforcements from England. "Up, then, brave Canadians!" he told them. "The promised land is now before us—up then, and take it!" He told all who would listen that a general uprising had been arranged across the entire province. When they marched on Toronto, half the city was prepared to join them. Even some important Tories were on their side, so disgusted were they with the policies of Sir Francis Bond Head. A new government would fairly distribute the great tracts of land held by the speculators of the Family Compact. Every man who joined the march on Toronto would receive 121 hectares (300 acres). They would not have to fight, Mackenzie said, but take part in an armed demonstration that would awe the governor and any die-hard Tories. Mackenzie warned that anyone who did not join risked having his land confiscated in the new scheme of things.

In the last week of December tensions were mounting in Upper Canada and rumours were flying fast. On Saturday, December 2, Fitzgibbon disturbed a meeting between Bond Head and some other officials. He desperately repeated his warning about a rebellion. Bond Head and the others laughed at him. But Bond Head finally agreed that on Monday he would order two militia regiments to be formed, and he would issue a warrant for Mackenzie's arrest.

Later that day Dr. Rolph heard rumours that Bond Head knew all about Mackenzie's plan and was mobilizing the militia. He sent out a message to other rebel leaders suggesting that the date of the march on Toronto be changed from December 7 to December 4. He thought they should seize the city before Bond Head had a chance to install the militia. Rolph did not know where Mackenzie was, but he was sure the message would reach his ears. Samuel Lount received the message, mistook it for an order, and sent word to his men to assemble at Montgomery's Tavern.

On Sunday Mackenzie was informed of the change of date. He was angry that such a step had been taken without his counsel. He gave orders to go back to the original plan, but by then it was too late. Groups of rebels were already on their way to Montgomery's Tavern. Mackenzie would have to try to make the best of a quickly deteriorating situation.

Montgomery's Tavern was a large frame building on the west side of Yonge Street. At the time that part of Yonge was just a country lane, with fields and forest on either side. Montgomery's was a popular stopover for people travelling to and from the city. Now it was to become the central command post for armed revolt.

Over the next two days hundreds of men converged on Montgomery's Tavern, and travellers on their way to Toronto were detained. There was not enough food for all those people, and muskets the rebels had been expecting did not arrive. Mackenzie sent foragers out to find food and seize arms from neighbouring houses. Then word came of the *Patriote* defeat at St-Charles. Rolph wanted to call the whole thing off, but Mackenzie said it was too late for that. On Monday night the first blood of the rebellion was spilled.

Mackenzie, Captain Anderson and some others had ridden south on Yonge Street to reconnoitre. They met Alderman John Powell, who had come north from Toronto on a similar mission. The rebels made Powell a prisoner, and Mackenzie accepted Powell's word that he was unarmed. Anderson and another man started back toward the tavern with Powell, while Mackenzie and his party continued with their scouting expedition. Meanwhile, Colonel Robert Moodie of York County was riding down Yonge Street with several companions, to warn Toronto of the rebel threat. As they approached the pickets at Montgomery's Tavern the sentries challenged them. Moodie drew his pistol and fired, hitting no one. Four rebels shot back, and Moodie fell from his horse, mortally wounded. His companions galloped on.

Further down the road they encountered the rebels escorting their prisoner, Alderman Powell. One of the York County men shouted, "The rebels have shot poor Colonel Moodie and are advancing on the city." Suddenly Powell drew a pair of loaded pistols. With one he shot Captain Anderson in the neck, killing him. Then he dashed back toward Toronto. Along the way he encountered Mackenzie's party. Powell aimed his other gun at Mackenzie and pulled the trigger, but the weapon misfired. Powell spurred his horse on to Toronto, and hurried to Government House to warn the governor.

Powell had to awaken Sir Francis Bond Head. When the governor finally understood that rebels really were marching on Toronto, he became panicky and, according to one witness, "completely terrified." He had his own family and that of Chief Justice John Beverley Robinson placed on a steamer for safety. He sent messages for all militia units to hurry to Toronto. Then he prepared himself to do battle with the forces of sedition. Those who saw Sir Francis armed to the teeth thought he looked absurd, though they admired his sense of duty.

North of Toronto the rebels camped outside Montgomery's Tavern waited in restless confusion for the leaders to decide what to do. Van Egmond had still not arrived. Should they proceed or not? Mackenzie and his lieutenants finally adopted a plan. They would move south to Gallows Hill, just south of what is now St. Clair Avenue. There, they would split up, with Samuel Lount continuing down Yonge with part of their force while Mackenzie took the rest down present-day Avenue Road. They would meet at Osgoode Hall. Mackenzie had about eight hundred men. Some of them had guns, but many carried nothing but pikes or pitchforks. The rebels had detained some fifty or sixty people at the tavern. These were made to march with the rebels, to make their numbers appear greater.

The rag-tag army started south on Yonge Street at about noon on December 5, with Mackenzie in the lead on a white pony. He wore several overcoats as protection against bullets. At Gallows Hill they were met by a delegation of known Reformers sent by Bond Head to parley. The message from the governor was that there would be an amnesty for all if the rebels would disperse and return to their homes. Mackenzie wanted the offer in writing, as well as a national convention to consider his demands for reforming the government. When this reply was taken to Bond Head, he refused to parley with the rebels any further. Quite likely he had just been buying time. While the rebel leaders were once more at loggerheads over what to do next, militia units were forming up in Toronto, and more were arriving by steamer from Hamilton.

At about six o'clock Samuel Lount and Mackenzie continued down Yonge with several hundred men. They passed Bloor Street, and just north of College they encountered a picket of twenty-seven loyalist militia commanded by Sheriff William Jarvis. What happened next was quite likely the most farcical "battle" in Canadian history.

The sheriff's men fired a volley, then turned and ran for Toronto. The rebels were lined up so that the men with muskets were in the front ranks. Behind them were men armed with pikes. To the rear were those who had nothing but sticks and cudgels. The rebels' front rank fired their muskets. Then, instead of stepping aside so the second rank could fire, they fell down on their faces. Those in the rear ranks thought the men in the front line had been cut down by bullets. They turned and ran, and nothing their leaders said could stop them. Soon the whole rebel army was in full retreat. It was later reported that they mistook a wagon load of cordwood on a hilltop for a cannon. The Sheriff's volley killed one man and mortally wounded two others, while the rebels' fire hit no one.

Once more the rebels congregated at Montgomery's Tavern. Mackenzie sent a party to waylay the mail coach, in hope of finding useful information in the correspondence. He found nothing of importance, but he did receive news from Toronto that Thomas Morrison had been arrested for high treason, and Dr. Rolph had fled. When this information reached the rebel ranks, men began to desert.

Toronto was in a state of panic. Angry citizens questioned the governor's wisdom in sending all of the province's garrisons to Lower Canada. City Hall, Government House, the Bank of Upper Canada, and many other buildings had their doors and windows boarded up with heavy planks that had been loopholed for guns. Almost every store was closed, and in those that remained open the price of food skyrocketed. A few known Mackenzie sympathizers were arrested and jailed. More volunteers arrived from nearby communities.

Colonel Van Egmond did not reach Montgomery's Tavern until eight o'clock on the morning of December 7, the day originally scheduled for the march on Toronto. By that time any chance of success for the rebels was long gone, but Mackenzie, Van Egmond, Lount and others held a council of war anyway. Van Egmond took one look at Mackenzie's sorry army and said it was hopeless. Mackenzie, according to legend, put a pistol to the Dutchman's head and told him to lead the army. Mackenzie and Van Egmond wanted to make a diversionary attack from the east, while the main force of rebels swept into the city from another quarter. Not everyone agreed, and the meeting was a stormy one.

Meanwhile, a group of sixty rebels led by "Captain" Peter Matthews entered the city from the east over the Don Bridge on King Street. They encountered a militia company who engaged them in a shootout, while the rebels attempted to set fire to several buildings. The hostler in a stable was killed by a stray bullet. The rebels withdrew. If this was to be the diversion, nobody took advantage of it.

While the rebel leadership bickered, and what was left of their army sat inactive, Colonel Fitzgibbon was organizing his militia. Early that afternoon some six hundred loyalist militia led by Fitzgibbon, Allan MacNab of the Family Compact, and Sir Francis Bond Head himself on a fine stallion, started up Yonge Street for the rebel position. They took along two nine-pounder field guns.

Of Mackenzie's five hundred men, two hundred did not have guns. They could do little more than stand around at the tavern. Van Egmond deployed the rest in the woods along the road and behind fences. A few men were stationed in the Paul Pry Inn on the east side of Yonge just to the south of Montgomery's Tavern. When the loyalist militia came into view over the brow of a hill, their bayonets gleaming in the sun, and bagpipes wailing, the rebels braced for the attack. Joseph Gould, one of Mackenzie's men, later recalled that day:

> "We soon got under arms and started down Yonge Street to meet them. The troops, however, turned to the west and made as though they wanted to get round the west side to our rear. We hastened through the woods, climbing over

dead hemlock trees and through the underbrush, and rushed to head them off. We had no arms but our rifles, and some had only rude pikes and pitchforks. The troops, besides their muskets and plenty of ammunition, had two small field pieces—one controlled by a friend of ours, and the other by an enemy. The friend fired grape-shot, and fired over us into the tops of the trees, cutting off the dead and dry limbs of the hemlocks, which, falling thickly amongst us, scared the boys as much as if cannon-balls had been rattling around us. The other gun was fired low, and so *careless* that I did not like it. One of the balls struck a sand-bank by my feet and filled my eyes with sand, nearly blinding me. Another one struck one of those dry hemlocks, scattering the bark and splinters about, and into my face. Captain Wideman was killed on my left side, and F. Shell was shot through the shoulder to the left of the fallen captain. But we got to the west of the troops. They then turned and crossed to Yonge Street behind us."

The Battle of Montgomery's Tavern lasted barely half an hour. A cannonball smashed through the roof of the Paul Pry Inn, and the defenders spilled out and ran for Montgomery's Tavern. Two cannonballs tore right through the tavern, and that building, too, quickly emptied. The men behind the fences and in the trees could not hold against the numerically superior, better armed loyalists, led by a professional like Fitzgibbon. They were soon running for their lives across the fields and into the woods. Many were taken prisoner. Bond Head let all but the leaders go free. Van Egmond, found hiding in a farmhouse, would be dead in a few weeks, victim of an illness he caught in a cold, damp jail cell. William Lyon

Mackenzie was not among those captured. The rebels had eleven casualties. The loyalist militia had five men wounded, four of whom died. Before Montgomery's Tavern was put to the torch, Bond Head had it searched. Among other things found was Mackenzie's carpet bag, which Bond Head called "The Devil's snuff-box." In it were papers with the names of many people connected to the rebel cause.

Though minor incidents occurred in various parts of the province, the defeat at Montgomery's Tavern marked the end of the Mackenzie Rebellion. Though Mackenzie and many other rebels escaped to the United States, most certainly with the help of admirers and sympathizers, some nine hundred others were arrested, including Samuel Lount. He tried to cross Lake Erie in a small boat, but was blown back to the Canadian shore where he was caught. Between ten and twelve thousand volunteers joined the militia to help track down and apprehend suspected rebels. Many of those, of course, were men who seized upon an opportunity to terrorize, plunder and settle old scores. Nonetheless, it indicated that although many people in Upper Canada were fed up with the self-serving corruption of the Family Compact, they could not condone taking up arms against the Crown. Two rebels, Samuel Lount and Peter Matthews, were hanged. Nearly a hundred were deported to Australia. Thousands left to escape the reprisals of their Tory-supporting neighbours.

Mackenzie, never one to say die, could not admit defeat. Four days after his army was routed, he crossed into the United States and was welcomed as a hero. With the help of both American and Canadian supporters he set up a "republic" on Navy Island, on the Canadian side of the Niagara River. Between three hundred and four hundred recruits joined him there under the banner of his new republic. The guns of the British fort at Chippawa bombarded the island. The Canadians also complained vigorously to the American government about the American steamer *Caroline*, which was keeping Mackenzie's rebels supplied from the United States shore. The Americans did nothing, so on the night of December 29, in a spectacular raid, a Captain Andrew Drew of the Royal Navy and a band of Canadian militiamen slipped across the border, cut the *Caroline* from her moorings and sent her down the Niagara River in flames. The steamer broke up before reaching the falls. The Americans withdrew all support for Mackenzie rather than risk provoking a war with Britain, and Mackenzie had to abandon his "republic."

Mackenzie spent a year in jail for breaking United States neutrality laws. Then he worked as a journalist in New York. For four years he covered American politics for the *New York Tribune*. He later said that if he had seen the American system of government at work sooner, he "would have been the last man to rebel."

Mackenzie was eventually pardoned, and returned to Canada and to politics. By that time responsible government had come to Canada, and the power of the Family Compact was broken. In 1858 Mackenzie moved into a house on Bond Street, and lived there until his death in 1861 at age sixty-six. The house is now a museum, and among the exhibits is Mackenzie's printing press. For a man like William Lyon Mackenzie, the press was always a more potent weapon than a gun.

The Battle of Ridgeway

The Fenians Attack

We are the Fenian Brotherhood
Skilled in the arts of war
And we're going to fight for Ireland
The land that we adore
Many battles we have won
Along with the boys in blue
And we'll go and capture Canada
For we've nothing else to do
—Fenian marching song

Tramp, tramp, tramp, the boys are marching
Cheer up, let the Fenians come
And beneath the Union Jack
We will drive the rabble back
And we'll fight for our beloved Canadian home
—Canadian militia marching song

Many factors led up to the bizarre clash at Ridgeway, Canada West (Ontario), in which the Canadians lost the battle but, in the end, won the "war." The principal cause was the situation in Ireland. For centuries Ireland had been festering under English misrule. One rebellion after another had been crushed. The potato famines of the mid-nineteenth century had seen millions of Irish people starve to death or immigrate, most of them to the United States. In the aftermath of the famines Irish nationalist groups arose, their goal being Ireland's independence. One was called the Fenian Movement, after the *Fianni,* a band of legendary warriors from ancient Irish mythology.

The Fenian Movement in Ireland was quickly suppressed by the British, but in 1859 an American branch called the Fenian Brotherhood was founded in New York City. It was a small group that attracted little attention. The members' original plan was to finance and equip rebels in Ireland.

Then in 1861 the American Civil War broke out and tens of thousands of Irish Americans enlisted in the Union Army. By war's end in 1865 they were well-trained, tough, battle-hardened soldiers. During those four brutal years the Fenian Brotherhood had grown; many of its members were now second-generation Irish Americans who had never set foot in Ireland. The Fenian leaders were quite vocal with their anti-British rhetoric, and much of what they had to say reached the ears of willing listeners in the Northern states.

While Britain had not officially recognized the Confederacy, she had shown sympathies toward the South and had done business with the Confederate government. British-built warships manned by Confederate crews had wreaked havoc with Union shipping. Confederate agents based in Canada had plotted and carried out raids against the North on both land and water. Many Americans, including some in high places, felt the time had come for what they had always believed to be an inevitability: the annexation of Canada by the United States and the final expulsion of Britain from North America.

Of course, the attempt to do just that in the War of 1812 had failed utterly. In the 1830s American invaders calling themselves "Hunters" and "Patriots" had attacked Canada, supposedly to liberate the colony from British tyranny. To their great surprise they found that the Canadians did not want to be "liberated."

But the Fenians were less interested in the liberation of Canada than they were in the liberation of Ireland. To them an invasion of Canada would be an opportunity to "flesh their bayonets in corpulent Mr. Bull." They would capture Canada, and then demand Ireland's independence as the price of ransom.

At a Fenian convention held in Pittsburgh early in 1866, "General" Thomas W. Sweeny, a former officer in the Union Army, proposed a three-pronged attack on British North America. One column would strike at Campobello Island along the Maine–New Brunswick border. Another would invade Canada East (Quebec) from Vermont. The third would cross the border somewhere in the vicinity of the Niagara Frontier to penetrate into what is now Southern Ontario.

Sweeny was certain that thousands of Irish Americans—and Irish Canadians, too—would flock to the Fenian banner. To Irish-American war veterans who had been mustered out of the army and were now unemployed, he offered bounties and free land in Canada. "Before the summer's sun kisses the hill tops of old Ireland," he said in one speech, "a territory will have been conquered on which the green flag, the sunburst of old Ireland, shall float in triumph, and a base be formed for some glorious operations."

The Fenians made no secret of their activities. They spoke openly of their intentions and recruited publicly. The government of President Andrew Johnson kept an eye on them, but did nothing to discourage them, just as a previous administration had done nothing to discourage the Hunters and the Patriots. There was always that possibility that the trouble the invaders stirred up could lead to a juicy plum like Canada falling into Uncle Sam's hands.

But Canadian authorities heard of the Fenian threat and infiltrated the movement with their own spies. Thomas D'Arcy McGee, the Irish-born firebrand who would become a Father of Confederation, was clear about where he stood on the matter of Fenianism:

"Either President Johnston [sic] must put it down in good earnest, with its ringleaders, or we ourselves must put it down in blood on Canadian soil. I need hardly add that my present politics for Canada are: plenty of breech-loaders for our volunteers, and complete union amongst our people."

Sometime after the Fenians' Pittsburgh convention, John A. Macdonald, Attorney General of Canada West, received information that the Fenians intended to attack on St. Patrick's Day. He instructed the adjutant-general of the militia, Colonel Patrick MacDougal, to call up ten thousand volunteers to support the small garrisons of regular British troops. Fourteen thousand men immediately responded to the call. For weeks there was great anticipation in the colony. Would a few British soldiers and the amateur Canadian militia be able to drive back a force of veterans who had helped defeat the armies the legendary Robert E. Lee?

But March 17 came and went without incident. Most of the Canadian volunteers went home.

Then in April the Fenians launched their attack at Campobello. It was a disaster. Due to the presence of a pair of British warships the invaders accomplished nothing more than the burning of a few warehouses before they were forced to withdraw. An embarrassed Washington sent General George Meade, the victor at Gettysburg, to Maine to disperse the Fenians and restore order. One positive result of the Fenian fiasco in New Brunswick was that it pushed the population of that colony closer to accepting Confederation.

Now Thomas Sweeny had to galvanize his forces for what he believed would be the real invasion of Canada. This would be the campaign that would bring the British in Canada to their knees and liberate Ireland. He even said he would make a gift of Canada to the United States, which begs the question of what Canada's fate would be in the event of a Fenian victory. Was Canada to be a bargaining chip in negotiations concerning Ireland, or was the country to be handed over to the Americans? No one seems to have thought these matters through. The only people who knew exactly where they stood were the Canadians. They did not want their country to be held for ransom or annexed by the Americans. But did they have the military strength to prevent either of these things from happening?

The man Sweeny chose to lead the Fenian attack on Canada was "General" John O'Neill. He was a thirty-two-year-old veteran of the Union Army who had fought in the Indian Wars and the Civil War, and had risen to the rank of colonel. He had resigned from the army in a fit of pique after being passed over for further promotion. Now he sought glory as a Fenian commander.

On May 28 O'Neill arrived in Cleveland, Ohio, with another Fenian officer, Colonel Owen Starr. On May 31 O'Neill and Starr received orders from Sweeny to assemble with their men at Black Rock, New York, a short distance down the Niagara River from Buffalo. Between eight hundred and a thousand Fenians armed with guns taken from American arsenals gathered at that small community. Some no doubt considered themselves the vanguard of a greater force that would win liberty for Ireland. Quite a few were very likely adventurers who had visions of plunder. Most wore civilian clothes with only their gun and ammunition belts revealing their paramilitary nature. A few wore bits and pieces of Union and even Confederate uniforms. The officers all wore Union army uniforms. This invading army was divided into five units: O'Neill's Thirteenth Tennessee Regiment, Starr's Seventeenth Kentucky, Colonel John Grace's Eighteenth Ohio, Colonel John Hoye's Seventh New York, and two companies of Indiana Fenians under a captain named Hagerty. In the early hours of June 1 they crossed the Niagara River in scows towed by tugs. American authorities did nothing to stop them. Within three hours the Fenians had entrenched themselves, unopposed, on Canadian soil.

The Fenians established their first camp on Thomas Newbigging's farm, near the mouth of Frenchman's Creek. Some erected breastworks, while others went in search of horses. Local farmers soon realized what was going on and drove their horses and other livestock into the woods. The Fenians were able to "requisition" only a few mounts.

Colonel Starr's first objective was the Erie and Ontario Railway yard in the village of Fort Erie. He and his regiment dashed for the terminal, but the alarm had been spread. Railway officials sent four locomotives and every car in the yard down the line and out of the Fenians' reach. Starr had to content himself with cutting the telegraph wires, burning a railway bridge, and forcing the reeve and town council to provide food for his men.

Meanwhile, O'Neill distributed the few stolen horses among men who were sent out as scouts. These scouts were to look for British troops and Canadian militia. They also carried a proclamation written by Sweeny that assured the Canadians the Fenians' war was not with them, but with the forces of England. The proclamation invited Irishmen, Frenchmen and Americans to take "the honest grasp of friendship." This invitation was not extended to English or Scots.

The Fenian scouts who rode in the direction of Chippawa encountered a group of farmers on horseback. They opened fire on them, putting the farmers to flight. The scouts went back and reported to O'Neill that they had driven off a Canadian cavalry patrol.

As O'Neill awaited the reinforcements he was certain would come across the river, word of the invasion spread across the Canadian countryside. There were no militia units within thirty-two kilometres (20 miles) of the Fenians' encampment, but everywhere men were rushing to volunteer. In Ottawa Governor General Lord Monk signed Order Number 1, calling up sixty-seven militia units in Canada West. "The soil of Canada has been invaded," Monk announced, "not in the practice of legitimate warfare, but by a lawless and piratical band, in defiance of all moral right, and in utter disregard of all the obligations which civilization imposes upon mankind. Upon the people of Canada the state of things imposes the duty of defending their altars, their homes, and their property, from desecration, pillage and spoilation." Some twenty thousand recruits swelled the ranks of militia units across the province. Many of them were under twenty years of age.

The commander of the British forces in Canada West was Major General George Napier. His first action was to secure the Welland Canal, which ran from Port Dalhousie on Lake Ontario to Port Colborne on Lake Erie. Responsibility for protecting the canal fell to Lieutenant-Colonel George Peacocke, a British officer who was given command of the Sixteenth Regiment from London, the Forty-Seventh Regiment from Toronto, and a battery of Royal Artillery. Peacocke assembled his men in St. Catharines, near Port Dalhousie, and then marched to Chippawa. His subordinate, Lieutenant-Colonel Alfred Booker, an English-born militia officer, took another force by rail to Port Colborne. It included his own Volunteer Militia Infantry of Hamilton, the Second Battalion of the Queen's Own Rifles of Toronto, the Caledonian Rifles and the York Rifles. One company of the Queen's Own Rifles had been issued lever-action Spencer repeating rifles; weapons with which they had never drilled. Everyone else carried the standard firearm of the British Army, the muzzle-loading Enfield rifle.

By this time the American government had taken belated action. The gunboat U.S.S. *Michigan* arrived on the scene and prevented Fenian reinforcements and ammunition from crossing the Niagara River. There was no longer any reason for O'Neill to keep his army camped by the river, so he moved inland to a place called Limestone Ridge near the village of Ridgeway. There the Fenians dug in and awaited the enemy.

Colonel Booker had no cavalry at his disposal. The only horse in his command was his own. Cavalry was essential for scouting and reconnoitring. Booker therefore did not know the Fenians had moved to Limestone Ridge. He thought they were still at Newbigging's farm. Booker wanted to cut the Fenians off from any escape to the United States. He had been given orders to patrol the Niagara River, so he sent his second-in-command, Lieutenant-Colonel Stoughton Dennis and a company of 110 men to Fort Erie on the steamer *W.T. Robb.*

Then Booker received orders from Peacocke to rendezvous with him and the main British-Canadian force at Stevensville, a village about twenty-four kilometres (15 miles) from Chippawa and eight kilometres (5 miles) from Ridgeway. Booker telegraphed Peacocke requesting permission to change those orders because he had his own ideas on how to contain and defeat the Fenians. He was genuinely surprised when forty-five minutes later he received a telegram from Peacocke telling him in no uncertain terms to obey his original orders. In the small hours of the morning of June 2, Booker put his 840 men—a somewhat reduced force with the departure of Dennis's men—on a train that would take them to Ridgeway. From there they would march to Stevensville to join Colonel Peacocke.

John O'Neill was surprisingly well-informed of the Canadian–British movements. His mounted scouts advised him of the large force under Peacocke marching toward Stevensville from Chippawa. He also knew about the smaller force on its way to Ridgeway. O'Neill decided to strike at Booker's column before it could hook up with Peacocke.

The Fenians broke camp at dawn June 2. They marched to a location on the Lime Ridge Road that the veteran commander knew was an excellent position at which to intercept Booker. It gave his men the cover of forest and orchards and the advantage of high ground, while forcing the foe to attack across dangerously open ground. O'Neill put his men to work building breastworks and a defensive zigzag barrier made from fence rails. From nearby Ridgeway the Fenians heard the whistle of the train carrying Booker's men, and then the sound of bugles as the Canadians fell into formation. O'Neill sent an advance guard of about 150 men under Starr to take up skirmishing positions about half a mile in front of his main force.

When Booker arrived in Ridgeway, local farmers who had seen the Fenians on the move reported to him that the enemy was just a few miles away. Booker dismissed this information as unreliable rumour. As far as he was concerned, the Fenians were still at Newbigging's farm. He was going to follow orders and meet Colonel Peacocke at Stevensville.

Alfred Booker had been in the militia for many years, but he had never been in a battle. Nor had the men—many of them quite young—whom he was leading. Because of a tight-fisted government, many of the militiamen lacked complete uniforms and proper equipment. Most of them were armed well enough, but were not well-trained in the use of their weapons. Some had never fired a round of live ammunition. These Canadians were not lacking in courage and enthusiasm, but they were otherwise ill-prepared for actual combat.

Though Booker did not believe the Fenians were in the immediate vicinity, he did take some sensible precautions. He ordered his men to load their weapons. He placed Number Five Company of the Queen's Own Rifles—the men who were armed with the repeating Spencers—as his advance guard. At about 7:00 a.m. the column was ready to move out. At the centre of the procession of mostly green coated militiamen rode Colonel Booker, resplendent in his red uniform.

The day promised to be hot and humid as the men trudged along the Lime Ridge Road. At about eight o'clock the Canadians came within sight of the invaders. Ensign Alexander Muir (future composer of "The Maple Leaf Forever") who was with the Queen's

Own Rifles, spotted some Fenian pickets in an orchard. He cried out, "I see three Fenians! There are the Fenians!"

Booker called a halt. He scanned the area with his field glasses, but could see only a few horses. He sent Number Five Company of the Queen's Own Rifles ahead as skirmishers. When those men saw the Fenians they waved their shakos (tall military hats) on the ends of their rifles as a signal that they had seen the enemy. At that moment, as Ensign Muir recalled later, "... a bullet came whistling from the direction of the orchard. This was the first shot, and came close to Captain (John) Gardner and myself."

The firing now began in earnest, but the two sides were still too far apart for it to be very effective. Booker began to deploy his companies, though he didn't seem to have much of a battle plan other than to advance and hopefully rout the enemy. He intended to hold the Thirteenth Militia from Hamilton in reserve, but instead had to send them in to support the advance company of the Queen's Own Rifles, who were already running low on ammunition for their Spencer Rifles. The men simply hadn't been issued an adequate supply of bullets for their rapid-firing weapons. One of them, Ensign Malcolm McEachran, took a Fenian bullet through the body while trying to position himself for a good shot. He was the first Canadian killed that day.

If the inexperienced Colonel Booker did not have a definite plan of battle—other than an exercise from a militia training manual—Colonel Starr of the Fenians evidently did have a strategy in mind. He intended to draw the Canadians into a trap where O'Neill could cut them to pieces. Starr made a slow withdrawal, and the Canadians advanced. One Fenian later said, "It was plain that fighting was new to them. They exposed themselves unnecessarily, which trained men never do."

238

Starr's tactic did not work entirely to his satisfaction, however. Though the Canadians thought they were pushing the Fenians back, they advanced cautiously and did not fall into the trap. But they were taking casualties.

John O'Neill was having troubles of his own. He did not know if British regulars were among the ranks of the foe. As an experienced officer he knew that regulars were to be feared much more than militia. Because the Canadians had not plunged into Starr's trap, O'Neill was now concerned about being outflanked. If that happened, it would be the Fenians and not the Canadians who would be trapped.

O'Neill had also been plagued by that bane of every military commander: desertion. For the rank and file Fenian soldiers, things were not going as they had expected. They'd had no reinforcements from the United States. They were out of food. They had not yet suffered many casualties, but they knew that a force larger than Booker's would soon be brought against them. It just didn't seem they would be doing Ireland much good by dying in Canada. If they were taken captive, they could not expect to be treated as prisoners of war. They would be tried as bandits and then sent off to prison or a penal colony—or hanged! Many of the men who only days earlier had boasted they would capture Canada had slipped away to find their way back across the border even before the fighting started.

O'Neill called in his skirmishers, and then withdrew his entire force to a secondary defensive position. There the Fenians put up a stiff fight. Their rate of fire was so rapid, the Canadians thought they must be armed with repeating rifles. The Fenians were actually fighting with single shot weapons. But they had been trained and could fire and reload much faster than the Canadians.

Nonetheless, the green Canadian troops were giving a good account of themselves against the veteran Fenians.

Then two twists of fate changed the whole direction of the battle and led to disaster for the Canadians. Colonel Booker was under the impression that Colonel Peacocke had left Chippawa at 5:00 a.m. and would reach Stevenville at any moment. From there he would hear the sounds of battle and would hurry to Borden's aid with his regulars and militia. At about 9:30 a messenger delivered two telegrams to Booker. Both were from Peacocke. The first advised Booker to be wary of "obstacles" as he advanced toward Stevenville. The second told the colonel that Peacocke was unable to leave Chippawa before 7:00 a.m. That meant Peacocke was nowhere near Stevenville. This was shattering news for Booker, who might well have already concluded that he was in over his head. The Canadians were still pressing the Fenians. Ensign Muir recalled later:

> "After passing through a bush we came to a wheat field on the opposite side of which we found the Fenians posted opposite our front and to our right. We commenced firing upon the enemy as soon as we saw them and they began to retreat. They were about 200 yards from us. We fired for some time, until ordered to advance and we leaped over the fence and entered the wheat field. We fired from the wheat field for some time. After entering the wheat field I saw the thirteenth battalion on my left, below me in skirmishing order, advancing toward the enemy."

It appeared to the Canadians that the Fenians were giving way. Then O'Neill decided to counterattack. Again, we have Ensign Muir's testimony:

"I distinctly saw the enemy retreating a long distance
before them towards a bush in the rear. Suddenly they
seemed to rally and came down upon the line of the 13th
yelling. At this moment I saw a wavering in the line of the
13th. The Fenians advanced in a loose manner but in great
strength; then the 13th retreated at the double, but I did not
hear the 'retire' sounded for that purpose."

The "retire" Muir referred to was caused by one of those
mishaps that so often change the course of a battle. At a crucial
moment in the struggle, some Canadian militiamen saw a few
Fenian scouts or officers on horseback and mistook them for cavalry. A cry went down the line, "Cavalry! Look out for cavalry!"

Booker heard the alarm and gave the order for his skirmishers
to retire and "Prepare for cavalry." The standard infantry defence
against a cavalry charge was to form a square, a rectangle of standing and kneeling riflemen firing in precision order to decimate the
oncoming horsemen. The "British Square" had become legendary
in the annals of warfare, and Colonel Booker was going by the
manual when he gave his order.

But the Fenians had no cavalry. Booker realized his mistake and
ordered his men back into their lines. This came hard on his order
for the skirmishers to retire. Now confusion ran through the
Canadian ranks just as the Fenians launched their counterattack.
The men thought they had been ordered to retreat. Soon they were
in a panic-stricken flight toward Ridgeway. The Tenth Highland
Company of the Queen's Own Rifles and the York Rifles formed
a rearguard to cover the retreat. Then they, too, had to withdraw
from the field. Booker later reported that he tried to check the
flight of the men:

"I entreated them to rally and implored them to halt, but
without effect. If I could form at Ridgeway I might regain
order. I there found Lieutenant Arthur of the Queen's Own
and other officers attempting to rally and form companies. I
called for 'Covers' for the men to form. I was answered that
the men could not find their officers. I then ordered the men
to fall in and show a good spirit. The attempt was made but
without success and I ordered the retreat upon Port
Colborne, toward which place many had previously turned
their step."

At Port Colborne Colonel Booker requested that a regular officer be sent to take over his command. The defeat at Ridgeway
would haunt him for the rest of his life, even though he would be
officially exonerated of any blame. Canadians needed a scapegoat,
and Booker was the officer in charge.

O'Neill did not pursue the fleeing Canadian militia. He was
concerned Colonel Peacocke would soon arrive with his superior
force. He did not know that Peacocke, lacking an accurate map,
had taken the long route from Chippawa. Moreover, he'd had to
call a halt because his men, marching in the June heat in their
warm uniforms and loaded with equipment, were dropping from
exhaustion. Peacocke received word of Booker's defeat, along
with a vastly exaggerated account of the number of Fenians. He
decided it would be the better part of valour for him to await reinforcements, especially cavalry.

O'Neill and his Fenians, who probably numbered between four
and five hundred men after all the desertions, headed in the direction of old Fort Erie, the remnant of the War of 1812 stronghold.
O'Neill wanted to find out if more Fenians were going to cross the

river or Lake Erie. He knew that thousands of them had gathered in Buffalo. If necessary, he would hold old Fort Erie in a heroic, Alamo-like stand until they could join him. He was unaware of Colonel Stoughton Dennis and the militiamen on the *W.T. Robb*.

Colonel Dennis had spent the day cruising up and down the river, sending companies of men ashore to search for and capture Fenian stragglers. They had rounded up eighty-nine prisoners when Dennis learned that a large force of Fenians was approaching Fort Erie. He knew nothing of what had happened at Ridgeway, and decided to put his men ashore to fight. At the south end of the village of Fort Erie, his little company encountered the Fenians' advance guard, commanded by a Colonel Bailey. The Canadians opened fire, and at first drove the Fenians back. Colonel Bailey was mortally wounded. Then O'Neill's main body of men arrived, and the Canadians began to fall back. Colonel Dennis said it was every man for himself, and took refuge in a private home. He eventually slipped away and made it to Peacocke's headquarters. A militia captain named King made a stand at the wharf with a small band of men. They fought for about twenty minutes, but then had to surrender when they ran out of ammunition. King received a wound that would cost him a leg. Another group of thirty took cover in a house, and they, too, fought until they were out of bullets. They had no choice but to surrender. However, their stand allowed eighteen other men to make it to the river, where they were picked up by the *Robb*.

While an audience on the American shore watched, the *Robb* headed upstream through a fusillade of Fenian gunfire. Several bullets smashed into the pilot house, but nobody was hit. The *Robb* reached Port Colborne safely at about 6:30.

243

That night O'Neill and his officers held a council of war. He still wanted to fight. He insisted they would be reinforced from Buffalo. The rest of the men did not agree. They had no more food, and they had no guarantees they would receive help from the American side. They had defeated an army of militia, but they had no desire to tangle with British regulars. To O'Neill's disgust they elected to get out while the getting was good. That night, as the Fenians crossed to the New York side they were taken into custody by the U.S.S. *Michigan*.

The following day more redcoat troops poured into the Niagara Peninsula, but the Fenians were gone. Two local farmers who had picked up cast-off Fenian rifles were mistaken for the enemy and shot. One died from his wounds. In their two battles with the Fenians the Canadians had twelve men killed and forty wounded. The Fenians were believed to have lost eighteen dead and twenty-four wounded.

In the United States no Fenians were punished for the invasion. Many were given train tickets home. Fenian leaders hailed Ridgeway as a great victory and promised future glories in the fight for Ireland. But though there were minor raids in Quebec and the West, the attack on the Niagara Frontier would prove to be the last time a foreign army attempted to invade Canada.

The Battle of Cypress Hills

Thirteen Kit Carsons

T he Battle of Cypress Hills in what is now Alberta, like the better known 1890 Battle of Wounded Knee in South Dakota, was not really a battle at all. It was a massacre. It achieved the status of "battle" only in the minds of the white men who participated in it, and in the tall tales and newspaper stories that circulated in its aftermath. This brief but bloody confrontation between Natives and white plainsmen was a tragic, drunken brawl. It was also, as far as the Canadian government was concerned, the final straw in a long list of atrocities that plagued the country Canadians then called the Northwest Territories.

Compared to the fabled "Wild West" era of the United States, which lasted from the end of the Civil War until the turn of the twentieth century, Canada's Wild West period was quite short, lasting less than a decade. There were no wild and woolly cow towns like Dodge City, no lawless mining towns like Tombstone. The Canadian West didn't have gunslinging lawmen like Wyatt Earp and Wild Bill Hickok shooting it out with the likes of the Clanton gang and Billy the Kid. The main reason was that the

Canadian West had not yet been settled by hordes of homesteaders and town builders, as had the American West. The Canadian prairies were still sparsely populated by the Natives who had lived there for thousands of years, and the white traders who did business with them in scattered posts.

This was the country that had once been called Rupert's Land, the domain of the Hudson's Bay Company. The "Honourable Company of Adventurers" had a charter, signed by Prince Rupert, cousin of King Charles II, giving it exclusive trading rights over a vast territory stretching from the shores of Hudson Bay to the Rocky Mountains. Any Native hunter who wanted to trade his furs for guns and ammunition, steel knives, copper cooking pots, or rum, had to go to the Hudson's Bay post. For a while the Northwest Fur Trading Company of Montreal challenged the Hudson's Bay Company, but eventually it was absorbed by the London-based giant.

For many years the only law in Rupert's Land—aside from the tribal laws of the various Native peoples—was the Hudson's Bay Company. Company governors held, on paper, considerable legal powers which they had the right to enforce at gunpoint if necessary. They could have criminals flogged, shot or hanged. Many a lawbreaker was brought before a Hudson's Bay governor for punishment. Often it was not necessary for someone to go after the culprit. Sooner or later, everybody showed up at a Hudson's Bay post. The trading posts were the social, economic and administrative centres of the Northwest. Company employees—trappers, traders and clerks—made up most of the white population. Many of them took Native wives. Their children, along with the children of earlier French–Native marriages, became the Métis: the mixed-blood buffalo hunters of the prairies.

Much of the stock in a typical Hudson's Bay post was made especially for the "Indian trade": blankets; steel hatchets and knives; cooking utensils; luxury items like sugar, salt, tea and flour. The guns were single-shot muzzle loaders. Then there was rum.

For generations alcohol had been a staple of the fur trade. Native hunters and trappers exchanged their pelts for English rum, French brandy and American whiskey. Not everyone approved. In the days of New France the Catholic Church had managed to outlaw the liquor trade, but when the Natives began taking their furs to the hated English, the colonial government in Quebec reinstated it—but kept it under a certain degree of control. Even so, a scoundrel like Antoine Cadillac, founder of the city of Detroit, proved that a man with no principles could make a fortune debauching the Natives with limitless supplies of booze. On the other hand, David Thompson, one of the Northwest Company's greatest explorers and map-makers, smashed kegs of rum rather than trade the stuff to the Natives. Hudson's Bay Company traders knew that unrestricted trade in alcohol hurt business in the long run because it demoralized and corrupted Native fur producers. The rum they traded was diluted, and some governors wouldn't deal in any drink stronger than tea.

Trouble began in 1864 when independent American traders began to encroach on Hudson's Bay territory. Some were honest traders—even if they *were* trespassing—who dealt in the domestic goods and wares the Natives sought. But others peddled whiskey and guns. They quickly discovered that Rupert's Land was an unpoliced paradise for outlaws.

In the United States selling alcohol or firearms to Natives was illegal, and the United States army did its best to enforce the law.

North of the border the whiskey and gun peddlers could operate with impunity. Hudson's Bay Company clerks just weren't equipped to deal with them. Many of the traders were veterans of the Civil War: tough and trained in the use of weapons. They would take their wares right to the Native camps, saving the customers the trouble of travelling to a Hudson's Bay post. At first they operated out of the backs of wagons. But in time they learned that a band of liquored up warriors could be dangerous, so they began to build their own "whiskey forts" from which they could conduct business with a degree of security. The names of some of these posts testify to the characters of the men who operated them. One was called Fort Stand Off, for the whiskey smugglers who had "stood off" an American marshal who pursued them over the border. Fort Slideout got its name after the occupants "slid out" one night to escape a war party of angry Blood warriors who were determined to kill the white men who had been poisoning their people. In the case of Robbers' Roost, the name says it all.

The brew these unscrupulous men offered for sale hardly deserved the name "whiskey." It was a concoction made strictly for the Indian trade, and was soon known far and wide as "firewater." There were many recipes for it, all of them starting with a base of raw alcohol. Other ingredients could include gunpowder, molasses, tobacco juice, Jamaica ginger, hot peppers, painkillers, laudanum, red ink, and fusel oil (a poisonous mixture of alcohols, usually used as a solvent). The peddlers often heated the drinks up so the customer could experience the ultimate blast. It was this devil's brew, more than anything else, that was responsible for the saying, "Indians can't hold their liquor."

The Natives traded pemmican (a staple food on the prairies) and the furs of a variety of animals, but the whiskey peddlers were mostly interested in buffalo hides, which at that time were in great demand in the east. They made excellent winter coats and robes, but even more importantly, tough buffalo leather was prized by industry. The steam-driven industrial machinery of the time was not driven by gears, but by wheels and belts. Buffalo skin made the very best belts.

Most people with an interest in the history of the West are familiar with the stories of the white hunters who went out to the plains and prairies with high-powered rifles and decimated the mighty buffalo herds, taking only the hides (and sometimes the tongues, which were considered a delicacy in fancy restaurants) and leaving the meat to rot. Sadly the scenario is all too accurate. But with the coming of the whiskey traders, some Natives, too, were involved in the slaughter, killing the animals not for the means of survival, but for whiskey.

Of all the whiskey forts that sprang up in the Northwest, none was more notorious—or financially successful—than Fort Whoop-Up, built in 1869 at the junction of the St. Mary and Oldman rivers, near present-day Lethbridge, Alberta. Fort Whoop-Up was founded by an adventurer named Johnny Healy, with money advanced to him by his pal Al Hamilton, nephew of a wealthy entrepreneur in Fort Benton, Montana. Fort Benton was the main base for most of those nineteenth-century western bootleggers, and was a popular town with outlaws, vagabonds and riff-raff of every sort. It was nicknamed "The Chicago of the Plains" and "The Sagebrush Sodom." Legend has it that when Healy headed north out of Fort Benton with his first wagonload of whiskey, a local resident shouted to him, "Don't let the Indians whoop you up!" Hence, the name of the fort. The road north became known as the Whoop-Up Trail.

Irish-born Johnny Healy was one of those characters around whom legends grew. He had travelled West with the American army, searched for gold in Indian country, and prospected as far north as present-day Edmonton. He could handle a gun, and boasted that he was ready to "fight anything from a grizzly bear to a circular saw." Healy was courageous, flamboyant, resourceful, and utterly ruthless when it came to making money. And make money he did. In its first six months of operation Fort Whoop-Up turned an incredible profit of fifty thousand dollars!

The first structure Healy built on the site of Fort Whoop-Up was nothing but a collection of rude huts surrounded by a flimsy stockade. It was burned down, either by accident or by angry Natives. A small setback for Healy. He returned and put up a small fortress that would have impressed an army engineer. The walls were made of heavy, thick timbers, loop-holed for rifles. The windows and chimneys were fitted with iron bars. The roofs of the buildings were covered with earth as a defence against flaming arrows. Healy placed a cannon in one bastion, and a howitzer in the other. Among the men who worked for Healy at one time or another were characters with names like Spring Heel Jack, Slippery Dick, Waxy Weatherwax, Toe String Joe, and Blood Chief Joe Healy, Johnny Healy's adopted Indian son.

With the exception of women whose sexual services were sometimes traded by intoxicated husbands and fathers who had run out of other means to buy whiskey, Natives were not allowed inside the fort. Business was done through three wickets near the gates. The Natives would push their buffalo hides and other trade items through the opening, and the whites inside would hand out firewater. Healy had his own brand called Whoop-Up Wallop. He bragged that it was so potent, an Indian who drank it could be shot through the heart, and wouldn't die until he sobered up.

A Native on a drinking binge might trade away everything he owned: furs, weapons, horses. If he ran out of things to trade for whiskey, he was cut off. Sometimes enraged, inebriated Natives who had been refused more whiskey tried to climb the walls of the fort. Gunmen patrolling the ramparts used long poles to push them off. If a Native was too persistent, he was liable to be shot.

As the Natives drank themselves senseless, violence usually erupted in the camps around the fort. At such times the whites did not dare venture outside, but stayed within the safety of their stockade. It was not uncommon for the guards on the walls to look out in the morning after a wild spree and see the ground littered with Native men—most dead drunk, but some dead.

Not all Natives who went to Fort Whoop-Up were looking for whiskey. Some went there to buy guns. Unlike the Hudson's Bay posts that traded only single-shot muzzle loaders, Johnny Healy dealt in repeating rifles. In the early years following the Civil War a lot of those weapons were available through army surplus and Healy knew that a Peigan, Blood or Blackfoot warrior would part with a lot of buffalo hides to get one.

Of course, there were some whites who took a dim view of traders like Healy who sold repeating rifles and ammunition to Natives. On the American plains, nations like the Sioux and Cheyenne were becoming increasingly resentful of American expansion into their lands, and rifles sold to Natives north of the border did not necessarily stay there. Moreover, even in the Canadian West certain parties did not like the idea of repeating rifles in Native hands. One such group was the wolfers.

Wolfers made their money collecting and selling wolf pelts, but they hardly deserved the name hunters. They had a relatively easy method of getting the pelts. They would shoot a buffalo, lace the carcass with strychnine, and then return to skin the bodies of the wolves that had been attracted to the bait. The poisoned buffalo carcasses also killed the Natives' camp dogs, which were valued as pack animals and as the night sentinels of almost every Native camp. The Natives hated the wolfers and killed them on sight. The wolfers, in turn, hated the white men who sold the warriors repeating rifles. In 1872 a band of wolfers calling themselves the Spitzee Cavalry, because their headquarters was an old whiskey post called Fort Spitzee, rode out to intimidate the traders into shutting down their gun business. They were led by a man named John Evans. At several of the whiskey posts the wolfers easily forced the proprietors to sign a pledge agreeing to stop selling guns to the Indians. Then they went after the biggest gunrunner of the lot, Johnny Healy.

But Johnny Healy did not scare easily. He invited the heavily armed wolfers to join him for supper, and after the meal he asked what their business was. They told him they intended to put an end to the gun trade and demanded that he sign the pledge. Healy refused, and called them a pack of mad dogs. As the wolfers hurled threats at him, Healy told them his men had a cannon aimed at the door, with orders to fire if they didn't listen to reason. He then sat down and explained to them that they were all in the same business, working for financial interests in Fort Benton, and that they had better co-operate and make as much money as possible.

That, at least, was one story. In another version Healy confronted the angry wolfers with an open keg of gunpowder and a lit cigar. He roared that if they didn't clear out, he'd blow himself, the fort and the Spitzee Cavalry straight to hell. Whatever actually happened, Healy subdued the wolfers. The Spitzee Cavalry rode no more, and the rifle trade continued.

Guns and liquor weren't the only causes of tragedy and trouble. Smallpox epidemics swept across the prairies, carrying off thousands and further weakening and demoralizing the tribes, making them all the more susceptible to the evils of predatory whites. A rumour spread that whiskey traders were selling the Natives disease-infected blankets. Sick warriors were said to have made suicidal attacks on whiskey posts, preferring a quick death in battle to the slow agony of the disease. And still the rotgut whiskey poured in from Fort Benton. A Methodist minister named John McDougall wrote:

"Many Indians were killed, and also quite a few white men. Within a few miles of us, 42 able bodied men were victims...all slain in drunken rows. Some terrible scenes occurred when whole camps went on the spree, as was frequently the case, shooting, stabbing, killing, freezing, dying. Mothers lost their children. These were either frozen to death, or devoured by the myriad dogs of the camp. The birth rate decreased, and the poor red man was in a fair way toward extinction, just because some white men, coming out of Christian countries, and themselves the evolution of Christian civilization, were now ruled by lust and greed."

Captain William Francis Butler, a British soldier who travelled through the country, wrote in his report, "The region is without law, order, or security of property; robbery and murder have for years gone unchecked; and all civil and legal institutions are unknown."

The Hudson's Bay Company could not compete with the unscrupulous, illegal business practices of the American whiskey men, and could no longer keep order in its vast domain. There was concern that the United States would send its cavalry north to root out the whiskey posts, and by its mere presence annex the country. In 1869, the Honourable Company sold Rupert's Land to the fledgling Dominion of Canada. The company advised Prime Minister John A. Macdonald to send a military force west to clean out the whiskey posts and establish law and order. Macdonald said he would do it. But Macdonald was a notorious procrastinator who had earned himself the nickname Old Tomorrow. It was not until 1873 that Macdonald finally took steps to do something about the deplorable situation in the West, and even then it took a tragedy to galvanize him into action.

Late in April 1873, a band of wolfers made camp on the banks of the Teton River near Fort Benton. They were returning from Canada with their season's haul of wolf pelts. The boss of this gang was Tom Hardwick, a ruffian known as the Green River Renegade. With him were John Evans (of Spitzee Cavalry notoriety), Trevanian Hale, Ed Grace, John Duval, Charlie Smith, Jeff Devereaux, Jim Hughes and Charlie Harper. These men were all Americans with the exception of Ed Grace, who was Canadian. That night Natives stole their horses, and the men had to walk the remaining few miles to Fort Benton. White frontiersmen never shared the Native perception of horse stealing being a sort of honourable sport. By the time the angry men reached Fort Benton their anger had turned to fury. They took their complaint to the army, where they received sympathy but no help. The thieves, they were told, had no doubt crossed the line into Canada, where the U.S. Cavalry could not go.

International boundaries meant nothing to the wolfers, so they acquired new horses and went after the rustlers themselves. They followed the trail north into the Cypress Hills on the Canadian side of the border, but then lost it. They were near a small whiskey post on Battle Creek, run by Abe Farwell, a man they all knew. The wolfers rode over to Fort Farwell to ask if anyone had seen their missing horses, and to indulge in some liquid refreshment.

Camped near the trading post was a band of Assiniboines led by Chief Little Soldier. Hardwick asked Farwell if he thought the Assiniboines might be the horse thieves they'd been tracking. Farwell said no. He told Hardwick the Assiniboines had only a few horses. Moreover, they had come down from further north where they'd spent the winter, and couldn't possibly have been stealing horses near Fort Benton. The wolfers decided to spend the night at the whiskey post.

The disgruntled wolfers had ridden into the Cypress Hills at a bad time, as trouble had been brewing there. Near Farwell's post was another whiskey fort run by a man named Moses Solomon. Farwell got along well with the Natives, but Solomon did not. The Natives resented Solomon's high-handed manner with them and believed he cheated them. A rumour had it that they planned to kill Solomon and burn down his post. Local Métis warned Farwell to keep out of the way when the shooting started. Every man in the area—white, Native and Métis—went around armed and ready for trouble.

That evening, while the wolfers and some other white men were drinking at Farwell's, Indian raiders slipped into his corral and made off with thirty horses. Farwell was stunned, because he had thought himself to be in good standing with all of the Natives. One of the stolen horses belonged to a Canadian named George Hammond, a man described as "an unsavoury loafer." A Native soon returned with Hammond's horse, demanding a jug of whiskey as a reward for "finding" the animal. Hammond reluctantly handed over the firewater.

A lot of whiskey was consumed that night, both in the white fort and the Indian camp. The following morning, June 1, the wolfers and their friends were enjoying a breakfast of whiskey, when George Hammond learned that his horse had been stolen *again*! All of the whites in the trading post were furious. Hammond swore that he would get his horse back, and take an Indian horse as well. He grabbed his gun and stormed off in the direction of Little Soldier's camp.

Farwell later claimed that he tried to stop Hammond. He argued that in all likelihood the horse thieves had not been the Assiniboines, but some Crees who were camped a few miles away. While Hammond fumed, Farwell dashed off to the Assiniboine camp to talk to Little Soldier. The Assiniboine chief was in the grip of a hangover, and impatiently told the trader that Hammond's horse had probably wandered off and was grazing on a hillside somewhere.

While Farwell was talking to Little Soldier, Hammond and the wolfers had come swaggering up to the edge of the Assiniboine camp. They were quickly joined by Moses Solomon and two other men from his post. All were armed, the wolfers with high-powered repeating Henry rifles. Some of the young Assiniboine men, edgy with hangovers or already emboldened by a few morning drinks, became angry at this intrusion. They began to taunt the white men. Farwell sensed an explosion coming, and tried to defuse the situation. He urged both parties to calm down, and called on Little Soldier to restrain his men. Frightened Native women hurried out of the camp with their children.

Little Soldier had awakened that morning in an alcoholic fog, but now he seemed to understand the danger of the moment. His camp consisted of some forty lodges, so his warriors outnumbered the whites. But those of his men who had guns were armed with the single-shot trade guns of the Hudson's Bay Company. The rest had bows and arrows. Little Soldier told his young men to stop goading the whites. Then he offered to give Hammond two of his own horses as a guarantee against the return of Hammond's missing horse.

Little Soldier's peace offering should have mollified the whites. But whiskey, injured pride, and long-simmering tension over the Solomon trouble had driven matters beyond the point of reason. Hammond and the wolfers, seeing they were outnumbered, began to back off toward a coulee that ran between Fort Farwell and the Assiniboine camp. The young warriors pressed forward, throwing off their blankets and robes as though preparing for a fight. Within moments Farwell was in the middle of a no-man's-land. The whites were in the coulee, crouched with guns at their shoulders. The Assiniboines were scrambling for cover, and demanding to know why the white men were behaving in such a way if they had not come looking for a fight. The wolfers shouted to him to get out of the way. Farwell repeated Little Soldier's offer of two horses for Hammond's missing horse. The wolfers rejected it. They said it was a trick.

Desperate to keep the two drunken sides from killing each other, Farwell said he would fetch his interpreter, Alex Lebompard, to confirm Little Soldier's offer. Once again the opportunity to avoid violence and bloodshed was lost. Farwell had taken but a few steps toward the trading post when Hammond fired. A split second later the rest of the whites in the coulee opened fire on the Assiniboines, and all became chaos.

The long-range, fast-shooting Henry rifles in the wolfers' hands had been made to kill buffalo. Their heavy slugs tore through men who had not found cover as though they were paper. Within moments, the ground was littered with Assiniboine bodies. The Natives fell back, then rallied and attacked with their muzzle loaders. That charge, and a second, were driven back by the heavy fire of the wolfers' powerful guns. Each time, warriors fell to Henry bullets, and so far not a single white man had been hit.

The surviving warriors retreated to a gully that afforded them some cover from the rifle bullets. From there they were able to keep up a steady fire that had the white men pinned down. Tom Hardwick and John Evans had an idea for placing the Assiniboines in a crossfire. They crept back to where they had left their horses, and galloped to the top of a hill that overlooked the Assiniboines' gully. They began to shoot down at the Natives, but the ploy backfired on them. Forced out of the protection of the gully, the Assiniboines dashed through the brush at the bottom of the hill, obviously trying to encircle it and surround the wolfers at the top.

The other whites saw what was happening. They grabbed their horses and charged to the rescue, firing from the saddle as they plunged through the brush. The Natives fell back to the gully, but one of them first took aim at Ed Grace and blew him out of the saddle. Shot through the heart, Grace was dead before he hit the ground. The rest of the whites made a dash for Fort Farwell. For several hours the two sides blasted away at each other. The whites were safe behind the walls of the whiskey post, and they had the superior weapons. The Assiniboines could not go into their lodges, which were directly under the white men's guns. At sunset they slipped away, leaving behind their possessions and over thirty dead.

As soon as the whites realized the Assiniboines had gone, they dashed into the camp looking for plunder. In one lodge they found Little Soldier, either wounded or drunk. They murdered him, decapitated the body, and mounted the head on a pole. According to one report they also found several women and children whom they abused and then murdered. The whites then went back to the post to celebrate their victory with a grand drunk.

The following day the wolfers burned the Indians' lodges and all of the possessions not worth stealing. Moses Solomon decided he'd had enough of the whiskey trade business, so the men emptied his post of its stock, buried Ed Grace under the floor, and burned the post to the ground. Then they mounted up and rode off, still looking for their stolen horses. Meanwhile, word of the one-sided "battle" was racing across the prairie like a grassfire.

Not long after the massacre the wolfers rode into Fort Whoop-Up. There they learned that a band of Bloods was camped nearby. Now considering themselves an invincible force that struck terror into Native hearts, the wolfers barged into the village and demanded to see the chief, so they could question him about their horses. The warriors in the camp caressed their weapons glared at the white men with unconcealed hostility. These Bloods were well-armed, and not drunk or hung over. The white men realized they had placed themselves in a precarious situation. The chief had but to give the word, and they would all be dead. To their relief, the chief simply said he knew nothing about their horses. The wolfers did not attempt to question him, and were glad to get out of the camp unmolested.

The wolfers now gave up the hunt for the missing horses and returned to Fort Benton. There they were hailed as heroes who had taught the bloodthirsty savages a lesson. One Fort Benton newspaper called them "Thirteen Kit Carsons," in reference to the famous mountain man. Everywhere men slapped them on the backs and bought them drinks. Not everybody, however, shared this view. Other people on both sides of the border were appalled.

In Abe Farwell's version of the story, he had tried to act as an intermediary. The wolfers, he said, fired first. But he was not the only witness. A Métis named Joseph Turcott claimed to have seen the whole affair. He told *Winnipeg Free Press* that Hammond did not shoot first. The Assiniboines started shooting their guns in the air, and then the whites, thinking they were being fired upon, shot at the Indians. One of the wolfers told a reporter for the Fort Benton *Record*:

> "We went to the camp for the purpose of assisting a neigh-
> bour in the peaceable recovery of a horse. We had no other
> object in going there, our own property was not in the camp
> and we could have no motive in commencing the fight.
> Four or five shots were fired at us before we pulled a trig-
> ger, and then the odds were so much against us that we
> acted only on the defensive, until one of our party was
> killed, when through sheer desperation we changed from
> the defensive to the attack and routed the whole five or six
> hundred warriors, killing some 30 or 40."

The fact that the narrator greatly exaggerated the number of warriors present makes the validity of the rest of his story rather suspect. But many people had reservations about Abe Farwell's version, too. For one thing, Farwell was suspected of dealing in stolen goods, including horses, and may have known more about the wolfers' missing mounts than he let on.

While the wolfers were doing the rounds of the Fort Benton saloons and bragging about their victory, news of the so-called battle was slowly making its way east. The United States Department of the Interior investigated the event and passed its findings on to the Secretary of State. That official handed the information over to the British consul in Washington, who in turn sent a brief to Ottawa. Prime Minister Macdonald gave Dominion Police Commissioner Gilbert McMicken the assignment of investigating the incident. Owing to the lateness of the season, McMicken could not leave for the West until the following spring.

Canadians were outraged that American desperadoes could violate their sovereignty, commit every sort of crime from bootlegging to mass murder, and get away with it. The public demanded that the wolfers be brought to justice. There was even concern that American settlers would simply move north, and claim the Northwest Territory as their own, as they had done with lands once owned by Mexico. Alexander Morris, the Lieutenant Governor of Manitoba and the Northwest Territories had been pleading with Macdonald since 1869 to send a police force west to bring about law and order. Macdonald procrastinated. Now, because of the Cypress Hills Massacre, the entire Native population of the West was restless, and the small white population feared a bloody retaliation. Morris wired Macdonald from Winnipeg, "What have you done as to Police Force. Their absence may lead to grave disaster." Within days recruiting began for the North West Mounted Police, and the first officers were appointed by order-in-council.

In 1874 the Mounties made their epic journey west. Rather than try to shoot it out with the red-coated policemen, most of the whiskey traders scooted back to their side of the border. When the Mounties arrived at Fort Whoop-Up, they fully expected to have a fight on their hands. They found the place abandoned by all but a single caretaker who invited them to a supper of buffalo steaks. Johnny Healy hadn't left behind a drop of Whoop-Up Wallop.

Now, instead of sending McMicken west, Macdonald turned the case over to the NWMP. In May of 1874 Lieutenant Colonel A.G. Irvine traveled to Fort Benton and interviewed Alex Lebompard and others. In a week he had enough evidence for the British government (which still dictated Canadian foreign policy) to make a request to Washington for the extradition of all thirteen wolfers, as well as George Hammond and Moses Solomon. Washington agreed to the request, and instructed law enforcement officers in Montana to arrest the men.

Residents of the American West who admired the Thirteen Kit Carsons were stunned. Arrest men and put them on trial for killing *Indians*? These were people who believed in the popular saying, "The only good Indian is a dead one." They rallied to the defense of their heroes, and protested the government's decision to hand them over to the tyrannical British. Johnny Healy, who by now ran a Fort Benton newspaper, called the wolfers true pioneers who had helped open the West to civilization. The Mounted Police, he wrote, were heralds of British tyranny and "grabbers of the spoil." John Donnelly, the one-time Fenian invader of Canada, ranted that the wolfers were being sacrificed to the British ogre, and would never get a fair trial in Canada. Tensions in Fort Benton were so high, the American government had to send in the army to keep order, and the extradition hearings were moved to Helena.

At those hearings Abe Farwell's testimony was generally discredited. One of the lawyers for the wolfers said in an outburst, "If your honour pleases, you are certainly not going to turn over to the tender mercies of the Canadian government these brave and hardy citizens of Montana upon the evidence of Abe Farwell, an informer who will hereafter be known as a man to whom the woods will deny shelter, the earth a grave and Heaven a God." The court decided that the evidence presented by the Canadian government was insufficient, and the defendants were released.

Jubilant crowds carried the wolfers through the streets in a torchlight parade, complete with brass band. Cannons were fired in salute, and the men were treated to rounds of whiskey in every saloon. John Evans would soon open a bar of his own and call it the Extradition Saloon. Abe Farwell received numerous death threats. He fled to Canada, and became a mail rider for the Mounted Police.

Sometime later former wolfer Jim Hughes and two men named Bell and Vogle, who were involved in the whiskey trade with Moses Solomon and were present at the massacre, were arrested on Canadian soil. They were tried in Winnipeg in 1876. They had the support of the American consul, and the United States government expressed concern for them. Their lawyer wanted the Thirteen Kit Carsons brought in as witnesses, but the Canadian government would not guarantee those men immunity from arrest. In the end, witnesses for the Crown changed their stories and testified for the defence. The three men were released. No one ever paid any penalty for the Cypress Hills Massacre.

Before Batoche

There have been three major, enigmatic "rebel" leaders in Canadian History: Louis-Joseph Papineau in Quebec, William Lyon Mackenzie in Ontario, and Louis Riel, who was born in 1844 in what is now Manitoba. Of the three Riel, arguably, was and remains the most controversial. Like Papineau and Mackenzie, Riel stood up against what he believed were injustices. Like the others he first tried to solve problems diplomatically, and when that failed, he turned to armed revolt. For their violent actions—or support of violent actions—all three men were admired as heroes by some, denounced as villains by others. All three were charged with treason, which to many people in nineteenth century society was a crime even more foul than murder, and rightly punishable by death. But even though followers of Papineau and Mackenzie died on the gallows, of the three leaders only Riel paid the supreme penalty. In death the persona of Riel was wrapped in a glowing cloak of martyrdom that not even Papineau or Mackenzie could achieve, and which many people still feel he does not deserve. Would Riel be so revered in French Canada, they ask, if his name had been Lount or Matthews, and his first language was English? To understand what happened at the Battle of Batoche, and why it happened, one must have at least some understanding of who Louis Riel was, and what took him to that final dramatic confrontation with his foes on the Canadian prairie.

Louis Riel's claim to being Métis was slim. He was one-eighth Native. He was born in St. Boniface, now part of Winnipeg, in 1844, in what was then the domain of the Hudson's Bay Company, Rupert's Land. At the age of thirteen he was sent to school in Montreal. He was a star student who at one time considered going into the priesthood, but then turned instead to law. Even as a youth, though he was bright and charismatic, he could also be moody and quarrelsome. He did not accept criticism well, and he hated contradiction. After spending a few years in the United States, Riel returned to St. Boniface in 1868.

Riel soon found himself in the midst of controversy. In 1869 the Hudson's Bay Company sold Rupert's land to the fledgling Dominion of Canada. A new community, the village of Winnipeg, had already been established in the Red River Valley, not far from St. Boniface. It had a population of about 1,500 settlers, most of them from Ontario and many of them Orange Protestant. The British government had delayed in officially transferring sovereignty, but an impatient Canadian government sent surveyors out anyway. The charts and guidelines the Canadian surveyors used did not coincide with already established Métis property lines. The Métis, who had not been consulted in the sale of the land they lived on, were afraid that their land rights and their way of life were in danger.

On October 11 a relative of Louis Riel found surveyors on his land. He did not speak English, so he sent for Louis, who was bilingual. Riel arrived with a party of eighteen Métis hunters. Riel put his foot on the surveying chain and said, "You go no farther!" He said the Canadian government had no right to make surveys on the land without the permission of the people. The surveyors withdrew and lodged a complaint. Riel went a step further and prevented the newly appointed governor, William McDougall, from entering the Territory. A furious McDougall, instead of going on to the old Hudson's Bay post at Fort Garry, had to content himself with taking up quarters in Fort Dufferin, an abandoned Hudson's Bay post just north of the United States border. Riel and 120 Métis took over Fort Garry.

Riel and most of the Métis were French-speaking Catholics. From Fort Garry he sent an invitation to the English-speaking Protestant Métis, and the English-speaking white settlers in Winnipeg to send delegates to attend the first Convention of the People of Rupert's Land. At that convention, and in other meetings that followed, Riel laid out the simple and reasonable conditions his people wanted met. If their country were to become part of Canada, they wanted certain things guaranteed by Ottawa and confirmed by London. In an eighteen-point List of Rights, Riel demanded a voice in government for the Métis, respect for their language and religious rights, and prior consultation before anything was done with their land.

The English-speaking Métis were hesitant. They agreed with the List of Rights, but they were afraid Riel had gone too far in barring the governor's entry and seizing Fort Garry. Riel angrily berated them as cowards.

Governor McDougall had sent a flurry of messages to Ottawa, demanding that something be done. Prime Minister John A. Macdonald advised waiting and letting things cool off. But

MacDougall was hotheaded and impatient. He decided to raise a militia force to kick Riel out of Fort Garry. One of those who answered the call was Dr. John Schultz, owner of a store in Winnipeg. He was leader of a group who called themselves Canada Firsters. They were contemptuous of the Métis and totally opposed to Riel. The idea of sharing political rights or anything else with "half-breeds" was completely unacceptable to them.

Schultz brought about seventy men with him, but McDougall knew he would need more than that to fight the French-speaking Métis. He sent his aide, Colonel John Stoughton Dennis, to recruit the English-speaking Métis. But those people refused to make war on "those who have been born and brought up among us, ate with us, slept with us, hunted with us, traded with us and are our own flesh and blood."

Dennis's failure to bring over the English-speaking Métis sank McDougall's plan to take Fort Garry by force. Schultz, however, was determined to fly in the face of common sense. He and forty-five men fortified his Winnipeg store, which was well-stocked with provisions. Métis who approached it saw guns pointed at them through the windows.

Just what Schultz planned to do from his personal fort is not known, but Riel considered it a threat. On December 7, Riel and two hundred Métis riders surrounded the store, aimed a pair of cannon at the doors, and gave Schultz and his men fifteen minutes to surrender. Schultz and his men came out, and were taken to Fort Garry as prisoners. The next day Riel declared that he and the *Comité National des Métis* had formed a provisional government. That government, he said, was the only legal authority in Rupert's Land until such time as an agreement was reached with Canada that would be favourable to the people.

John A. Macdonald was livid over the goings on in Red River, but he knew better than to act rashly. He sent Donald Smith, chief officer of the Hudson's Bay Company in Canada, to talk to Riel. Smith had long conversations with Riel, and extended Macdonald's invitation for the Métis to send at least two residents (not delegates of the provisional government) to go to Ottawa and state the case for the Métis. The Métis did so, and returned with Ottawa's promises that all the government wanted was a peaceful annexation, and that the wishes of the Métis would be met. Of course, the government would have to send troops to the new territory to establish sovereignty and law and order, and to help with the building of roads.

That satisfied Riel, especially since it was acceptable to both English- and French-speaking Métis. The Métis held another convention on February 10, 1870, and elected twenty-five-year-old Louis Riel president of their provisional government. As an act of good faith, Riel released the Canadian prisoners he'd taken at Schultz's store. However, several of the prisoners had already escaped, including John Schultz and Thomas Scott. Schultz made his way back to Ontario. Thomas Scott went to Portage La Prairie where he put together another gang of Canada Firsters who were determined to defy Riel.

Born in Northern Ireland about 1842, Thomas Scott arrived in Canada West (Ontario) about 1863. In 1869 he went west to work as a labourer. He was an Orangeman who was outspoken in his hatred of Catholics, the French and the Métis. He quickly gained a reputation as a brawler and a bully. He was arrested on at least one occasion for assault, and fined.

On February 17 Scott and his roughnecks were intercepted on their way to Fort Garry, and taken prisoner. They were jailed in the

Fort Garry guardhouse. There, Scott was a difficult prisoner. He allegedly attacked his guards, and loudly vented his hatred for Riel and all of his people. Riel went to speak to him personally. What was said between the two men is not known, but Riel had Scott tried for insubordination. He was found guilty, and shot by a Métis firing squad. To justify his action, Riel said, "We must make Canada respect us."

Protestant Ontario was outraged. John Schultz toured the province, calling on Orangemen and other Protestants to avenge Scott. When a military force of 1,200 men under Colonel Garnet Wolseley left Toronto on May 21, bound for the West, it included eight hundred volunteers, each of them anxious to be the man who killed Louis Riel.

The United States would not allow a foreign military force to pass through its territory, so the Canadian troops had to take a ship across Lake Superior, and then spend ninety-one brutal days crossing the rough country to Fort Garry. Ottawa had assured Riel that the soldiers' purposes were peaceful, but as the army approached Fort Garry, a white Canadian friend warned him to get away if he didn't want to be charged with murder. As the soldiers marched through the front gates, Riel slipped out the back. Wolseley wrote to Ottawa, "I was glad that Riel did not come out and surrender, for I could not then have hanged him."

A few days later when a friend gave the fugitive some food, Riel said, "Tell the people that he who ruled in Fort Garry only yesterday is now a homeless wanderer with nothing to eat but two dried fish."

Riel had got what he wanted for the new province of Manitoba, so in that sense his "Red River Rebellion" was a success. But the execution of Thomas Scott was a colossal blunder. It made a fugitive of Riel at a time when the people of Manitoba could have used a man of his talents in Ottawa, and it earned him the undying hatred of Protestant Ontario. Riel won elections to Parliament in 1873 and 1874, but could not take his seat. After the 1874 election he went to Ottawa, signed the register of members and took the oath of allegiance, but then fled before he could be arrested. In 1875 he was granted amnesty on the condition that he stay out of Canada for five years. When Riel returned to Canada, it would be to lead another rebellion, and this one would not be quite as bloodless.

The Battle of Batoche

Last Stand of Louis Riel

O n June 4, 1884, four Métis horsemen rode into St. Peter's Mission in Judith Basin, Montana. Their leader was Gabriel Dumont, a stocky, powerfully built man of forty-seven who was known among his people as "The Prince of the Prairies." Dumont was a superb rider, a crack shot, and for many years had been the chief of the buffalo hunt, the harvest of meat and hides that was the mainstay of the Métis economy. Dumont was known to fill the Red River carts of all those people who could not hunt for themselves before he put meat into his own carts. Sam Steele, the pride of the North West Mounted Police said of him, "One might travel the plains from one end to the other and never hear an unkind word said of Dumont...When in trouble the cry of all was for Gabriel." Dumont was a man you wanted as a friend if you were in trouble. And he was no stranger to fighting. While still in his early teens in 1851, he was with a small band of Métis who were attacked by a large party of Yankton Sioux in the Missouri River country. The Métis dug rifle pits and drove off the Sioux. The Indians suffered many losses, while the Métis had but one

271

man killed. Dumont would remember the Battle of Grand Couteau years later, in the face of a different foe.

The enemy Dumont and the Métis had been struggling with since the Red River Colony became the province of Manitoba was not Native warriors, but the Canadian government. In almost a decade and a half since 1870, white settlers had swarmed into Manitoba, overrunning the land that had been the hunting grounds of the Natives and the Métis. The government had promised the Indians food, but had not lived up to those promises, and the Natives were starving. The Métis were just as badly off, if not worse. Because they were not full-blooded Natives, they were not entitled to the annuities—however small—the Indians received. They had to register the land holdings that had been theirs for generations as though they were new settlers, and then wait three years before being granted deeds. The government was slow to send out surveyors to chart plots of land, and when the surveyors did arrive, they insisted on charting square plots instead of the long, narrow ones with river fronting that the Métis were accustomed to. And there were always slick speculators ready to cheat unschooled Métis farmers.

To make matters worse, the buffalo were rapidly disappearing. Overhunting by Native, Métis and white hunters had driven the once mighty herds almost to extinction. Many Métis had left Manitoba and moved to the north and south branches of the Saskatchewan River where there were still enough buffalo for a season or two of hunting, but soon they, too, would be gone. The Métis needed the federal government to recognize their problems and take action. But the Canadian government was too busy with the construction of the new transcontinental railroad to pay much attention to the needs of a few thousand Métis. Moreover, Sir John

A. Macdonald had said back in 1870 that he expected the Métis to be "swamped by the influx of settlers."

The Métis were indeed being swamped. Gabriel Dumont was a leader of his people, but he was no diplomat and he spoke no English. So he and his companions had ridden 1,095 kilometres (680 miles) to speak to the one man they believed could help them: Louis Riel!

Riel had never met Dumont, but he had kept in touch with people in the Métis community and he knew Gabriel by reputation. He was also aware of the difficulties his people had been experiencing. Since leaving Canada Riel had become an American citizen. He had married and had two children, and was teaching at a mission school. Riel was a dedicated teacher, but the responsibilities of parenthood and teaching were suffocating him. He was certain God had some greater purpose for him.

Riel had, in fact, spent some time in an asylum. He suffered from fits of depression and was sometimes delusional. He had always been a devout Catholic, but now he believed God spoke directly to him and sent him visions. When Dumont explained why he and his companions were there, Riel said he needed a day to think about it. The following day he agreed to return to Canada with them. God had finally revealed Riel's great mission to him. Louis Riel was to be the messiah of the Métis people! He packed up his wife, children, and few belongings and set off with Dumont on the trail to the Saskatchewan River. Along the way, he claimed to have had a vision of a gallows, with himself hanging from it.

By the end of June the little party reached the village of Batoche on the South Saskatchewan River. This was the capital of the Métis community. During the journey, God had revealed more of his grand plan to Riel. If the Canadian government refused to recognize the land rights of the people of the prairies, and would not live up to its promises, then Riel was to lead the people in rebellion, and create a new republic of Indians and Métis.

Riel, now 39, spent the summer and autumn of 1884 travelling through the Saskatchewan River Valley talking to the people and listening to their grievances. More than anything they were afraid of losing their land, because the government had not sent out surveyors and had not even opened a land registry office. Technically they were "squatters" on their own property. That meant the first white man who came along with a formal deed to the land could take it. That had happened in Manitoba.

Riel wrote a petition outlining the needs of Métis, Indians and whites, and sent it to Ottawa in December. The secretary of state acknowledged receipt of the petition, but did nothing else. John A. Macdonald denied ever having seen it. Macdonald's only action was to send extra North West Mounted Police constables west.

As the early weeks of 1885 passed with no indication that Ottawa would do a thing, Riel became increasingly agitated. Finally on March 5 he, Dumont and other Métis leader swore an oath to "Save our souls by making ourselves live in righteousness night and day [and] to save our country from wicked government by taking up arms whenever it shall be necessary." Riel made Dumont commander of a cavalry force of about four hundred Métis riders. On March 18 Riel rode into Batoche with a group of armed men. They occupied the Catholic church, and Riel proclaimed a provisional government.

English-speaking settlers who had welcomed Riel as a man who might get things done with the indifferent government in Ottawa, now withdrew their support, fearful that he would lead them into open rebellion. The local clergy, worried that Riel would undermine their authority, denounced him as a fanatic. But Riel was certain that Native leaders who had reached the end of their patience with Ottawa would join his cause.

The Métis cut the telegraph wire at Batoche. Then they went into a government store and carried off everything, including guns and ammunition. They did the same thing at a privately owned store. Riel told the proprietor, "Give my men what they want and charge it." The Indian agent and several other people were made prisoners.

Riel then called a public meeting in the church, much to the anger of the priest. When the clergyman tried to stop Riel from entering the building, Riel said to his men, "Rome has fallen. Take him away."

Inside the church, Dumont spoke first. "The police are coming to take Riel. What are you going to do? Here is a man who has done so much for us. Are we going to let him slide through our hands? Let us make a plan."

Then Riel spoke. "We send petitions, they send police to take us—Gabriel and me. But I know very well how this works. It is I who have done wrong. The government hates me because I have already made them give in once. This time they will give up nothing. I also think it would be better for me to go now. I must leave you and I feel I should go now. Once I am gone you may be able to get what you want more easily. Yes—I really think that it would be better if I went back to Montana."

At that, the whole crowd interrupted and told Riel they wouldn't let him go. They said he couldn't quit. Then Dumont asked the crowd, "All in favour of taking up arms, raise your hands."

The people leapt from their seats and cried, "If we are to die for our country, we will die together."

The Métis' first objective was Fort Carlton on the south bank of the North Saskatchewan River. It was a Hudson's Bay Company post that was in temporary use as a NWMP fort. Riel and Dumont wanted to make it their own fortified base. Some of the Métis leaders were in favour of attacking the post in force and killing any Mounties who didn't surrender. Riel wanted to avoid bloodshed if at all possible. He sent a message to the senior officer, Superintendent Leif Crozier. Riel offered the Mounties safe conduct out of the territory if they would surrender and lay down their arms. Otherwise he would "commence without delay a war of extermination upon all those who have shown themselves hostile to our rights."

Crozier, of course, ignored the demand. He had fifty-six Mounties in the fort, plus a number of civilian volunteers. He was expecting to be reinforced by another hundred constables. Riel did not try to attack Fort Carlton. Both men played a waiting game.

Supplies in the fort were running low, so on March 26 Crozier sent fifteen Mounties and seven volunteers with a dozen sleighs to a post at Duck Lake, between Batoche and Fort Carlton, to load up with provisions. Before they reached Duck Lake, the police sleighs were intercepted by Gabriel Dumont and a company of his Métis cavalry. Riel had told Dumont not to shoot unless the Mounties shot first. There was some shouting between the Mounties and the Métis, but the Mounties withdrew without any gunfire.

Superintendent Crozier was now in a dilemma. He knew he should wait until reinforcements arrived, but he was afraid the NWMP would loose face with the Métis and the Indians if he did not respond immediately to this insult to the force. The civilian volunteers were goading him, telling him he was a coward if he didn't lead his men out against "a parcel of half-breeds." Against his better judgment, Crozier told the entire company to fall in. He set out for Duck Lake with fifty-six Mounties, forty-three volunteers and a seven-pounder cannon. Some were mounted; others rode in sleighs. Crozier thought he could outmanoeuvre the Métis by taking a trail through the reserve of the Cree Chief Beardy.

When the police stopped at Beardy's house, the chief told Crozier they were trespassing on his reserve, and that he had nothing to do with the Riel trouble. He offered the services of an elderly, almost blind man named Assiyiwin as a mediator. Even as Chief Beardy was talking to Crozier, the Métis were moving in.

Dumont had about two dozen men with him when he turned back the Mountie supply detail. When his scouts told him the police had marched out of Fort Carlton in force, he sent word for every available Métis to join him. Then Dumont led his men to the Cree reserve. He told his brother Isidore, who rode with him that day, "I don't want to start killing them, I want to take prisoners. But if they try to kill us, then we will kill them."

Dumont knew the Mounties were better armed than his men, and had professional training and discipline. But he had the advantage of knowing the country like the back of his hand. As a master of the buffalo hunt, he knew the ploy of drawing the herd into a "pound" where they could be slaughtered. Now he allowed Crozier to lead his men into a hollow that had little protection, which the Métis could surround.

Crozier's scouts told him there was a possible ambush up ahead. The superintendent halted his troops, then had sleighs pulled up in front as a barricade. Assiyiwin went to speak to the Métis. He returned with Isidore Dumont, who was waving a white blanket, Crozier asked Isidore what he wanted. Before he could answer, an English Métis interpreter named Joseph McKay suddenly moved his horse forward, startling the old Indian. McKay had a rifle in his hand and a pistol in his belt. Assiyiwin asked him what he was doing with so many guns, and grabbed at the rifle. They struggled briefly, and then McKay shot Assiyiwin dead. Immediately Crozier shouted, "Fire away, boys!"

It was the wrong order for the superintendent to give, because the Métis, whose numbers had grown to as many as three hundred, had formed a semicircle around the Mounties. They had the high ground and the cover of trees and Beardy's cabin. Isidore Dumont, however, was right in front of the Mounties and still holding the white blanket. He hadn't fired a shot, but he was the first of the Métis to be killed by police bullets.

The Mounties quickly realized they were in a trap, taking fire from three sides. They got their cannon into position, but then couldn't fire it because Crozier was in the way. "Bullets fell like hail," one policeman said later.

Riel did not take part in the fighting, but sat on his horse in a small hollow, praying. Because he was mounted, the upper part of his body was exposed. Bullets flew around him, but he was not hit. This gave rise to the belief among the Métis that Riel was protected by God.

After twenty minutes Crozier realized he was in a hopeless position. He had twelve dead and eleven wounded. There was nothing for him to do but retreat back to the fort. It was a humiliating defeat for the vaunted NWMP.

Dumont, who had a head wound, wanted to pursue them and finish them off. But Riel would not allow it. "For the love of God, kill no more of them," he cried. Riel also stopped Dumont from shooting a wounded volunteer who had been left behind. The Métis had five dead, including Dumont's brother and a cousin.

Riel sent word to Crozier that if the Mounties wanted to come and pick up their dead, they would not be harmed. Métis even helped the police load the bodies into a wagon.

One hour after Crozier's battered column limped into Fort Carlton, Colonel A.G. Irvine arrived from Regina with reinforcements of 108 men. Irvine decided that Fort Carlton was not worth defending. It was built for trade, not war, and its interior was exposed to sniper fire from a hilltop. He ordered an evacuation to Prince Albert, 120 kilometres (75 miles) away. As the Mounties and volunteers were preparing for the journey, some hay accidentally caught fire and the fort burned down.

The Mounties moved out at night. Of course, Dumont's spies were watching them the whole time. Dumont wanted to attack them right away, but Riel would not allow it. He said it would be "too savage" to attack them at night. Dumont became angry and said, "If you are going to give them the advantage like that, we cannot win."

This was the beginning of a rift between the two leaders. Dumont might even have started to suspect Riel's sanity. Because he believed himself to be a prophet sent to the Métis, Riel had given himself the middle name "David." He told his people the Ten Commandments would be the law of the Provisional Government, and that a local bishop would be recognized as the Pope of the New World.

After his victory at Duck Lake, Riel sent messages to the white settlers on the prairies that he meant them no harm. His war, he said, was against the Canadian government and the Hudson's Bay Company. Riel's assurances fell on deaf ears. Already stories were circulating about atrocities committed by the Métis. In Prince Albert 1,800 people were crowded into a small stockade, and every man kept a gun loaded and ready.

Riel pleaded with the English-speaking Métis to join him as comrades in arms. They said they sympathized with the French-speaking Métis on the land claims problem, but they would not support armed rebellion. They chose to remain neutral. That left only the Natives as potential allies.

The Blackfoot Confederacy would have been a powerful friend to have in the Métis camp, but Chief Crowfoot kept them out of it. However, Riel's attempt to draw Natives into the conflict met with some success. A few hundred Crees under chiefs Poundmaker and Big Bear, weary of poverty, disease and starvation on the reservations, struck out against the whites. Poundmaker's warriors sacked the settlement of Battleford while the townspeople watched from the safety of their fort. At the tiny community of Frog Lake, a party of Big Bear's warriors led by Little Big Man and Wandering Spirit massacred nine whites, including two priests. Then they burned down Fort Pitt.

Elsewhere there were individual acts of retribution. A farm instructor named James Payne, whom the Natives hated because of his strict manner with them, was murdered by a Stoney Indian. The Stoneys also killed a rancher named Barney Tremont, who had made no secret of his hatred for Indians and had often threatened them.

Back in Ottawa, Prime Minister John A. Macdonald may have been slow to respond to the problems of Natives and Métis—when he responded at all. But he lost no time in summoning the military to go and put down the rebellion for which his government was largely to blame. He called up the militia, and all across Canada men flocked to enlist. It seemed that every man who could shoulder a gun was eager to go west and teach the half-breeds and Indians a lesson. Macdonald was delighted not only with the response, but also with the fact that his new transcontinental railroad—though incomplete—would be instrumental in hastening the army to the trouble spot. That, in turn, would enable him to squeeze more money out of Parliament for the almost bankrupt Canadian Pacific Railway.

The commander of the northwest expedition was General Frederick D. Middleton, a fifty-nine-year-old Anglo-Irish career soldier who had been educated at Sandhurst and had served all over the British Empire. Middleton was a rotund man with a walrus moustache and the haughty air of an English aristocrat. He accepted the position as commander of the Canadian militia only eight months before the rebellion in the west because he needed a paying job. He did not particularly like "colonials," and now he was about to lead three thousand amateur soldiers against fewer than a thousand tough Métis guerrilla fighters.

The first units of the Canadian militia started west on March 30. Because there was not yet a continuous length of track across the rugged country north of Lake Superior, the troops had to travel by foot and by sleigh across the gaps in the line in sub-zero temperatures. For one leg of the journey they had to cross thirty-two kilometres (20 miles) of the frozen surface of Lake Superior. Even where they could travel by train, the men were often crowded onto flatcars, where they were exposed to the cold and driving sleet. Many suffered frostbite or became ill with pneumonia or bronchitis. Nonetheless, it took them only twelve days to reach the Saskatchewan country. General Middleton did not share the gruelling journey with the troops. He had a comfortable train ride through the United States.

As soon as Riel and Dumont learned that a Canadian army was coming, they concentrated their forces around Batoche. As the soldiers began arriving at Qu'Appelle, Dumont's scouts kept him informed of everything they did. He even had spies in the Canadian camp. One of them worked as a teamster for General Middleton himself.

Dumont had plans to make life very miserable indeed for the invading army. He wanted to blow up bridges and sections of track to slow down the troop trains. He wanted to send bands of raiders swooping down on the outposts where food for the soldiers and hay for their horses were being stockpiled. Dumont knew most of the Canadian soldiers were green troops who had never been west before. He wanted to harass them on the trail and when they camped at night, depriving them of sleep. He believed "this was a good way to demoralize them and make them lose heart," he wrote later.

But Riel would not allow it. He was concerned about Dumont's head wound, which had not healed properly. Riel wanted his men kept close to Batoche because he was worried about the Mounties at Prince Albert; the same Mounties Dumont had wanted to ambush before they could even reach Prince Albert. No doubt Dumont was also thinking of all the guns and ammunition that would have fallen into his men's hands if he had been permitted to make that attack. Riel would not allow his men to make night raids, because he felt that was too barbaric, like Indian warfare. He knew, too, that there were French Canadians in Middleton's army, and Riel did not want to make war on them. Most of all, Riel clung to the hope that Ottawa would see the light and negotiate with him. On April 29 he wrote in his diary:

"O my God, for the love of Jesus, Mary, Joseph and Saint
John the Baptist, grant me the favour of speedily reaching a

good arrangement, a good agreement with the Dominion of Canada. Guide me, help me to secure for the Métis and Indians all the advantages which can now be obtained through negotiations."

But General Middleton had not travelled west to negotiate, and he was making plans of his own. When all of the troops had arrived at Qu'Appelle, Middleton took some time to drill them—though in his estimation they would never be "real" soldiers. Then he put his plans in motion. Major General Thomas Bland Strange would take six hundred men north to deal with Big Bear. Lieutenant-Colonel William Otter's seven hundred troops would advance on Battleford, which was besieged by Poundmaker's warriors. Middleton himself would move on the rebel stronghold at Batoche. He would take eight hundred men plus his artillery, which included nine cannon and two Gatling guns that fired 1,200 rounds a minute. Middleton was a strong believer in infantry, so he left most of his cavalry behind to guard supply depots and protect the railway. That would seriously hamper his army's mobility.

Middleton's column left Qu'Appelle on April 6. With it went a plodding train of 120 wagons. By April 13 they were at Humboldt, still 161 kilometres (100 miles) from Batoche. Dumont's scouts brought him regular reports of Middleton's advance, but this news also reached the ears of his men. Some became unnerved when they were told the size of the redcoat army coming their way, and deserted. Dumont finally ran out of patience with Riel. To Dumont, it made no sense at all to allow this foreign army to march across his country unchallenged. He told Riel he intended to go out "and shoot at the invaders."

Riel finally let Dumont have his way. "Very well," he said. "Do what you wish." Then he warned Dumont to be mindful of his own reckless courage and not expose himself needlessly. Dumont replied that he and his men would deal with the soldiers "as we would the buffalo." Dumont chose a place called Fish Creek to give the British general a taste of prairie warfare.

Middleton's men had captured some Indians who told the general that the Métis rebels had only 250 men. Middleton was afraid the enemy would run away without even a fight. For some inexplicable reason he split his force in two, sending 370 men to the other side of the South Saskatchewan River under the command of his Chief of Staff, Gilbert Elliot, Lord Melgund. Now, with the turbulent river between the two columns, communications were difficult and it would be almost impossible for one to go to the relief of the other in case of attack.

Dumont had about 130 Métis and Indians hidden in the bushes at Fish Creek, at a place where the trail turned inland from the Saskatchewan River. He had told his Métis not to leave any signs that would give them away, but some of them ignored his order and left the remains of campfires in plain view. He told them not to fire until Middleton's advance guard had passed.

On the gray, rainy morning of April 24, the Canadian troops came in sight. Their scouts spotted the ashes of fires and then the Métis. There would be no surprise attack. The Winnipeg Ninetieth Rifles were the first company to make contact with Riel's men. They had the high ground, but the Métis and Indians fought from the cover of ravines and trees. The Canadians fired their cannon, but could not depress the muzzles of the guns low enough to be effective. The cannon fire roared harmlessly through the treetops. Dumont seemed to be everywhere, encouraging his men. "Don't be afraid of bullets," he told them. "They won't hurt you." Some of the Métis began singing a song they considered their anthem, Pierre Falcon's song about the Battle of Seven Oaks.

Even though the Métis and Indians were giving Middleton's troops all they could handle, many of them were discouraged by the numbers of the redcoats and the superiority of their weapons. The Canadians had the very latest rifles, and all the ammunition they wanted. Dumont's men had a few rifles, but most of them were armed with old muzzle-loaders, and their ammunition was in critically short supply. Many of Dumont's men fled.

When his remaining fighters were down to their last few bullets, Dumont started a brush fire in front of the redcoat lines. The wind was blowing in their direction, and the soldiers had to retreat as a wall of flame roared toward them. Dumont and his men followed in the wake of the fire, yelling and screaming. When the fire hit a patch of wet woods and went out, the soldiers were gone. The victorious Métis searched the bodies of the dead for ammunition, but found none.

The Métis had five men dead and two wounded. They had also lost fifty-five horses. Middleton had ten dead and forty-eight wounded. The general halted his advance on Batoche to tend to the wounded and re-think his strategy. He telegraphed Ottawa:

"The troops behaved well on the occasion of their first meeting with the enemy, but I confess to you that it was very near being otherwise, and if it had not been for myself and A.D.C's it would have been a disaster."

Middleton gave serious though to telling Prime Minister Macdonald that this was a job for British regulars. But then he had another idea. He would attack Batoche with a combined infantry and naval assault.

In Batoche, Riel prayed while the other men fought at Fish Creek. He knelt with his arms outstretched as though he were on a cross, and when he could no longer hold them up, the women held them up for him. When the men returned with news of their victory, Riel ordered four days of fasting, penance and prayer. He wrote in his journal, "Properly performed, four days of fasting is enough to turn a nation of dwarves into a nation of giants." Riel quarrelled with the local clergy, who would not administer the sacraments to men bearing arms. He told the Métis that their horses had been killed at Fish Creek as God's punishment for their sin of gambling on horse races. Riel also decided that in his new utopia, the old pagan names of the days of the week would be changed to something with a more Christian sound to them. While Riel seemed to sink deeper into madness, Dumont prepared Batoche for the battle he knew was coming.

On the same day that General Middleton's men were fighting at Fish Creek, Colonel Otter's column arrived at Battleford. The besieging Indians had fled before the army's approach, after torching the Hudson's Bay Company warehouse. The haggard people were grateful to get out of the stockade, but now they wanted to go after Poundmaker and his warriors. Colonel Otter's men were disappointed that it had been so easy. They, too, were eager for a fight. Otter himself had had but one battlefield experience in his lifetime as a soldier. Nineteen years earlier he'd been with the Canadian militia that fled in disorder from the Fenian invaders. Now he wanted a victory on his record. Otter telegraphed General Middleton, requesting orders. Middleton was vague in his response—which was a way of escaping blame if things went wrong. He told Otter to do whatever was necessary. "You have sole command." Otter interpreted that as permission to chase down Poundmaker. He rested his troops for a few days, and then marched them out of Fort Otter, the post he had established on the outskirts of the town.

Otter left half his force to garrison Battleford in case Poundmaker doubled back. The three hundred men he took with him were a mixed collection of Canadian militia, Mounties and local volunteers. He had a Gatling gun and two seven-pounder cannon that belonged to the NWMP; fifty wagons hauled provisions and gear. The column moved slowly, circling the wagons for rest and meal stops. By the early morning of May 1, the men had covered only thirty kilometres (18 miles). But scouts told Otter that the Cree camp was on the east side of Cut Knife Creek, just a day's march away.

Otter rested the troops, and then moved on. At about 4:00 a.m. on May 2, they crossed Cut Knife Creek in a single file. There was plenty of evidence that an Indian camp *had* been there, but the Natives had evidently moved to another location. Colonel Otter ordered the men to proceed to the top of a rise where they would stop for breakfast. When they reached that hill, they were surprised to see Poundmaker's camp spread out before them. Most of the people in the camp were asleep, but an elderly man who was awake saw the soldiers and raised the alarm.

People now streamed out of the teepees, the men hurrying the women and children to the safety of nearby woods. The Canadians hauled up their artillery and opened fire. Cannonballs and Gatling gun bullets tore through the empty teepees. A white prisoner in the village, Robert Jefferson, ran to Poundmaker's teepee. He found the chief putting on a patchwork quilt. This was Poundmaker's war cloak, which he believed would make him invisible to the enemy.

However, Poundmaker did no fighting that day. He was a political leader. The war chief of his band was a man named Fine Day. This battle-savvy leader was about to give Colonel Otter a lesson in tactical fighting.

As soon as the women and children and the elderly were out of firing range, Fine Day sent his men in squads of four or five into the ravines that surrounded the Canadians' position. He used a small hand mirror to signal his orders to them. The warriors would pop up in one place, fire at the soldiers, then duck down and reappear somewhere else. This completely confused the soldiers and gave the impression the Indians' numbers were greater than they actually were. The Gatling gun and cannon made no difference. The gun carriages for both cannon collapsed, and the Gatling gun bullets were whistling over the warrior's heads. If Colonel Otter had ordered an attack on the enemy position, he probably could have scattered them by sheer force of numbers. But he kept his force in one spot, until he finally decided to retreat. With eight dead and fourteen wounded, Colonel Otter had had enough. Fine Day's warriors wanted to pursue the Canadians and kill as many as they could, but Poundmaker would not allow it. He did not want a massacre. He remembered what had happened to the Sioux and Cheyenne after the Custer massacre at the Little Bighorn nine years earlier. When Colonel Otter and his men got back to Battleford, reporters wrote glowing stories about his "victory" over the savages, stating that the brave Canadian lads had killed at least a hundred warriors. Actually, the Cree had six killed and three wounded.

At the end of the first week of May General Middleton was ready to move. As the redcoat army marched along the South Saskatchewan, it was accompanied by the Hudson's Bay

Company's flat-bottomed river steamer *Northcote*. The vessel had been converted into a gunboat, with a cannon, a Gatling gun and thirty-five soldiers on board. Middleton's plan was to have the *Northcote* fire on Batoche from the river and create a diversion while the main army struck the settlement from land.

As the Canadians advanced through the river valley they behaved more like marauders than a disciplined army. They looted and burned every farmhouse they came to. They slaughtered cattle and stole horses. The men took particular delight in destroying Gabriel Dumont's house and stable.

Middleton moved slowly and cautiously, expecting an ambush at every bend in the river. For that reason, the *Northcote* was well ahead of the army when it came within sight of Batoche on May 9. Middleton had expected the Métis would be unpleasantly surprised by his "warship," but Dumont knew exactly what the general was up to, and was prepared for it. He wanted the guns and ammunition that were on the *Northcote*.

As the boat neared Batoche, Métis on both sides of the river suddenly opened fire. The helmsman dove for cover. Then the riverboat struck a sandbar and was suddenly caught in the main current. Dumont jumped on his horse and dashed along the riverbank, shouting to his men to get to the ferry cable at the town landing. He hoped to snare the *Northcote* so his men could board it. The Métis tried to lower the cable to hold the boat, but instead it scraped along the top of the pilot house and sheared off the smokestack, whistle, mast and spars. The whole lot fell into a tangled mess on the deck and burst into flames. With Métis bullets smashing into the timbers all around them, the crew manned a bucket brigade and doused the fire. Still out of control, the *Northcote* drifted another three-and-a-half kilometres (two miles) downstream before it finally came to a stop. It sat there for the duration of the battle, out of Dumont's reach now, because bugle calls announced the enemy's approach.

In the two weeks since he had fought the Canadian army to a standstill at Fish Creek, Dumont had put his men to work digging trenches and rifle pits. These were so well concealed, the crews manning the cannon and Gatling gun could not even see anything to shoot at. Nor could the infantrymen who were ordered to advance on the village. As they started out, not a Métis was in sight. Suddenly the ground in front of them erupted with smoke and flame as the Métis opened fire on the exposed soldiers. One group of Métis made a dash to try to capture one of the field guns, but was driven back into their rifle pits.

Then a white flag was seen flying from the church. The village priest, Father Moulin, wanted to give up. The Canadians held their fire until the priest reached their lines. The Métis were certain Father Moulin gave General Middleton information about their defences. They would regard him ever after as a traitor.

The shooting resumed and kept up for most of the afternoon. Then General Middleton realized his men were doing nothing but waste ammunition. He called them back, and set up a camp about a mile from the village. He surrounded it with a *zareba,* a type of stockade, and had men dig rifle pits of their own. His well-equipped army of eight hundred had just been stood off by about 175 Métis, most of them armed with ancient guns. Had it not been for the presence of the Gatling gun and the cannon, those Métis would have rushed the Canadians and might well have routed them.

That night the Métis harassed the invaders. They let out blood-curdling war cries and fired into the camp from the darkness. Soldiers had to take turns risking their necks to keep the horses calm.

The following day the fighting was much the same. The Canadians could not see anything to shoot at, but they made perfect targets if they advanced too close to the hidden Métis. The gunners and the men on the Gatling gun could only blast away and hope to hit something. At dusk Middleton called them back to the *zareba*. They spent another night listening to the taunts of the Métis and dodging sniper fire.

For Dumont's fighters the ammunition situation was now critical. They were shooting nails, bits of scrap metal and even stones out of their muzzle-loaders. After dark they crawled out to where the Canadian soldiers had been standing, and picked up bullets that had been dropped while the men reloaded. They even found discarded Gatling gun ammunition belts that still had bullets in them. Dumont was outraged when he learned that some of the bullets the Canadians were using were an exploding type, designed to inflict the maximum damage on a human body. The Canadian government denied equipping its troops with such bullets, but many of the surviving Métis swore they saw them.

By day four one might have said the routine had become monotonous, but for the fact that blood was being spilled. The Canadians continued to pound the village with artillery fire, but by now the return fire from the Métis was sporadic. They had to make every shot count. Some of the men in the rifle pits hadn't slept since the battle began. Riel moved from one weary fighter to another, reading from the Bible and offering prayers. On one occasion when General Middleton was preoccupied, Lieutenant Colonel Arthur Williams and a small group of men rushed a Métis trench. The defenders quickly retreated, and the Canadians returned to their lines with cooking utensils, tools, blankets and other plunder they had scooped up. This action showed that the trenches could be taken. Moreover, the priest had evidently told General Middleton about the shortage of ammunition in Batoche. The general decided that the following day, May 12, he would risk an assault on the village. It helped, too, that 150 North West Mounted Police had joined in the fight, so Middleton had 950 men to Dumont's 175.

Middleton's plan was simple. He would lead an attack from the northeast, supported by cannon and the Gatling gun. With the rebels diverted, Lieutenant Colonel Bowen van Straubenzie would lead the main attack from the south and overrun the enemy's defenses. The troops took up their positions in the morning and waited for the signal, the sound of Middleton's cannon. However, when the big gun roared, the wind carried the sound away from the place where van Straubenzie was waiting. He didn't hear it, and, assuming something had gone wrong, didn't order his men to advance.

At noon a furious General Middleton gave his officers a dressing down and told them he wanted Batoche taken that afternoon. He didn't realize the confusion in the Canadian army had caused Dumont to make a mistake. When he saw General Middleton and his men at the northeast approach to Batoche, Dumont thought the attack would come from there. He reinforced that section of his defences, taking men away from the southern sector.

After lunch the general again ordered a cautious approach to the Métis defences. Lieutenant Colonel Arthur Williams ignored the order. He led his men in a charge at the south end of the village and soon occupied the church where the prisoners were kept. Middleton wanted to follow up that success with a careful reconnaissance probe. Again the men ignored him. Screaming out battle cries, they rushed the rifle pits. The Métis defenders didn't have the firepower to stop them, and they fell back to the village. One

Canadian soldier bayoneted a Métis, only to learn later the man was ninety-three years old.

In the village the fighting was house to house, with the Métis resisting to the bitter end. But they were too few, and their ammunition was gone. In a little over an hour the Battle of Batoche was over. The Métis had twelve dead and three wounded. Two of the slain were children. They had suffered all their casualties in that final attack. General Middleton had ten dead and thirty-six wounded.

The victorious Canadians then went on a rampage, breaking into houses and destroying everything they could not carry off. A reporter for the Toronto *Mail* called them "raving maniacs." The surviving Métis made their way to General Middleton's tent, carrying white flags of surrender. The Riel Rebellion was over.

Middleton held members of Riel's provisional government prisoner, but told the rest of the Métis to return to their homes. Gabriel Dumont escaped to the United States where he would live in exile until his eventual return to Canada. On May 15 Riel gave himself up to General Middleton. Within a matter of weeks Poundmaker surrendered rather than have his people annihilated. Big Bear tried to escape with his band into desolate country, but was run to earth and forced to surrender. Both chiefs would serve prison terms, and die soon after being released.

Riel went on trial for high treason in Regina on July 28. His lawyers tried to save his life with a plea of insanity, but Riel refused to cooperate with that tactic. He was sane, he insisted, and he believed he had done the right thing for his people, who were suffering under a neglectful government. He was found guilty and sentenced to hang. Catholic Quebec cried out for clemency. Protestant Ontario wanted him dead. John A. Macdonald said, "He shall hang though every dog in Quebec bark in his favour." On November 16, 1885, Louis Riel died on the gallows in Regina. Some people said he was executed not because of the rebellion that had ended at Batoche, but because fifteen years earlier he had ordered the death of Thomas Scott.

Bibliography

Berton, Pierre, *The Invasion of Canada, 1812–1813,* McClelland & Stewart, Toronto, 1980

———. *Flames Across the Border, 1813–1814,* McLelland & Stewart, Toronto, 1981

Butts, Ed & Horwood, Harold, *Pirates & Outlaws of Canada, 1610–1932,* Doubleday Canada Ltd., Toronto, 1984

Carroll, Joy, *Wolfe and Montcalm: Their Lives, Their Times, and the Fate of a Continent,* Firefly Books, Richmond Hill, 2004

Fryer, Mary Beacock, *Battlefields of Canada,* Dundurn Press, Toronto, 1986

———. *More Battlefields of Canada,* Dundurn Press, Toronto, 1993

Garrett, Richard, *General Wolfe,* Arthur Baker Ltd., London, 1975

Graves, Donald E., *Fighting For Canada: Seven Battles, 1758–1945,* Robin Brass Studio, Toronto, 1998

———. *Field of Glory: The Battle of Crysler's Farm, 1813,* Robin Brass Studio, Toronto, 1999

Gray, John Morgan, *Lord Selkirk of Red River,* Macmillan Co., Toronto, 1963

Guillet, Edwin, *The Lives and Times of the Patriots,* Thomas Nelson & Sons, Toronto, 1938

Hannon, Leslie F., *Forts of Canada,* McLelland & Stewart, Toronto, 1969

Hitsman, J. Mackay, *The Incredible War of 1812: A Military History,* University of Toronto Press, Toronto, 1965

Jenish, D'Arcy, *Indian Fall,* Viking Books, 1999

Lanctot, Gustave, *Canada and the American Revolution, 1774–1783,* Clarke Irwin &

Co., Toronto, 1967

Mckenzie, Ruth, *James Fitzgibbon: Defender of Upper Canada,* Dundurn Press, Toronto, 1983

O'Neill, Paul, *The Oldest City: The Story of St. John's, Newfoundland,* Press Porcepic, Don Mills, ON, 1975

Paterson, T.W., *Canadian Battles and Massacres,* Stagecoach Publishing, Langley, BC, 1977

Schull, Joseph, *Rebellion: The Rising in French Canada, 1837,* Macmillan of Canada, Toronto, 1971

Senior, Hereward, *The Last Invasion of Canada: The Fenian Raids, 1866–1870,* Dundurn Press, Toronto, 1991

Siggins, Maggie, *Riel: A Life of Revolution,* Harper Collins Ltd., Toronto, 1994

Sugden, John, *Tecumseh: A Life,* Henrey Holt & Co., New York, 1997

Tanner, Ogden, *The Canadians,* Time Life Books, Alexandria, VA, 1977

The Dictionary of Canadian Biography